Understanding Violence

Understanding Violence

Elizabeth Kandel Englander
Bridgewater State College

LEA LAWRENCE ERLBAUM ASSOCIATES, PUBLISHERS
1997   Mahwah, New Jersey

Lawrence Erlbaum Associates, Inc., Publishers
10 Industrial Avenue
Mahwah, New Jersey 07430

Library of Congress Cataloging-in-Publication Data

Englander, Elizabeth Kandel.
    Understanding violence / Elizabeth Kandel Englander.
        p.   cm.
    Includes bibliographical references and indexes.
    ISBN 0-8058-1939-8 (cloth). — ISBN 0-8058-1940-1 (pbk.)
        1. Violent crimes—United States. 2. Violent crimes—United
States—Psychological aspects. 3. Criminal psychology—United
States. 4. Violence—United States. I. Title.
    HV6789.K364   1997
    364.1'5'0973—dc20   96-34117
                                                                              CIP

Books published by Lawrence Erlbaum Associates are printed on acid-free paper,
and their bindings are chosen for strength and durability.

Printed in the United States of America
10 9 8 7 6 5 4 3 2 1

For Michael,
without whom it would never have been possible.

Contents

Preface   ix

1   Introduction   1

PART I: GENERAL ISSUES

2   The Numbers: How Common Is Violent
    Behavior Today?   11

3   Social Causes of Violence   33

4   Individual Causes of Violent Behavior   49

5   Television and Violence   79

6   The Biosocial Model   85

PART II: SPECIAL ISSUES

7   Substance Abuse and Violent Behavior   99

8   Gangs   105

9   Sexual Assault   110

10 Spouse Homicide   116

11 Child Abuse and Physical Punishment   124

12 Victims: The Consequences of Family Violence   140

Epilogue: Preventing and Controlling Violence   152

References   156

Author Index   177

Subject Index   185

Preface

This book was born on a beach in Truro, Massachusetts, and is the brain-child of my husband, Michael. In 1993 I was teaching a course called the Psychology of Criminal Behavior, with no text available that spanned the breadth of the fields which have contributed to our knowledge about crime, and about violent crime in particular. Instead of letting me complain, Michael merely pointed out that if no such book existed, then I should write it.

Several years later, I have completed a manuscript that, I hope, reflects my years working with colleagues in psychology, biology, sociology, and criminal justice. The study of violent crime has frequently been reduced to the study of very specific characteristics hypothesized to be causally related to violent behavior. As absolutely invaluable as knowledge of specific relationships is, it is critical to remember the forest, and not merely the trees. I explain this dilemma to my students in the following way: Suppose you were assigned a jigsaw puzzle to complete, and the pieces were hidden all over a house. First, you would need to locate each individual piece, but after you had these pieces, you would need to put them all together in order to complete the puzzle—just having the pieces in a heap wouldn't be helpful at all. You need to assemble them in order to form a general picture which you could then interpret usefully. The purpose of this book is to begin to form that picture, even while it is obvious that we have not yet found all the individual jigsaw pieces. Although many pieces are still hidden, I believe we have enough information now that if we assemble it, we can begin to understand how violence happens in a way that can be pragmatically useful to us as a society.

There is no doubt that this book has been influenced by all of my years of training and work. It is most appropriate that I thank first of all Sarnoff Mednick, whose advice was so valuable to me during my years of graduate training. David Finkelhor and Murray Straus also offered invaluable help during my postdoctoral training. I particularly appreciated their broad view of violence.

A great deal of this book is also due to the diligence and hard work of my editor, Susan Milmoe, who did her best to transform my often-confusing thoughts into clear and concise prose, and deserves much credit. My father, Stephen Kandel, has also been very helpful in his contributions to the book, particularly in the area of television violence, but also in a series of general comments and suggestions.

I am most grateful, however, to my husband Michael, whose confidence in me and whose gently pressuring style and calm equanimity kept this project alive—to say nothing of the many hours he kept our son out of my hair. Last, but not least, this book was written for Joshua, who is the representative of a generation which I hope fervently will benefit from the effort to control violence.

—Elizabeth Kandel Englander

"Thus with violence shall the city be thrown down. . . . thus with violence shall a great city Babylon be thrown down."

—Revelation 18:21

Introduction:
The Problem of Violence

In Texas, a young woman is shot to death outside the elementary school where she taught. Her killer was her former boyfriend, who was able to commit the homicide because he was freed on bail earlier in the month, after he had put a gun to her head and tried to kill her once before.

— Associated Press (1995j)

About 1.3 million U.S. residents faced an assailant armed with a gun during 1993.

—Associated Press (1995a)

No longer rare in the experience of most Americans, violence hits us where we live—literally. It is little wonder that few other social issues inspire such passion. However, violence must be distinguished from aggressive behavior. *Violence* is aggressive behavior with the intent to cause harm (physical or psychological). The word *intent* is central; physical or psychological harm that occurs by accident, in the absence of intent, is not violence.

All aggressive behavior can be divided into two fundamentally different types: instrumental aggression and hostile aggression. *Instrumental aggression* has as its purpose the achievement of a separate goal. For example, hitting a woman over the head in order to steal her purse is instrumental aggression. The motive is not to harm, but to gain the purse.

By contrast, *hostile aggression* more closely fits our definition of *violence*: It is performed for the purpose of harming (physically or psychologically) another person. Human beings and other animals differ in their use of *hostile* versus *instrumental* aggression: Whereas human beings engage in both types of aggression, other animals primarily, if not exclusively, engage

1

in instrumental aggression. They may use threats of violence to psychologically intimidate a competitor, but these threats are made for an instrumental purpose: to gain what the competitor is also seeking (as in competition for a mate; Bandura, 1989).

Family violence is hostile aggression between people who are intimately involved with each other—by traditional definition, between those who are married or related to one another, but in current practice, between all those who are intimately involved, such as cohabitating or dating couples (Straus & Gelles, 1990; Straus, Gelles, & Steinmetz, 1980). There is not universal agreement about what the term *family violence* means. For example, the terms *family violence* and *domestic violence* are sometimes seen as synonymous with wife-beating, although spouse abuse is only one type of family violence. Other types are child abuse, incest or child sexual abuse, marital and date rape, and elder abuse.

Until relatively recently, the causes of violent behavior were not widely studied. Shared social values constrained aggressive behavior in public; domestic abuse was concealed as a private family problem. Today, however, violence is among the most pressing problems with which behavioral experts must cope. It is clear that violence is neither so rare nor so private as it once was, or was popularly supposed to be. One recent survey of children in a Boston-area health clinic, for example, found that 1 in 10 had, by age 6, witnessed a knifing or a shooting; half of these shootings and three quarters of the knifings had been witnessed by the children in their own homes (Cohen, 1992).

The increasing significance of violence can be seen in a cost analysis of the problem. Even when one ignores the cost to the victim in suffering and pain, and the emotional cost to family relationships, substantial financial costs can be identified as follows:

1. Medical expenses to victims.
2. Lost productivity due to injuries.
3. Expenditures for mental health services.
4. Expenditures for police, social services, and investigations.
5. Financial support of victims (e.g., through public assistance, battered women's shelters, etc.)
6. Expenditures for prosecution and/or incarceration of the offenders.

It is very difficult, if not impossible, to estimate all these costs exactly. However, the figures we do know precisely are staggering enough. For example, in 1990 the U.S. federal and state prison systems alone spent $11.5 billion—an average of about $15,603 per inmate (Greenfeld, 1992). Popular media have estimated that crime in the United States costs hundreds of billions of dollars every year. Official numbers report that the nation spent $75 billion for all criminal justice expenditures (Lindgren, 1990). The National Crime Victimization Survey of 1992 found that crime victims lost a staggering $17.6 billion, which included both property and cash losses, wage losses, and medical expenses (Klaus, 1994). More than two thirds of personal crimes involve an economic loss to the victim, as do almost one in four violent crimes (Klaus, 1994). Rape, robbery, and assault alone cost victims almost $1.5 billion in 1992 (Klaus, 1994). Approximately 8% of all victims counted in 1992 lost time from work as the result of a violent crime (Klaus, 1994). Statistics such as these do not typically include costs such as long-term medical costs, psychological counseling, decreased productivity at work, higher insurance premiums, or moving costs. Additionally, as large as these numbers are, they do not represent the total cost of violent crime because not all violent crime is detected.

The secrecy that surrounds most cases of family violence makes them particularly difficult to detect, which means that most of the statistics cited here probably do not include domestic violence and are thus likely to be underestimates. It is not known how many women stay home from work each day to hide injuries caused by abusive spouses. Because most cases of family violence are never reported to the authorities, we have no way of knowing how many women call in sick to work when in fact they have been injured by a spouse or partner. Similarly, how can we estimate the costs of mental health services? Presumably, some violence and abuse is revealed to mental health service workers and not to law enforcement authorities, but we cannot tell what proportion of these services goes to victims and/or abusive families.

However, some estimates do help to clarify the costs of family violence. For example, the cost of family homicide in 1984 alone was estimated to be $1.7 billion (Straus & Gelles, 1986). We also know that severely battered women average almost twice as many days in bed as other women (Straus & Gelles, 1990). Three times as many battered women as unbattered women reported being in "poor" health during a 1985 survey of Americans (Straus & Gelles, 1990). Battered women appear to have higher rates of all types of illnesses, including depression, headaches, and suicidal thoughts. Abused children have higher rates of all types of social and medical problems, such as difficulty in making friends, learning problems, or aggressive behavior (Straus & Gelles, 1990). How can we possibly estimate the costs associated with a child who might have succeeded in school but failed because of victimization? Finally, it is well known that abused children are more likely to be arrested (Spatz Widom, 1989a), which costs police, judicial, prison, and social services resources.

Although each of these costs are ultimately borne by taxpayers, most of us have only recently become aware of the scope and seriousness of violent behavior in society. Experts in a variety of fields have, however, been trying for years to understand why human beings become, on occasion, violent with each other. Psychologists, sociologists, biologists, and criminologists have all been studying human violence from different perspectives, and each group has a valuable contribution to make.

Sometimes a multiperspective approach seems tiresome and irrelevant to readers who can often "see" the causes of violence quite easily. Gain seems to be the motive in cases of instrumental aggression; there are other obvious motives in cases of hostile aggression. For example, when you read in the newspaper about a young man who kills another man in a gunfight for "no apparent reason," the story will often describe the perpetrator as having been the victim of abuse, a broken family, or poverty. What else do you need to know? The answer to the question of why this young man is violent seems self-evident: All the reader has to do is consider his early deprivation. If he had been born into wealth and privilege, if he had been raised in a loving, nurturing, nonviolent environment, we all feel sure that he would not have so easily committed murder. In fact, our analysis may be correct.

But consider, for a moment, the possibility that this perpetrator has a brother. Perhaps this brother is not violent; perhaps there are other siblings who are not violent. Yet all the offspring in this family shared a psychosocially impoverished and troubled childhood. Why was this one man so vulnerable, when his siblings managed to stay out of trouble? Many individuals are exposed to early stress or neglect, even to violent abuse, yet most of them do not grow up to become violent themselves (Spatz Widom, 1989b). There are individual differences in vulnerability; in other words, factors other than the young man's environment must be at work. To the student who asks why, when a history of victimization is so clearly important as a precursor of violence, it is necessary even to study biology, I reply that no one factor, no matter how compelling, can completely explain why some individuals are violent and others are not. It is clear that a person's situation is vitally important in understanding his or her violent behavior. But there are always reasons why one individual was influenced by a situation when others were not.[1] In chapter 6, I develop a model of violent behavior that attempts to account for a variety of influences in assessing the potential of an individual for violence.

The first step in understanding risk for violence must be understanding where and when violence occurs. We are coming to realize that by far the most common type of violent behavior may occur not on the street, but in the family (Cervi, 1991; Hotaling, Straus, & Lincoln, 1989; Kandel-Eng-

---

[1]No matter how many factors one takes into account, it is impossible to predict with complete precision who will act violently and who will not. Nevertheless, a multidisciplinary approach enhances understanding of why some people become violent and others do not in a way that no single-discipline approach can.

lander, 1992; Pittman & Handy, 1964; Shields, McCall, & Hanneke, 1988; Straus, 1992b). Although historically family violence has been seen as fundamentally "different" from "traditional" criminal violence, in the second half of the 20th century the U.S. judicial and criminal justice systems began to undergo a significant change of attitude: Attacks on family members began to be viewed as violent crimes, and victims of family violence began to be recognized by law enforcement authorities as being in need of protection. Thus, family violence came to be located squarely within the jurisdiction of the criminal justice system. One survey found that by 1986, most police officers considered violence between spouses to be "criminal and unacceptable" (Saunders & Size, 1986).

Even so, new ideas and beliefs gain wide acceptance at a very slow pace. Thus, criminal justice authorities have very uneven knowledge of, sophistication about, and training in the recognition of the seriousness of family violence. Even today some do not see it as the expensive and potentially lethal threat that it is—despite its prevalence in Western nations (which is discussed in detail in subsequent chapters). It is startling that a crime of such widespread proportions could have escaped public concern for so long.

When domestic violence has been detected, most societies have been reluctant to take action against it. In the United States we have abhorred child abuse and the beating of women, but many have also been reluctant to label incidences as *crimes*. It is as though cultural blinders were in place; to be murdered by a burglar breaking into your house is terrible, but to be murdered by your own husband, although shocking, is not so clearly a heinous crime.

Some of the reluctance to criminalize family abuse can be traced to the roots of the U.S. legal system. Under English Common Law (the basis for much of the U.S. legal system), a man could not be punished for beating his wife or children. In fact, the legal system operated specifically to protect a man's right to chastise his wife and children by physical means (Paterson, 1979). However, there were limits: The law stipulated that a man should not, when beating his wife, use a rod thicker than his own thumb (Paterson, 1979). It is from this centuries-old law that we get our modern saying "by rule of thumb."

Although it was illegal for a man to beat his wife with a rod thicker than his thumb, fewer, if any, limits were placed on how severely parents could beat their children. Children could be starved, tortured, abandoned; children were property and parents had the right to do with them as they pleased (Paterson, 1979). The first time the U.S. public rallied to the defense of an abused child was around the turn of the 20th century, when a horribly abused little girl was rescued by the American Society for the Prevention of Cruelty to Animals—because although Americans had begun to object to the abuse of animals, they had not yet begun to object to the abuse of children! (The American Society for the Prevention of Cruelty to Children was subsequently formed and remains in existence today.)

Until recently, our personal behavior was guided by two conflicting principles: first, the right of privacy to decide how to treat family members—abusively or kindly; second, the right to protection by the government from physical violence. Many U.S. scholars (and others) recognized that these two principles were in conflict. In theory, a government cannot tell its citizens that they have the right not to be assaulted while telling certain citizens that they have the right to assault others without interference. An example of this conflict can be seen in a session of the Washington State Legislature in the mid-1980s, where, while attempting to assure children that they would be protected from assault by their parents, the Legislature could not agree if it should ban "kicking" or "punching" as abusive (Berliner, 1988).

To the U.S. public, the right to treat family members as they pleased, without interference, often outweighed the right of spouses and children not to be abused. Americans did not believe that it was acceptable for a man to strike his wife or for a parent to assault a child, but were nevertheless squeamish about interfering in family affairs, including a man's or woman's right to treat his or her family as he or she wishes without interference. In Boston as late as 1986, for example, when a woman named Pamela Dunn sought protection from her abusive husband, she was told by a judge that she was just taking up the court's time when it had many more serious "crimes" to cope with. Ms. Dunn was refused police escort and told to "act as an adult"; approximately 5 months later, her body was found in a dumpster and her husband, who had abducted her, was charged with first-degree murder. Many similar cases have occurred in the United States.

Despite tragedies such as these, some Americans still believe that family violence is not a serious enough offense to warrant official interference. Nonfamily violence is frequently perceived as more serious, more potentially lethal, and more common. However, many others no longer believe that family violence is insignificant enough to simply tolerate. Legally, no state in the Union now permits a husband to hit his wife (Browne, 1987). Although states began changing their laws as early as the end of the last century, U.S. social beliefs did not begin to really change until much more recently. It was only a few decades ago that a profound shift in public attitude began to change the criminal justice systems of the Western world. People in many countries now recognize that private relationships do not give a person the right to victimize family members and other intimate acquaintances and that such violence should be regarded as criminal. We have begun to fundamentally change our willingness to tolerate assault, regardless of the presence or absence of a relationship between perpetrator and victim.

Although almost all Americans would agree that family violence is a tragedy, not everyone agrees that the criminal justice system is the correct agency for dealing with it. Criminalizing family violence has been controversial for at least the following four reasons:

1. All families have conflicts, and we all sympathize when families fight. Violence between a husband and wife, however unjustified, is undoubtedly one type of family fight.

2. Members of a family may feel humiliated or embarrassed by the existence of violence within their family. Most of us would like to keep our family problems private, and may feel we can best help those in conflict by pretending that we do not notice the violence. Designating family fighting as a *crime* means bringing in outsiders (e.g., police officers, attorneys, judges, psychological and psychiatric experts), and potential witnesses may feel that such legal scrutiny would only be an embarrassing invasion of an already troubled family.

3. Some aggression between family members is clearly legal and (to many) acceptable. Two examples of legal aggression are parent-to-child physical punishment for discipline purposes and physical fighting between siblings (which is regarded as naughty but clearly not a case for the criminal justice system). The fact that some types of illegal violence (e.g., child abuse) are legal in milder forms (spanking) may make it difficult for both experts and the general public to know where to draw the line. Is hitting a child with a leather belt discipline or abuse? Many Americans are confused about what constitutes child abuse or child discipline. As recently as 1988, a pastor whose daughter was beaten to death said that the beatings were nothing more than "tough discipline" (United Press, 1988)—despite the fact that they were ultimately lethal.

These three factors—the common fact that families fight, the natural urge to respect the privacy of family problems, and the fact that some degree of family aggression is clearly legal—all work together to make some members of society fearful of labeling family violence a *crime*.

4. The fourth factor affecting our attitudes toward family violence is that most publicized cases have dealt with male perpetrators and female and child victims. As future chapters discuss, men are the primary, but not the only, perpetrators of violence (Ageton, 1983; Shanok & Lewis, 1981; Stets & Straus, 1990b; Straus & Gelles, 1990; Wolfgang, 1983). Many societies are struggling to redefine their conceptions of male and female roles. In past generations, men essentially owned their families and therefore were permitted relative freedom of behavior with wives, parents, and children. Under the influence of the feminist movement, women and children have ceased to be considered

possessions; they have increasingly fought for the legal right not to be violently victimized by family members. As support for women's rights grows, some men may feel that their rights are shrinking—including their "right" to treat their families however they wish.

Criminalization of street violence has not presented the same psychological barriers. However, other issues have presented themselves as obstacles to an accurate understanding of this problem. U.S. prisons and jails currently overflow with offenders, yet the public perception is that violent crime is constantly and alarmingly increasing. Governments have responded to this concern by increasing spending on crime; in fact, between 1985 and 1990 spending on the criminal justice system increased twice as much as spending on all other government expenditures (Lindgren, 1990). Despite public concern, or in part because of it, the fact is that the overcrowded conditions in U.S. prisons are primarily due to the enormous increase in drug offenders, rather than to the violent convict population (Bureau of Justice Statistics, 1992; Lesnik-Oberstein, Koers, & Cohen, 1995; Snell, 1992). In addition, rates of violent crimes are actually decreasing overall, rather than increasing (Lesnik-Oberstein et al., 1995). Despite these facts, Americans perceive violent street crime to be the threat of the century (ABC News, 1982; Arends, 1996; DeFrances & Smith, 1994). It may be that the quality of violent street crime is changing even more than its quantity. For example, youth violence is without a doubt dramatically increasing (Freeh, 1995). In Portland, Oregon, a 9-year-old boy shot and killed his 5-year-old sister, allegedly because she refused to go to her room (Reuters, 1995a). Despite the boy's youth, he is facing homicide charges and if convicted can be held until his 25th birthday. In many states, such young children are traditionally conceived of as incapable of comprehending the meaning of death and thus unable to form homicidal intent—in fact, Brandon Roses is the youngest child to ever face homicide charges in Oregon. The fact that this child is being formally charged demonstrates society's decreasing tolerance of youth violence. It may be this changing tolerance, rather than a change in the level of violent crime per se, which feeds our impression that America's streets, as well as her homes, are becoming more dangerous all the time.

*   *   *

Violent behavior is a serious problem with many social costs. As such, it provokes many questions. What constitutes a violent crime? What should we, as a society, do with violent offenders? How should victims best cope with the trauma? How do we prevent children from growing up to become violent? All of these questions are important, and are dealt with in this book.

Part I

GENERAL ISSUES

The Numbers: How Common
Is Violent Behavior Today?

METHODOLOGICAL ISSUES
IN COUNTING VIOLENCE

On Friday, August 6, 1993, the most popular newspaper in one major U.S. city reported on three murders in the metropolitan area. All three murders were referred to as "domestic" homicides. Two of these homicides involved the murder of women by their husbands; the third case involved the murder of a young woman by her estranged boyfriend.

There is little doubt that "domestic" murders, once routinely given little or no attention, are now considered to be good newsmakers. However, despite the mass media's increasing recognition of the toll (and frequency) of domestic violence, most Americans still believe that the violence that we are most likely to encounter (i.e., the majority of U.S. violence) occurs on our streets. Women are often taught to defend themselves against street crime; for example, a woman may attend a self-defense class, or may carefully check her car before getting into it at night. When she thinks of being attacked, raped, or beaten, she may imagine that the city streets hold the greatest threat.

Actually, a typical U.S. woman is much more likely to be assaulted in her own home than in the streets of her neighborhood. In fact, the leading cause of injury to U.S. women is domestic, not street, violence (J. Jones, 1990). The most recent National Family Violence Survey (NFVS) estimates that 1.8 million women are beaten domestically each year, compared to the National Crime Survey's most recent (1992–1993) estimate of 660,000 women assaulted by strangers on the street—numbers that suggest that

11

women may be three times more likely to be assaulted in their homes than on the street (National Archive of Criminal Justice Data, 1991; Straus & Gelles, 1990). People are often unaware of these facts, although the public's knowledge about domestic violence is increasing every day.

Our perceptions about the sources of danger around us are based largely on how we count violent crime. "How much child abuse is there in America?" I was recently asked. As is seen here, the answer depends on who does the counting, and how.

SOURCES OF CRIME STATISTICS

We glean most of our knowledge about crime from government and the mass media (e.g., newspapers and television). Thus, most of the misconceptions about the frequency of domestic violence can be traced to the way in which government authorities compile and release statistics about violent crime. Although official statistics about domestic violence are not a deliberate attempt to mislead the public, they can be easily misinterpreted. How does this happen?

There are three sources of statistics on crime:

1. Official statistics, based on police reports of arrests and convictions.
2. Statistics based on government surveys of victims of crime.
3. Self-report surveys, in which people are asked to report on their own criminal activity.

At first glance, many make the error of assuming that "official statistics" are the only reliable, valid, and legitimate measures of crime. Many people, when questioning the value of self-report surveys, ask: "Why would any violent person voluntarily report his own criminal activities to anyone?" However, as is seen here, the job of gathering statistics on crime is not as simple as it may seem.

The Uniform Crime Reports. The "official" source of crime statistics in the United States are the Uniform Crime Reports (UCR), which are compiled by the FBI and are based on local police reports. The FBI uses the UCR to form estimates on the frequency of a variety of crimes in the United States. In theory, local police detect all crime in their jurisdiction, record that crime, and send these records to the FBI, who compile them into the UCR. However, in reality, we know that the UCR is only an estimate because there are several steps in this process that may fail. First, the local police are rarely able to detect all crime that occurs in their jurisdiction;

and second, for a variety of reasons, local police probably fail to record all the crime that they do detect.

Why Don't Police Record All Crime?

At first, it may seem shocking that police do not record, and send on to the FBI, all the crime that they encounter in their district. It is easy to understand that police simply do not detect all crime, but it is more difficult to understand why they would fail to report crime which they do detect.

However, there are several logical and understandable reasons why local police might not record all the crime they encounter on their job. First, the officer(s) may be unable to identify the offender, which may make recording the crime irrelevant. For example, if a minor vandalism is reported to the police but there are no clues as to the identity of the offender, both the victim and the officer may see no good reason to record the crime officially.

In other cases, crime may not be officially recorded because it is not possible to prosecute the case. For example, all records of a crime may be discarded if there is no evidence that is strong enough to support the prosecution of a suspect. Third, sometimes the victims themselves urge the court to drop all charges in a case, thus dismissing the case. In some cases, the court will go along with the victim's wishes in these matters. For example, one reason that official statistics are a poor reflection of domestic violence is that victims of battering husbands, fearing retaliation or other consequences, may choose to drop charges rather than pursue them.

Finally, police see a great deal of crime in the United States today. They are aware that their time is best spent on the most serious crimes. Therefore, if a case appears to be "not serious," then police may choose not to bother recording that crime. There is no doubt that this is illegal; but psychologically, it is understandable.

At best, the UCR fails to reflect only the crime undetected by police. At worst, it omits both the undetected crime and the unrecorded crime. It is important to remember, however, that the UCR has significant advantages; for example, the information it contains tends to be very reliable and accurate. For some types of crime, the UCR is the best statistic available.

However, for two major reasons its weaknesses make it a poor choice for understanding the incidence of domestic violence. First, domestic violence often occurs in the privacy of the family home. As a "hidden" crime, it may be detected by police only in relatively extreme cases. In contrast, street crime occurs in public and is thus much more easily detectable. (Remember, the UCR only reflects detected and recorded crime.) Second, police are often reluctant to take official action, such as arresting the offender, because of a variety of concerns. Even if the police do arrest the offender, the victim may refuse to press charges, thus dropping the case from official statistics.

National Crime Survey. Fortunately, the UCR is not the only source of statistics on crime. The federal government, recognizing that the UCR reflects only detected and recorded crime, provides a different source for some statistics, called the National Crime Survey (NCS). Rather than counting the criminals, as the UCR does, the NCS counts the victims. The NCS is a large-scale survey that asks Americans about their criminal victimization experiences; by counting the victims instead of the criminals, it avoids restricting itself to detected and reported crime. The presumption is that victims will report their criminal victimization experiences, even if the crime was never reported to the police or the criminal never caught.

However, the NCS (and other victimization surveys) are also, unfortunately, less than ideal in the case of domestic violence. For victimization surveys to be successful in accounting for all criminal behavior, several factors must be present:

1. The victim must be able fully and accurately to recall the crime.
2. The victim must be aware that the behavior of the offender constituted a criminal offense.
3. The victim must be willing to disclose the crime (i.e., the victim must not be motivated to protect the offender and/or must not be ashamed of the crime).

In the case of domestic violence, all three factors may not be present in many cases. The accuracy of human recall is frequently poor (Bartol, 1991; Reiss, 1975), and may be especially so for traumatic events such as violent encounters. Furthermore, it is not uncommon for female victims of domestic violence to believe that their male partners were not committing any crime (Finkelhor & Yllo, 1985); many Americans believe that it is legal for a man to hit his wife. In addition, the NCS asks about assault in general, rather than assault specifically at the hands of a partner; many victims may be unaware that being beaten by one's partner constitutes the crime of "assault." Finally, intense fear of repercussions and shame over domestic violence increases the probability that victims of domestic violence may fail to admit their own victimization. Female victims of domestic violence often believe that they are at fault for the failure of the relationship (Langhinrichsen-Rohling, Neidig, & Thorn, 1995) and, as such, they may be motivated to conceal the crime. Their dependence on their partners (including financial dependence) may also motivate them to remain silent, even in the face of what may be brutal violence (Saunders & Size, 1986; Straus, 1992b).

National Family Violence Surveys. Self-report surveys share some of the problems of victimization surveys, especially those of fallible memory and reluctance to report on account of shame. However, some self-report surveys use improved methods of interviewing that are much more likely to elicit frank information about family violence from an otherwise reluctant respondent. In the area of domestic violence, these surveys stand out above the rest, and have provided the nation with the most accurate statistics on domestic violence to date. These surveys are called the National Family Violence Surveys of 1975 and 1985, and they are conducted by the researchers from the Family Research Laboratory at the University of New Hampshire.

These surveys include thousands of American households, and they address the problems of estimating the frequency of domestic violence in an unique manner. Rather than speaking to either perpetrators or victims only, the researchers surveyed husbands half of the time, and wives half of the time. For each household, either the husband or the wife was chosen at random and asked to report the frequency of violence in the household. However, because the researchers were interested in gaining as much information as possible, they did not ask respondents questions like, "Are you criminally violent with your wife?" Rather, the interviewers pointed out that all families had conflicts, and then gave each individual a list of specific behaviors and asked him or her if that behavior was engaged in during conflicts. The list included benign items such as "discussions," but also violent items such as "shoving," "pushing," and "punching."

Because no one was interviewed using legal terms such as *assault,* a respondent did not need to know that punching a spouse is a crime in order to report it to the interviewer. Both respondents who thought the violence was legal, and those who knew it was criminal, could equally report the violence. In addition, the way in which the question was asked tended to minimize any feelings of shame that might have prevented someone from admitting to the violence. The violent items were presented in the context of a list of possible responses, and were not emphasized by the researchers. In addition, the researchers reminded respondents that "all" families fight; therefore, conflict was not made to seem deviant.

Most of what we know today about the types and frequencies of U.S. domestic violence is the result of studies such as those conducted at the University of New Hampshire. The UCR and the NCS may be better estimates of street violence. What are the different types of street and domestic violence, and how common are they?

STREET VIOLENCE

Assault

The Bureau of Justice Statistics at the National Institute of Justice releases crime statistics gathered by the UCR and the NCS. For example, in 1992 there were 1,848,520 cases of assault reported in the NCS.[1] How many of these occurred between strangers? Two thirds (67%) of the victims reported that they did not know the perpetrator. Approximately half of these victims were women. Only one third of the respondents of assault reported knowing their attackers. Despite these numbers, most criminologists believe, on the basis of the majority of victimization research, that most assaults occur between people who know each other (Cervi, 1991; Kandel-Englander, 1992). The NCS numbers seem to suggest that many victims of domestic assault are either unwilling or unable to report it to interviewers from the National Institute of Justice, or do not conceptualize their domestic victimization as a case of "assault" (Kandel-Englander, 1992). In any case, 1,232,340 cases of stranger assault extrapolate to one half of 1% of the U.S. population being the victim of assault by strangers. Stranger assault seems to occur to both men and women, in roughly equal numbers; simple assault is approximately 1.5 times more common than aggravated assault on the streets.

Assault using firearms is becoming increasingly common, including the use of automatic and semiautomatic weapons (Associated Press, 1995e). Almost all victims of perpetrators carrying a gun reported that the weapon was a handgun. Despite these numbers, Americans remain ambivalent about gun control. They are more in agreement about the seemingly increasingly bizarre nature of assault in the United States. For example, a magazine salesman in Texas recently assaulted an 88-year-old woman because she refused to buy a subscription (Associated Press, 1995g). In an assault that allegedly mimicked a movie scene, two robbers set a New York subway clerk on fire by squirting flammable liquid into his booth (Reuters, 1995b). Finally, two sisters in Stratford, Connecticut, assaulted a woman with a jar of sauce when she moved their grocery cart without asking (Associated Press, 1995h). Although rates of assault are increasing, it seems to be these type of attacks—provoked by seemingly trivial issues—that frighten Americans most, in addition to the perception that when assault is not punished, it escalates to more serious violent crimes. A case in point is that of Gerald Craffey, a 29-year-old cleaning man, who had assaulted

---

[1] I used the 1992 NCS here because the UCR does not divide crime into categories reflecting type of victim (stranger vs. nonstranger), and the 1993 NCS has not yet been calculated by type of victim.

women in 1989, 1991, and 1992 without significant punishment before he was ultimately arraigned for murder in 1995 (Ellement, 1995).

Homicide

Homicide is counted only by the UCR because the NCS is a victim survey and, obviously, homicide victims are unavailable for interviewing. In 1993, 24,526 murders were recorded by authorities. Of these, approximately 13.5% were known to occur between "strangers." It is likely that a somewhat higher proportion did actually occur between strangers because more than one third of the homicides had no information recorded on the relationship or lack of relationship between perpetrator and victim. In any case, it seems probable that the majority of homicides occurred in 1993 between people who knew each other. Again, this is consistent with the hypothesis that most violence occurs intrafamily (Cervi, 1991; Kandel-Englander, 1992). Although Americans tend to believe that they are increasingly likely to be the victim of stranger homicide, the UCR numbers actually suggest that it is relatively rare.

In general, homicide rates in the United States appear to be declining; in the first half of 1995, the FBI reported a decrease of 12%—a substantial drop (Ostrow, 1995). Homicide declines also occurred in cities of more than 1 million citizens. Despite such decreases, however, Americans remained concerned about stranger homicide, for three major reasons: First, juveniles are increasingly responsible for killings (Freeh, 1995); second, homicides seem to be increasingly gruesome and unnecessarily violent (Associated Press, 1995m); and third, killings appear to happen at times in response to trivial provocations. One example of the latter is the case of Donald Graham, a 56-year-old Rhode Island man. Graham, who has been described as a "self-appointed highway vigilante," was driving at night on a highway when he was flashed by another car's headlights. When both cars pulled over and the other driver approached Graham's car, Graham shot and killed the man with a crossbow. Although he later maintained that he was "threatened" by the victim's approaching him, Graham was convicted of murder (Associated Press, 1995k).

Gruesome murders have always existed, but their scope and intensity appear to have increased. One of the most shocking cases happened recently in Illinois, where a woman and two men killed a pregnant woman and sliced open her body to retrieve a baby the killer had wanted; the murderers also killed the pregnant victim's two other children. The killing was described as "unimaginable" by local authorities and was publicized around the country (Associated Press, 1995a). Such publications probably serve to increase the public's fear of stranger homicide, although the risk of it may actually be decreasing.

Sexual Assault

Apart from assault and homicide, one of the most commonly perpetrated violent crimes is sexual assault. The 1992 NCS counted sexual assault in two ways: For half of the sample, it retained the traditional NCS wording by not asking respondents directly if they had been sexually assaulted. Rather, they asked respondents if they had been physically assaulted or assaulted in "some other way." Not surprisingly, very few respondents volunteered the information that they had been sexually assaulted, and the numbers from this half of the sample yielded the estimate that only 140,930 sexual assaults had occurred in the United States in 1992. Of these, approximately half of the victims reported that they did not know their perpetrator. These numbers suggested that 68,140 rapes took place between strangers in 1992.

However, the second half of the respondents was given a newer version of the NCS, and the numbers obtained here show how misleading the traditional version of the NCS was when estimating rates of sexual assault. These respondents were asked directly about sexual assault: "Incidents involving forced or unwanted sexual acts are often difficult to talk about. Have you ever been forced or coerced to engage in unwanted sexual activity by (a) someone you didn't know before; (b) a casual acquaintance; or (c) someone you know well." This newer version yielded a much higher estimate of sexual assault incidence: It suggested that fully 607,000 sexual assaults had occurred in the United States in 1992. Unfortunately, the data on the type of victim (stranger vs. nonstranger) have not yet been released.

By 1993, 100% of the sample was interviewed using the new wording, and this yielded an estimate of 485,000 sexual assaults for that year. This was a significant drop from the estimate of 607,000 for 1992, suggesting that the incidence of sexual assault decreased between 1992 and 1993. Again, however, data on type of victim are not yet available. If we extrapolate from the sample who were given the traditional wording in 1992, it could be estimated that in 1993 approximately 240,000 stranger rapes took place. This estimate should be considered extremely tentative, however, because the proportion of stranger rape victims who volunteer information may be different from the proportion of stranger rape victims who admit to the assault when directly asked.

As with assault and homicide, however, the public fears sexual assault, particularly by strangers. Cases such as Lisa Rene's also serve to fan that flame. Lisa Rene was a 16-year-old girl, staying in her own apartment, when it was broken into by several men claiming to be from the FBI. She called 911 and was recorded begging for help and screaming in terror as they dragged her away; they spent the next 2 days raping her repeatedly before finally burying her alive (Associated Press, 1995c). Although the data suggest that sexual assault rates are actually decreasing, such cases enliven the public's fear that strangers are apt to commit sexual torture.

Juvenile Violence

Almost half of all persons arrested in 1994 were under the age of 25 (Freeh, 1995). Greenwood (1995) provided an excellent review of violent street crime among juveniles. For example, he pointed out that 3 to 4 out of every 10 boys growing up today in urban America will be arrested before their 18th birthdays. Greenwood also pointed out that the UCR may be the best indicator of youth violence because victim surveys depend on the victims' abilities to determine that their attackers are juvenile. Recent UCR data reviewed by Greenwood reveals that juveniles aged 10 to 17 account for 11% of the U.S. population, but fully 16% of violent felonies. Although the juvenile index arrest rate increased by only 9% between 1985 and 1990—a slower increase than the adult arrest rate (15%)—the decline in juvenile rates is accounted for by property offenses, not by violent offenses. In 1980, juveniles committed 10% of homicides; by 1990 they were committing 13.6%. Between 1984 and 1992, the number of juveniles arrested for homicide who were under age 15 increased by 50%. Although these numbers are theoretically for all juvenile crimes, domestic violence by teenagers is less frequently recorded and prosecuted than domestic violence by adults; thus, the UCR for juveniles is probably a reasonable estimate of their rates of street crime.

Why do juveniles commit violent crimes? Sometimes the motive seems more clear, as in the case of Reiko Imazaki, a high school star athlete who had publicly apologized to his father for "not becoming all that his father wanted him to be" before killing him 2 years later—while telling him he loved him (Associated Press, 1995i). Many cases of youths killing family members are attributed to abuse; Gerard McCra, a 15-year-old, allegedly shot and killed his entire family because of abuse he claimed to have suffered for many years (Associated Press, 1995l). Reporters frequently find that perpetrators often give banal justifications for juvenile violent crimes; John Claypool, who admitted to two murders when he was 14 years old, said he did it "to see what it was like to kill" (Taus, 1995). A 17-year-old high school student punched an elderly teacher as his classmates cheered, claiming later that the 78-year-old man had "bumped him" (Hart, 1995). Despite this, the causes of juvenile violence run deep, and such offenders usually demonstrate a variety of risk factors for early aggression (as is discussed in the biosocial model of chapter 6).

DOMESTIC VIOLENCE

Child Abuse

Child abuse is usually separated into four subtypes: physical abuse; sexual abuse; neglect; and verbal, psychological, or emotional abuse. Each of these four subtypes has its own definition and incidence rate. The identity of the victims as children is the common thread.

Physical Abuse. The consequences of physical abuse were originally termed *battered child syndrome* (Kempe, Silverman, & Steele, 1962). Battered child syndrome was identifiable only by x-ray because it was characterized by the presence of several fractured bones in various stages of healing, suggesting ongoing severe physical abuse. However, it became increasingly recognized that the physical abuse of children can take many less severe forms. Today, our knowledge is still evolving, and even definitions can be difficult. Some consider that any physical aggression toward a child constitutes physical abuse; however, most U.S. parents believe that mild physical punishment, such as spanking, is actually good for children. Many who disapprove of more severe violence against children would state that physical punishment could not possibly constitute "abuse." Others would agree that spanking children with the hand is not abusive, whereas spanking them with any object is, because using objects greatly increases the risk of injury to the child. Still others would differentiate belts from other objects in cases in which children are not permanently injured.

As you can see, it is difficult, if not impossible, to arrive at a definition on which everyone would agree. However, for the purposes of this chapter, and with the understanding that there are other definitions, *physical abuse* is defined as "physically hitting children severely enough to cause injuries, including relatively mild ones such as bruises or cuts." According to this definition, spanking a child on the buttocks without leaving any marks or injuries would not be abusive. However, shaking a child, which can result in serious internal injuries, would be considered abusive. Similarly, whipping a child or spanking a child and leaving bruises or cuts would be abusive.

How frequently does child physical abuse occur? In 1985, the National Family Survey asked parents in more than 8,000 households how they behaved toward their children. Specifically, the researchers asked parents if they ever engaged in any of the following: kicking, biting, or punching; hitting or trying to hit with an object; beating up; choking, burning, or scalding; threatening with a knife or gun; or using a knife or gun. The rates of "serious" child physical abuse subsequently reported did not include minor violence (such as slapping a child). Furthermore, hitting with an object was kept in a separate category because although it substantially increases the risk of real injury, many parents hit with objects in a strictly disciplinary context.

The NFVS found that 2.3% of U.S. children (23 per 1,000 children) were seriously physically abused in 1985. This percentage suggests that approximately 1.5 million children per year are physically abused in the United States (Straus & Gelles, 1990). Of course, the actual rate of physical child abuse is almost certainly significantly higher than these estimates because many abusive parents may be reluctant to admit that they assault their children. When the rate was recalculated to include children who were hit with objects, the NFVS found that fully 11% of children were physically abused, suggesting that as many as 6.9 million U.S. children may be physically abused each year, depending on the definition used.

Child physical abuse can begin in infancy. Michael Bertrand, a 22-year-old father from Warwick, Rhode Island, "beat his 5½-week-old baby son so savagely that the boy suffered brain damage, broken ribs, and spinal cord injuries" (Associated Press, 1995f). Child physical abuse does not end at puberty. As the NFVS showed, many teenagers are also physically abused. Furthermore, even minor violence, such as slapping, carries increased psychological significance during adolescence. Although most parents view slapping small children as normal, the percentage of parents who view slapping, spanking, or shoving teenage children as normal is much smaller. In our culture, it is generally acceptable to hit small children but not adolescent children. Despite these widely shared cultural values, the NFVS found that one third of parents admitted having hit their teenage child at least once during 1985. Further, 7% of U.S. teenagers were victims of severe physical abuse during that year. Adolescents may be better able to defend themselves physically, but because the vast majority remain generally obedient to and dependent on their parents, they remain vulnerable, and thus these rates of physical abuse do indicate a serious problem. Even famous teenagers have been beaten by their parents, as in the case of tennis star Steffi Graf, who was allegedly beaten and kicked by her father while training (Associated Press, 1995d).

The NFVS may be one of the best sources, but there are other sources of statistics on child abuse. The best known is the number of child abuse cases reported by Child Protective Services (CPS); these numbers reflect the cases of child abuse that are detected and treated. In 1984, CPS found that almost 3% of U.S. children were reported to the authorities as victims of abuse; this number includes all types of abuse, such as physical abuse, sexual abuse, and neglect. Only about .68% of the reported cases reflected strictly physical abuse. This small percentage, in contrast to the percentage found by the NFVS, suggests that most victims of child physical abuse are not being detected and treated by CPS. This is undoubtedly due not only to the difficulty in detecting such cases, but also to the limited funding CPS receives and its consequently overworked social workers.

Sexual Abuse. This type of child abuse involves using a child in a sexual manner to arouse or satisfy an adult. Sexual abuse includes a wide range of behaviors, including (but not limited to) exposure, inappropriate touching, sexual contact, and intercourse. In one court, a father was convicted of child sexual abuse for paying another man to rape his 9-year-old daughter while he watched, although he did not molest the girl himself (Milne, 1995). The child's compliance, coercion, or the degree of force used is not relevant in the determination of child sexual abuse (although it may be important in determining the seriousness of the offense). Children, by nature of their inexperience and lack of maturity, are not capable of consent and thus any sexual contact with a child constitutes sexual abuse on the part of the adult, even if the adult claims that the child "enjoyed" the abuse or "wanted" it. In fact, claims that the child wanted or enjoyed the sexual contact are legally and psychologically irrelevant; sexual abuse is abusive even if there was in fact enjoyment (Hazzard, Celano, Gould, Lawry, & Webb, 1995).

How frequently does child sexual abuse occur in the United States? As in the cases of other crimes against children and other sexual crimes, many victims are too young to report, too ashamed to report, reluctant to report a family member (e.g., a stepfather), or all three. The UCR does not list child sexual abuse as a separate crime, but rather, includes it in a group of other violent sexual offenses. Finkelhor (1988), of the University of New Hampshire, is one of the preeminent researchers in the field of child sexual abuse. His studies indicate that approximately 25% to 33% of women recall being sexually abused as children. Men admit victimization at lesser rates: approximately 10% report that they were molested as children. In 1983, Russell found similar results in a study of San Francisco women; of these women, 28% reported some sexual victimization during childhood (before age 14). Finkelhor, and other researchers, have found that most victims never report the offense to authorities (Finkelhor, 1988; Russell, 1983).

Neglect. Neglect occurs when a custodial adult fails to see that a child's basic needs are provided for. Basic needs include (but may not be limited to) the need for food, clothing, shelter, schooling, and affection. The precise definition of *neglect* is still evolving. For example, a custodian may feel that a child is not neglected if he or she is fed and clothed; however, a court may rule that custodians who do not force a child to attend school are guilty of neglect.

Adults are not considered to be guilty of neglect when they are unable (rather than unwilling) to meet a child's basic needs; for example, a mother who is starving herself, with no food sources, is not neglectful because she fails to feed her child. Whether or not an adult is neglectful when they choose to meet their own needs rather than their child's (assuming that they only have enough resources for one) is a matter of controversy and individual judgment.

The incidence of child neglect rises with poverty (Baumrind, 1994; Jones, 1992). The exact number of neglected children is difficult to estimate because at least some neglected children may never be noticed by authorities (National Research Council, 1993). Generally, gross neglect of children is categorized with child physical abuse of various sorts, and thus is included in physical abuse statistics.

Emotional, Psychological, and Verbal Abuse. Like physical abuse, emotional abuse can be difficult, if not impossible, to define specifically. *Emotional abuse* generally refers to "the persistent degradation or humiliation of children" (Bartol, 1995). A child who is routinely made to feel stupid, ugly, worthless, ashamed, unlovable, or of no value is considered to be emotionally abused. Emotional abuse does not include physical or sexual abuse. However, all child abuse involves the degradation and humiliation of children emotionally (to some degree), and it may be that the "key ingredient" in the damaging affects of abuse is the emotional abuse that is always present. That is, there may be children who are "only" emotionally abused, but all children who are physically or sexually abused are also emotionally abused and damaged.

SPOUSE ABUSE

> Certain women should be struck regularly, like gongs.
> —Noel Coward (*Private Lives*)

For the purposes of studying abuse between spouses, little distinction (if any) is typically drawn between married couples and cohabitating couples. Violence between couples who are not living together is typically termed *dating violence*, although the terms *spouse* or *marital* may be used if the couple has a long-standing relationship (e.g., if the couple does not live together but has been dating for many years, or once lived together in the same household).

Like child abuse, spouse abuse can be roughly divided into different categories: physical abuse and sexual abuse. Neglect is not typically an issue between adults, except possibly in the case of dependent adults (such as those who are ill) or elderly adults (who may be dependent on another person for their basic needs). In this section, I describe physical abuse and sexual abuse between "spouses" (married and cohabitating couples) and between dating couples.

Physical Abuse

Unlike child abuse, the physical abuse of women includes even minor violence, such as shoving and slapping. Although it may be legal to use minor violence with a child, any violence (minor or severe) against an adult constitutes assault. However, the distinction is not crucial; however common (or controversial) minor violence against women may be, severe violence is most definitely too typical an event in many women's lives. Domestic violence is the single largest cause of injury to U.S. women, and four women are killed every day by men who batter them to death (J. Jones, 1990).

What is the frequency of physical spouse abuse in the United States? The 1985 NFVS found that approximately 16% of U.S. couples had some type of physical, aggressive encounter with each other during the previous year. Of course, the survey also differentiated between all violence, minor and severe, and severe violence (kicking, punching, stabbing, shooting, etc.) only. Across the United States, the rate of severe violence between spouses is, of course, somewhat lower: 6.3% of couples were severely violent with each other during 1985.

Although child abuse is typically studied as a parent-to-child phenomenon, spouse abuse is a two-way street: that is, it can consist of either husband-to-wife abuse or wife-to-husband abuse. The 1985 NFVS asked about both types of abuse. However, the results are not simple to interpret, because the two types of abuse are potentially different in many ways. First, men are usually physically larger than women and thus their aggression is more likely to result in the woman being injured. Whereas a man hitting a woman is likely to cause injury, a woman hitting a man is less likely to do so. Both men and women are typically aware of this different potential for injury, and this awareness is a factor in the determination of abuse. That is, violence is more abusive if perpetrators know that they will probably injure their victims; it is less abusive if the perpetrators believe that they are not capable of injuring their victims.

Perhaps the most significant difference between male and female spousal violence is, however, intent. Women and men may behave violently toward their mates for very different reasons. Most notably, men are more likely to hit offensively; women, self-defensively (Adler, 1991; Cazenave & Zahn, 1992; Mann, 1992).

It is easier to interpret the 1985 NFVS findings when these facts are understood. Interestingly, although 3.4% of couples were characterized by "wife beating" (husband-to-wife violence), 4.8% of couples were characterized by wife-to-husband violence. This means that at least 1.8 million women were being beaten in 1985, and at least 2.6 million men were being assaulted by their wives. It is probable, however, that these numbers are not strictly comparable. As discussed previously, most severe husband-to-wife violence results in injury, whereas much of the wife-to-husband violence does not. This is one reason why beaten wives are more likely to be noticed: Their injuries are apparent, or force them to seek medical or police attention. Second, much of the wife-to-husband violence appears to be an attempt at self-defense. (Much more about the use of violence as self-defense by beaten wives is discussed in later chapters.) These arguments are not intended to deny that there are males who are truly victimized and beaten by their female partners, and wife-to-husband violence should not be merely dismissed. Of course, reciprocal blows may escalate a physical fight to the point where real injury may occur. However, evidence does suggest that most of the wife-to-husband cases of violence involve either attempts to strike without expecting to cause any serious injury or attempts at self-defense (Adler, 1991; Cazenave & Zahn, 1992; Mann, 1992). In any case, because couples may understandably be reluctant to admit to violence, these numbers should be considered a probable underestimate of the true incidence.

Sexual Abuse (Marital Rape)

Some scholars in this area have called the marriage license a "license to rape" (Finkelhor & Yllo, 1985). It is true that historically, in the Judeo-Christian culture (among others), the fact that a woman was his wife gave a man full rights to sexual contact with her—her consent, or lack of it, was legally irrelevant. Certainly many moral and ethical people have deplored forced sexual contact, even between spouses. Legally, however, until very recently, a man has had the right to force his wife to have any sexual contact he wanted. In fact, the definition of *sexual assault* has typically been phrased as something similar to: forced sexual intercourse with a woman who is not his wife. Forced intercourse with a spouse, therefore, could not be legally termed *rape* or *sexual assault*. Today, many states have rewritten statutes to include spouses in the pool of potential victims of sexual assault.

It is extremely difficult to estimate the incidence of sexual assault between spouses. Most, if not all, victims believe that it is not possible, technically, to be "raped" by one's spouse. Therefore, merely asking women if they have ever been raped by their husband is likely to elicit an answer of "no," even if forced sexual interaction has occurred. Asking women if their husbands have ever "forced them to have sex" (thereby avoiding the confusion spawned by the word *rape*) is more productive. Of course, a victim of marital rape may decline to admit forced sexual interaction with her spouse because of intense shame; such an admission is tantamount to admitting a disturbed marital relationship. Thus, any statistics on marital rape should be considered underestimates of the true frequency.

The United States has a very high rate of sexual assault. Because it is a crime that is frequently unreported, victimization statistics (rather than statistics reflecting the number of arrests or convictions for rape) probably provide the most accurate estimates. In 1983, Russell reported on a sample of 930 women living in California. Her study and others suggest that 25% to 35% of women experience either a completed or attempted rape. Kilpatrick's (1993) data suggest that 40% of all rapes are perpetrated by husbands or other male companions. We can extrapolate from these numbers to estimate that 36 million women are rape victims each year, 14.4 million of them victims of marital rape. Official statistics based on the number of cases reported to the authorities would seem to indicate much lower numbers: that only .07% of U.S. women (only 840,000) are sexually assaulted each year. It is difficult to avoid the conclusion that these official numbers tell us a lot more about the reporting rate of sexual assault than they do about the rate of actual victimization.

Dating Violence

Although dating is usually considered an innocent and exciting form of socializing, it all too often also includes violence between dating partners. In the 1980s and 1990s media-publicized cases of date rape began to highlight this issue.

Violence is not confined to the marital relationship. Some evidence has suggested that unmarried dating couples may even be more violent than those who are married (Lane & Gwartney-Gibbs, 1985). College students have been asked about the violence in their relationships; about 20% admit to some degree of physical victimization. The studies usually have made no distinction between male versus female victimization; this makes comparisons with married couple data difficult. One study, in which responses from males and females *were* analyzed separately, found that the use of violence changes with the progression from dating to cohabitation and marriage. That is, males were least likely to be violent in dating relationships and most likely to be violent in marital relationships. Females, on the other hand, were most likely to be violent in dating relationships, less likely to be violent in marital relationships, and least likely to be violent in cohabitating relationships (Stets & Straus, 1990b). The percentage of couples in which both partners were violent was highest among cohabitating couples, compared to dating and married couples.

When severity of violence is considered, a different pattern emerges. When both partners engage in only minor assaults, there appears to be little difference among dating, cohabitating, and married couples. However, in the case of severe assaults, there is a difference. Fully 22% of cohabitating couples are severely violent, in comparison to 10.5% of dating couples and 10.5% of married couples (Stets & Straus, 1990b). When you consider how common cohabitating is today, it is astonishing to think of that figure.

Date Rape. Date rape, as its name implies, involves the sexual assault of a women by a man, not her husband, with whom she is involved in a social, or dating, relationship—sexual or nonsexual. The incidence of date rape has been investigated in two ways: by surveying young, dating women (typically college women) about sexual assaults they may have experienced, and by interviewing young men about whether or not they have ever forced a date to have sex. (Asking a man if he has ever "committed rape" is likely to result in a negative answer; many males may not consider forcing a date to have sex as "rape.") Surveys of college women generally find that approximately 20% to 28% report having been forced to have some sort of sexual encounter, such as forced intercourse, forced oral sex, and so on (Koss, Gidycz, & Wisniewski, 1987; Yegidis, 1986). The number of males who admit to forcing a date to have sex is, predictably, somewhat smaller: About 5% to 15% of males generally admit to this type of behavior (Koss et al., 1987; Rapaport & Burkhart, 1984). Again, because it is so rare for date rape to be reported, official crime statistics do not, at this time, provide useful information.

ELDER ABUSE

Estimates of the frequency of elder abuse have only recently become a cause for concern. It is difficult to measure elder abuse for two reasons. First, what constitutes abuse of the elderly? Older adults may have varying degrees of physical dependency, but psychologically (unless disease intervenes), they are adults. Therefore, they are probably less vulnerable to verbal and psychological abuse, compared to children. Second, elder abuse is difficult to measure because it is so hidden. Young children are regularly seen in public places: They frequently attend school or day care, for example. These external contacts give society opportunities to discover child abuse. However, apart from medical care, older adults may be entirely housebound.

Despite these difficulties, official data on violent crimes against older Americans suggests a rate of approximately 132,000 crimes in 1994 (U.S. Department of Justice, 1994). A survey of older Americans in the Boston area yielded a much higher estimate: Pillemer and Finkelhor (1988) estimated that there are approximately 1 million cases of elder abuse in the United States each year, suggesting that many such cases may never be reported. The cruelty of elder abuse may be compounded by the victim's complete financial and physical dependence on the abuser. Because older victims (unlike children) are usually dependent for the remainder of their lives, escape is improbable and defense a physical impossibility. Of course, as adults, these victims have advantages that children totally lack, such as a greater psychological ability to withstand stressors and trauma.

PAN-VIOLENCE

Pan-violence is a term that describes violent individuals who are violent both in the home (with family members) and outside the home (violent in the streets). How common is pan-violence? Are most violent street criminals also abusive toward their families? Are most domestic abusers also violent street criminals? Alternatively, are we discussing two distinct, separate types of individuals: those who offend only against family, and those who offend only in the streets?

These may seem to be obvious questions. However, very little research has actually addressed them. The reason for this "blind spot" is probably overspecialization among researchers. Although criminologists and psychologists have tended to focus on street or stranger violence, sociologists have (until recently) made up the most important group of researchers studying family violence. Because the two groups of researchers often publish in different journals and attend different conventions, the two kinds of violence are usually not examined simultaneously in the same research study (Cervi, 1991; Fagan, Stewart, & Hansen, 1983; Fagan & Wexler, 1987; Hotaling et al., 1989; Kandel-Englander, 1992; Shields, McCall, & Hanneke, 1988). This leaves a fundamental gap in what we know about violent behavior. Are people who are violent, violent everywhere and with anyone? Or do violent people choose their victims, and confine their violence to one arena?

A few studies have compared the arrest rates for street violence of wife batterers and nonviolent husbands (Graff, 1979; Straus, 1985). These studies found that those who are violent inside the home (i.e., batterers) are significantly more likely to be violent toward nonfamily persons, compared to nonviolent husbands (Browne, 1984; Fagan et al., 1983; Faulk, 1974; Flynn, 1977; Gayford, 1975; Rounsaville, 1978; Stacey & Shupe, 1983; Walker, 1979). It is difficult to draw any firm conclusions from these studies, however.

First, some of these studies examine only "clinical" samples (samples of people who seek psychological help). Although such samples do give some information, we cannot assume that all violent perpetrators are similar to those who actually seek help for their violence. Second, some studies did not look at violent behavior per se; because it can be difficult to measure violent behavior directly, researchers chose to assess attitudes toward violence, or use other indirect indices. Again, although this approach can yield interesting information, it cannot substitute for a direct approach. Finally, although the rate of street violence in batterers was considered, the researchers failed to ask the opposite question: What is the incidence of family violence among street offenders? Only by examining both sides of this coin can we understand the relationship between family violence and street violence, and estimate the frequency of pan-violence.

One study has focused more specifically on the issue of pan-violence (Kandel-Englander, 1992). This study examined, in a representative sample of unincarcerated U.S. males, the proportion of men who offend only outside their families ("street-violent" males); the proportion of men who are violent only toward their wives ("batterers"); and the proportion of men who are violent in both spheres ("pan-violent" individuals).

This study was part of the 1985 NFVS, which included 6,002 U.S. households, chosen randomly (Straus & Gelles, 1990). Half of the time wives were interviewed, and half of the time husbands were interviewed, yielding about 3,000 interviews with men. Of these 3,000 interviews, approximately 2,300 men answered questions about their violent behaviors both inside and outside the home. These 2,300 interviews are the basis for the study.

Each household was contacted by telephone and interviewed for an average of 35 minutes. The researchers set certain criteria that a household had to meet in order to be included in the survey. For example, households had to include adults who were either presently married or cohabitating, or who had been divorced or separated within the last 2 years; single-parent households were also included if they had a child under 18 years of age living in the household. Most of the eligible households agreed to cooperate with the survey; only 16% refused to respond to the interview (Straus & Gelles, 1990).

Violent behavior within the marriage was assessed as part of the Conflict Tactics Scale (CTS). The CTS is a scale that estimates the level of husband-to-wife violence by asking each husband to reject or endorse any of a list of specific behaviors that he may have committed during "fights" with his wife. This list of behaviors ranges from calm discussion to serious violence. Subjects who were considered "batterers" were those who admitted doing any or all of the following: throwing something, pushing, grabbing, shoving, slapping, kicking, biting, hitting with a fist, trying to hit with an object, beating up, choking, threatening with or using a knife or gun.

Street violence was assessed by asking the men if they had physically fought with and/or injured anyone who was not in their family. Those men who admitted to this behavior were considered to be men who did have some violent tendencies outside the family.

Sample Characteristics

Before the results of these interviews on pan-violence are examined, we must determine what the sample of U.S. males "looked like." Seventy-one percent was White; 11.4% was Black, 9.6% was Hispanic, and the remaining 1.8% was "other" (e.g., Pacific Islanders). Half of the sample was blue-collar workers, or farm workers with a high school education or less; the remaining half was white-collar workers, or farm workers, owners, or managers who had more than a high school education. The ages of the men sampled ranged from 18 to 90 years old, with an average age of 42.923 years (SD = 14.53). These numbers tell us that the men in this sample were not just "high-risk," inner-city, poorly educated or unemployed; rather, they represented a broad range of U.S. men.

Most (95%) of the men interviewed were married or cohabitating with a woman. The remaining 5% were divorced, separated, or widowed, all within the last 2 years. Thus, this study examined primarily married or cohabitating men.

Results of the Study

Of the men in this sample, 311 (15%) admitted assaulting either a spouse, someone outside their family, or both. Figure 2.1 shows the proportion of violent men who were batterers, street-violent, and pan-violent.

Batterers. Most of the violent men in this representative sample were men who beat their wives. Although fully three quarters (240) of the 311 violent men admitted assaulting their wives, only 13% (32) of these wife beaters also assaulted individuals outside of their families (i.e., were pan-violent). Most of the batterers (87%) denied that they ever used violence against nonfamily persons.

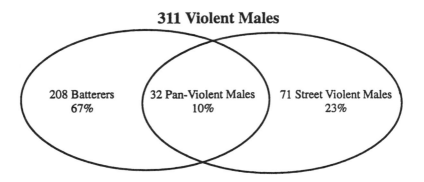

FIG. 2.1. Proportion of men who are batterers, street-violent, and pan-violent.

This pattern suggests that most criminal violence by U.S. men may be perpetrated in the home, and against families, rather than on the street (Gelles, 1985; Saunders, 1992; Shields et al., 1988).

Street Offenders. Of the 311 violent men, one third admitted to assaulting persons outside their family. Of all these offenders, almost one third were pan-violent (i.e., they also assaulted their wives). Nonetheless, it was still true that more than two thirds of the nonfamily offenders assaulted only extrafamilial victims. Like the batterers, most street offenders "specialized."

One interesting difference between batterers and nonfamily offenders emerged, however. Recall that of the batterers, a mere 13% were pan-violent. In contrast, almost one third of street-violent males were pan-violent. Thus, the chances of being pan-violent are much higher if a man admits to street violence than if he admits to family violence.

Pan-Violent Offenders. Thirty-two men (10% of the violent men, or 1.5% of the entire sample) admitted assaulting both their wives and people outside their homes. As just noted, the remaining 90% were violent either inside or outside of the family, but not in both spheres. Thus, pan violence was an unusual phenomenon in this representative sample of U.S. men.

In the debate on the causes of violence, this is an important finding. It suggests that the vast majority (here, 90%) of violent men choose to confine their violence to one arena, either the street or their home. This, in turn, suggests that even if individuals do have marked personality or biological tendencies toward violence, most are still able to control their impulses well enough to choose their victims.

Violent and Nonviolent Men and Their Characteristics. The four groups of men (batterers, street offenders, pan-violent men, and nonviolent men) were compared across several demographic variables: age, race (White vs. non-White), and social class (defined as white-collar vs. blue-collar employment). The comparisons revealed the following findings:

1. *Age:* Although the violent men were significantly younger than the nonviolent ones, the three groups of violent men (batterers, street offenders, and pan-violent men) did not differ from each other.

2. *Race:* The pan-violent men were different from the other violent men. Although 51.5% of the pan-violent men were non-White, only 35.5% of the batterers and 34% of the street offenders were non-White. The nonviolent group had the lowest proportion of non-White men (28%).

3. *Social Class:* Here, the subjects divided into two major groups: the batterers and nonviolent men, versus the pan-violent men and the street offenders. The batterers and the nonviolent men were almost equally likely

to have white-collar as blue-collar jobs. The pan-violent men and street offenders were different; these two groups were disproportionately blue-collar (71% and 76.9%, respectively). This finding suggests that although social class may be an important correlate of both pan-violence or street violence, it is much less strongly associated with domestic violence. It echoes the findings of many previous studies that family violence occurs across all social classes, whereas street violence tends to be more confined to lower income groups (Bartol, 1991).

Why Are Batterers Less Likely to Be Pan-Violent? One explanation for this pattern of violence can be inferred from the social class of the men sampled. In comparison to pan-violent and street offenders, batterers were more likely to be white-collar workers. Perhaps they are motivated to confine their violence to the family because they stand to lose status and income; in contrast, the primarily blue-collar street offenders have less to lose and thus may behave violently wherever they choose.

Why Do Violent Men Tend to Specialize? Remember, fully 90% of violent men specialized. Why is pan-violence apparently the exception?

A spouse or other family member is a relatively "safe" target to assault. Domestic violence is the least likely type of violence to be detected and prosecuted, as can be seen from official statistics reporting that most convicted violent felons are not convicted for family violence (although most violence in the United States is family violence; Straus, 1976). Assault outside the family is a much riskier crime.

Street offenders, already exposed to the risk of societal punishment, do not have the same motive as batterers to confine their violence to the family. However, they may have other motives. For example, some street offenders who have no moral scruples about engaging in bar brawls or fist fights with other men may be repulsed by the prospect of striking a woman or a child. (Recall that all street offenders in this study had families.) In addition, it is possible that men who engage in street violence spend little time at home, thereby lessening their opportunity to assault their families.

Clearly, more research needs to be done to understand the differences among the four groups, batterers, street offenders, pan-violent men, and nonviolent men, and many questions will remain.

Social Causes of Violence

Probably the most compelling question asked by those who study violence is, "Why?" Why do individuals engage in such horrifying and destructive behavior? Why do parents beat, and sometimes kill, their helpless children? What motivates sexual assault? Why do once-happy marriages deteriorate into violence? Why would an individual randomly kill dozens of people in a fast-food restaurant? What are the causes of violence? In this chapter, I discuss the major theoretical approaches to this question and begin to consider some of the research findings.

Some basic questions:

1. Are people born violent?
2. Do people learn to be violent?
3. Are violent people "mentally ill"?
4. Are violent people different from other people, apart from their aggressive behavior?

Psychologists and criminologists have studied not only the causes of violence that occur in individuals, but patterns of the incidence of violent crime. For example, they have looked at the question of whether violent people tend to have certain income levels. Income is one factor that is external to individuals, but closely related to their life and choices and thus possibly relevant in the cause of their behaviors. Because external factors can be so important in the causes of all types of behavior, including violence, I begin to examine the causes of violence by looking at factors that are outside the individual. In the next chapters, I examine factors that are internal to the individual and present a model that combines these factors to more accurately explain and predict violent behavior.

External factors can seem deceptively obvious. For example, almost everyone assumes that poverty breeds crime. In fact, this seems like a pretty safe assumption. But in the history of science, many safe assumptions have had to be tested and qualified or discarded. In the study of violent crime, it is critical to remember that there are many different types of crime with different causes. Perhaps poverty breeds some kinds of crime, but not others. Perhaps poverty is not so important in violent crime as in other types of crime. Perhaps it is more important. Furthermore, personal observations can seductively convince us that relationships are much simpler than they really are. Most of us probably feel that we have personally observed that poverty breeds crime—it may appear "obvious" to us that poorer neighborhoods have more crime—yet it is critical to remember that personal observations can be skewed and are therefore not nearly so powerful as empirical evidence.

SOCIAL CLASS, POVERTY, AND VIOLENCE

Many of the causal factors examined in this book are internal, but are nevertheless related to social class and personal income. For example, prenatal health (pregnancy and delivery complications), medical care during childhood (especially regarding head injuries), and similar health outcomes may clearly be influenced by poverty. Although some level of medical care is available to nearly all citizens, there is little doubt that in the United States those with lower incomes are less likely to have high-quality, comprehensive (especially preventative) medical care.

Health is not the only relevant factor related to poverty. For example, children of lower-income parents may be exposed to higher levels of violence in their neighborhoods. That exposure, in turn, enhances their learning of aggressive behavior patterns.

But let us start with the most basic assumption. How clear is it that lower income persons are more likely to be violent than people in higher socioeconomic classes? Is income inversely related to violence, and to domestic violence?

Tittle, Villemez, and Smith (1978) reviewed 53 studies and concluded that there was no compelling evidence of an inverse relationship between social class and criminal behavior, despite some assumption to the contrary. Most of the studies did not support the hypothesis that crime is more common among people with lower incomes. Since their findings were published (Tittle, Villemez, & Smith, 1978), a number of researchers have convincingly demonstrated that the conclusions were premature (e.g., Braithwaite, 1981). Nevertheless, their work was important because it motivated the research community to re-examine the relationship between social class and criminal and violent behavior, instead of merely assuming that an inverse relationship existed.

We are particularly interested in the relationship between social class and violent criminal behavior, including domestic violence. Although Tittle et al. did not specifically address violence, several of their critics did. For example, Braithwaite (1981) pointed out that Tittle et al. failed to consider the relationship between social class and different types of criminal behavior (e.g., domestic vs. street violence, or even violent vs. property crime). Thornberry and Farnworth (1982) reviewed many studies and did consider different types of offending. They concluded that there was compelling evidence of an inverse relationship between adult crime and social status— the higher the crime rate, the lower the social status. They also provided an interesting explanation for the difference between their conclusions and Tittle et al.'s. Thornberry and Farnworth found that although there was an inverse relationship among adult offenders, juvenile crime did not show this relationship—and most of the 53 studies that Tittle et al. reviewed focused on juvenile male offenders. Another intriguing conclusion was that the criminal's own social class was much more strongly related to criminal behavior than the social status of his father. So, perhaps the social class of the families in which offenders grow up is less crucial; perhaps more important is the social class they attain for themselves.

Thornberry and Farnworth also noted the importance of considering White and non-White subjects separately, because the strongest inverse relationship between social class and crime was seen in non-White adults in their study. Clelland and Carter (1980) noted that Thornberry and Farnworth's work is important in interpreting Tittle et al.'s because it emphasized that social class may be more strongly related to the criminality of certain types of offenders and offenses than to that of others. In summary, non-Whites, violent offenders, and adults (vs. juvenile offenders) are most likely to be poor.

The studies discussed here all focused on crime outside of the family. However, researchers have also examined the relationship between social class and family violence. Studies suggest that men of lower socioeconomic class are more likely to engage in wife abuse than are men of higher socioeconomic class (Kaufman Kantor & Straus, 1987/1990). Of 11 studies examining the husband's educational attainment (one commonly used measure of social class) and the risk of his being abusive toward his wife (Hotaling & Sugarman, 1986), the results were as follows:

1. Eight found a significant inverse relationship (i.e., the lower the social status, the greater the violence).
2. Two found no relationship between family violence and social status.
3. One found a curvilinear relationship (with more family violence at the poorest and richest ends of the social status spectrum, and less in the middle class).

Thus, the majority of the research reviewed indicated that the lower the social class, the greater the chance of at least one type of family violence (spouse abuse). None of these studies, however, addressed the question of how, or if, the social class of these domestically violent men was related to their violent criminality outside the home.

Research on social class and both criminal behavior in general and family violence in particular suffers from a significant, yet common, limitation: To date, only violence inside or outside the family setting tends to be the focus (Fagan & Wexler, 1987). As pointed out earlier (Hotaling & Sugarman, 1986), researchers tend to look at either family violence, or at crime and violence outside the family—not both. Given the findings of the study by Kandel-Englander (1992) discussed earlier, that domestic and street-violent men may be very different groups of offenders, it is of interest to consider the differences in social class between family and nonfamily-violent offenders.

The social class backgrounds of the four groups of men identified in Kandel-Englander's (1992) study—family offenders, street offenders, pan-violent offenders, and nonviolent men—were examined. Scores on two measures of social class or social status—prestige of occupation and income level—were combined to estimate the social class of each individual. When different types of violence are considered, many similarities between White and non-White violent men appear. First, among all ethnic groups, street-violent men were from a lower social class than nonviolent men, but family-violent men were not different from nonviolent men in social class. Further, pan-violent men did come from a lower social class than family-violent men. In other words, street-violent and pan-violent men seem to come from lower social classes, but family-violent men do not necessarily come from lower social classes in comparison to nonviolent men. This finding makes it apparent why it is important not to just assume that poverty breeds crime. It may breed some kinds of crime, but not others. This does not mean that family violence is unrelated to social class, but is merely less strongly related to social class, when compared to street and pan-violence. Other studies do suggest that there is at least some relationship between social class and domestic violence (Kaufman Kantor et al., 1987/1990).

The summary here is a good one for all offenders in the study, but how valid is it for different racial and ethnic groups? Social class scores suggest two major groups of White subjects: pan-violent and street-violent men, who come from lower social classes; and family-violent and nonviolent men, who come from higher social classes.

For non-White subjects, the pattern is more complex. In some ways, non-White men were similar to White men: the street-violent are from a lower social class; the nonviolent and the family-violent, from a higher (and are similar to each other).

For the pan-violent non-White men, however, the picture looked different when occupational prestige and income, the two measures of social class that had covaried in the other subjects were considered separately. Although the pan-violent non-White men were lowest of all in income, they were actually very high in occupational prestige. It is precisely such puzzling findings as this that demonstrate why experts do not make simple assumptions about social class and violent crime. One possible explanation is that pan-violent non-White men may cluster in low-income high-prestige occupations, such as those associated with some types of crime (e.g., drug sales); however, this is purely speculative because this study did not have the data to address the question of precise field of occupation.

EDUCATION AND VIOLENCE

Does the level of education an individual achieves have an impact on his tendency to be violent, either across the board, with his family, or on the street? One approach to this question is to compare the number of years of school completed by violent and nonviolent men. In my 1992 study, I began by lumping all three groups of violent men (street, family, and pan) into one "violent" group, and comparing them to nonviolent men. It is interesting to note that although violent and nonviolent men did not differ in the average number of years of school completed, nonviolent men showed a wider distribution than their violent counterparts. In other words, they were more likely to have either very little education or a great deal of education, whereas violent men tended to complete a "middle" number of years of school; they did not tend to drop out of school very early and they did not tend to complete many years.

What might account for this pattern? Perhaps one difference between violent and nonviolent men is how their cultures view education. In some cultures, such as those in more remote rural regions, education is viewed as less necessary, yet there remain strong social controls on violence. Perhaps one group of nonviolent men come from cultures such as these. On the other hand, nonviolent men were also more likely to have attained a great deal of education (e.g., they were more likely to have gone to college). In most cultures, more education means more investment in society, and more to lose by prosecution as a criminal; thus, it is not surprising that more education should be associated with less violence. Finally, perhaps violent men tended to cluster in the "middle" area of educational attainment because they did not succeed in school, on the one hand, but also did not come from cultures that would de-emphasize education while strongly controlling their violent behaviors. Further research will have to investigate these possibilities more closely.

Interesting as this picture is, as we know by now, these patterns may be very different for White and non-White violent men. When the two groups were considered separately, it became apparent that the violent versus nonviolent education differences hold only for non-White subjects—and are sufficiently marked in them to cause the differences found in the group as a whole. Violent and nonviolent White subjects, it turned out, did not differ much in years of schooling completed. Violent and nonviolent non-White men did. Education, therefore, may be a more important contributor to violence among non-White, than among White, men.

As we have seen, there are real differences between those men who are street- and pan-violent, and those who are violent only with their families. These differences were correlated with differences in education. Overall, family-violent men stayed in school as long, or longer, than nonviolent men. The pan- and street-violent attained, on the average, much less education. When only White men are considered, however, education appeared not to differ between the family-, pan-, and street-violent males. (Note that this analysis only considers the years in school, not the quality of school experiences.) A very different pattern characterized non-White violent men. The family-violent and nonviolent had completed a similar number of years in school; the street- and pan-violent had completed significantly fewer years.

To summarize, then, educational achievement is one indicator of the social status attained by a person. The number of years a child goes to school may be important in determining whether or not that child will become violent, but if this is the case, it is less true for White men than for non-White men. And different types of violent behavior are associated with different levels of education, particularly among non-White men.

Summary: Social Class, Education, and Crime

A variety of evidence does suggest that we should question Thornberry and Farnworth's (1982) finding that social status is strongly related to criminal behavior in non-White populations only. It is true that a number of studies seemed to converge on the conclusion that social class is related to violent crime in non-White populations.

However, it is Thornberry's corollary finding that White violent crime is unrelated to social class that requires a second look. Just as violent crime is different from property crime, we have begun to see that family-violent crime may be very different from street-violent crime. When I (Kandel-Englander, 1992) compared all three types of White violent subjects, I did find differences. Specifically, the family-violent were similar in social class to the nonviolent, and the street- and pan-violent were from lower classes.

When we look at education, a slightly different pattern emerges. Among Whites, there were no differences among street-, pan-, family-violent, and nonviolent offenders. Among non-Whites, family-violent and nonviolent offenders were similarly highly educated, whereas pan-violent and street-violent offenders were less educated.

It is interesting to note that although non-White subjects in the study achieved less education than White subjects, they were similar to the U.S. population as a whole. For example, 12% of the U.S. population drops out of school before high school; this is in comparison to 14% of the non-White study sample, and only 5% of the White study sample. Thus, non-White subjects were not characterized by extremely low educational achievement; rather, White subjects were characterized by higher educational achievement. Other research has suggested that longer stays in school may actually protect otherwise high-risk children from developing antisocial behavior (Kandel et al., 1988).

In any case, the statement that lower social class is simply related to higher violent crime appears to be inaccurate. For example, among non-White men, the significant and most interesting social class differences were found between family-only offenders and those men who were violent outside of their families. When considering the relationship of social class and education to violence, it is very important to remember potential differences between different groups of criminals and between different types of crimes.

Other research has found that the social class of violent and nonviolent subjects differs in studies drawing on official criminal data, but not in studies drawing on self-reported data (Bridges, 1978, 1981; Hindelang, 1978). Recall that official criminal data includes only criminals who are caught by the police; in contrast, self-report data includes a random sample of people, whether or not they have been caught, who respond to questions about violent behavior.

Officially detected violent criminals (i.e., those who are apprehended) are almost universally violent outside of the home; it is much rarer for family-only violent offenders to be arrested. Therefore, studies utilizing official data probably, in truth, involve a comparison of street- and pan-violent men versus family-violent and nonviolent men. We have seen that these two groups are indeed different in social class. In contrast, self-report studies typically involve a comparison of all violent (street-, pan-, and family-violent) men versus nonviolent men. As we have also seen, social class differs less in this comparison. Comparing the four groups of men (street-, pan-, family-, and nonviolent) helps us understand why different studies produce different findings.

Why would family-violent offenders be as highly educated as nonviolent men? One possibility is that violent men who are as highly educated as nonviolent men may be "protected" from involvement in street violence by their investment in their status. Thus, if they stayed in school, they choose only family victims because doing so is less risky than choosing outside victims. This interpretation rests on the social truism that violence against the family is less often regarded as a "crime" than is violence in the streets. It certainly seems very likely that battering is seen as more socially acceptable (and thus is less socially controlled) than street violence (Straus, 1976). Because of such cultural beliefs, men may perceive that street violence carries much more risk of official detection and punishment than does the commission of family violence.

Those men who have managed to stay in school and achieve a higher social class may not wish to jeopardize their gains by assaulting outsiders, when they feel able to assault family members more easily and with relatively greater impunity.

RACE AND VIOLENCE

Although we have discussed the importance of considering race when analyzing crime and violence patterns, there are basic questions left. Are members of some races or ethnic groups more likely to be violent than members of other groups? Are some types of violence related to race, whereas other types are not?

White-dominated media may have fostered the perception that race is a key factor in violent crime. In 1988, when George Bush was running against Michael Dukakis for president, he accused Dukakis, then governor of Massachusetts, of being "soft" on crime and of releasing hardened criminals before they had served their full prison terms. To illustrate the accusation, he ran an advertisement telling the story of the early release of a dangerous-looking, violent inmate named Willie Horton.

Horton evoked an emotional response from many viewers of the advertisement for a variety of different reasons. Some people felt that Horton perfectly matched their stereotype of an African-American violent felon—his frightening face evoked profound fears of crime and violent victimization. Others felt that the Horton campaign was an attempt to manipulate voters into being so afraid of racially motivated crime that they would vote for Bush. In any case, the campaign left open some basic questions about race and crime.

The evidence that Blacks in the United States are involved in criminal activity to a much greater extent than their proportion in the population is consistent (Block, 1977; Hewitt, 1988; Humphrey & Palmer, 1987; Wolfgang, 1958). However, the extent of involvement may vary depending on the crime. For example, in the 1970s the National Youth Survey (completed on 1,700 male and female adolescents) found no difference between the races when only low-frequency, minor offenders were examined. In sharp contrast to this is the picture of homicide, the most serious violent crime in our society. Although Blacks comprise only 12% of the U.S. population, it is estimated that more than half of all homicides are committed by Black individuals (Conklin, 1986; Freeh, 1995; Greenfeld, 1992). Similarly, about 4 in 10 assaults are perpetrated by Blacks. Most victims of Black violence are Black as well, a fact that has led many African-American community leaders to seek an end to Black-on-Black violence.

That said, a number of experts have noted that Blacks and Hispanics are more likely than Whites to be suspected, arrested, and, if charged, convicted of violent crimes (Elliot, 1980; Freeh, 1995). There is little doubt that racism plays at least some role in the U.S. criminal justice system, and at least part of the impression that African Americans are more violent than other ethnic and racial groups is probably due to the prejudicial handling of minorities within it.

On the other hand, it seems unlikely that prejudicial handling accounts for the entire ethnic discrepancy in crime rates. What other factors cause violence to be more prevalent in minority communities and among minority individuals? Biological variables that have been linked to crime appear to apply equally to different races. For example, several studies have found that the relationship between abuse and violence and health during pregnancy and delivery remains valid even when race is controlled for (Kandel & Mednick, 1991; Shanok & Lewis, 1981). It seems most likely that minority individuals and communities are under social pressures and stresses that increase their vulnerability to violence in general: They are more likely to live in violent neighborhoods, to have larger families without social support, to have fewer financial resources, fewer job opportunities, and so on.

OTHER FAMILY CHARACTERISTICS AND VIOLENCE

Social class, education, and race are not the only areas of interest in the development of street and family violence. For example, does marital status (being single, married, or divorced) affect the likelihood that someone will become violent with his or her family? And what about family size (coming from a family with many vs. fewer children)?

There is little doubt that pressures like financial distress can increase the probability of family abuse, whereas support can decrease at least child abuse (Cicchetti, 1990). Support is usually found in the presence of a helpful spouse, family, and/or friends. Even studies of mothers who were abused as children find that if they have good support as adults, they are unlikely to abuse their own children (Egeland, Jacobvitz, & Sroufe, 1988). Other research points out that parents who have unstable relationships (i.e., they shift from relationship to relationship) may be at greater risk of being abusive (Belsky, 1988; Cicchetti, 1990). Therefore, it is important to study not just the existence of a marital relationship, but also its quality.

Similarly, a large family size may increase the risk of violence in the offspring. Parents with many children generally are under more stress and have more responsibilities, and almost any factor that increases stress levels in a family also increases the probability of violence. One researcher examined family size and family violence to see if there was a link between the two, and found that larger families did indeed display more family violence (Gil, 1971). In addition, another researcher studying biological factors in violence noted an interesting pattern: he found that low monoamine oxidase (MAO) levels in humans are associated both with violent criminality and with larger family size (Ellis, 1991). This research suggests that having many children may actually have an impact on the physical status of those children, and that it may be these physical changes— in addition to the psychological pressures of a large family—that are responsible for an increase in violent behavior. Other research has noted that the children from larger families appear to have an increased risk for a number of developmental problems (Wagner, Schubert, & Schubert, 1985), including scholastic and achievement problems (specifically, lower SAT scores; Zajonc & Bargh, 1980). Clearly, different parents cope differently with large families, and having many children does not inevitably lead to problems in their behavior. It is not simply the presence of many children that is important, but how family size affects stress that determines the relationship to abuse and violence. Furthermore, the mechanism by which larger families develop this increased risk status may be biological, social, intellectual, or academic.

How do these family characteristics affect the probability that someone will become violent on the street or at home? It is clear that single people are more likely than married people to be involved in street crime; however, this difference probably has to do with age rather than marital status per se. The relationship between youth and violent crime is indisputable; people younger than 29 commit most violent street crimes (U.S. Department of Justice, 1988), and are also less likely than are older age groups to be married.

Little research has focused directly on the relationship between the number of children a person has and his or her propensity for violent street crime; however, the research on crowding in the home may be related to this issue. Although densely populated neighborhoods are not necessarily more high crime, densely populated households do produce more violent criminals (Mueller, 1983). This finding suggests that a large family living under stressful conditions, in a limited space, may contribute to the development of a violent street criminal.

SOCIOLOGICAL PERSPECTIVES

Sociological models emphasize the social characteristics or the social environment of a person, rather than that individual's biology, personality, or developmental history. Sociologists note that an increase in violence within a society is often accompanied by extreme social change, such as cultural conflict, when a dominant society imposes its values, structure, educational methods, and so on, on a politically or economically subordinate culture (Lee, 1995). Generally, sociology emphasizes causal factors that are close in time to the target violence and are external to the individual (Nagin & Paternoster, 1994). One major sociological theory pertaining to antisocial behavior is social control theory (Heimer & Matsueda, 1994; Hirschi, 1990; Nagin & Paternoster, 1994). The premise of social control theory is that individuals who are adequately invested in a society will be deterred from behaving antisocially by their investment. In other words, people who are invested in and committed to a society will not misbehave because if they do, they stand to lose their investment (Nagin & Paternoster, 1994). The most obvious example of this is property crime: People with more money are less likely than poor people to become involved in property crime. Presumably, becoming a criminal is simply not worth the risk of being apprehended if you already have substantial material gains. Researchers have suggested that if people need to be more invested in society in order for crime to decrease, then the current emphasis on incarceration is not the answer to today's violent crime problem in the United States (Gottfredson & Hirschi, 1995). Despite the popularity of social control theory, some researchers have argued that antisocial behavior is not particularly related to attachment and/or commitment to mainstream society (Heimer & Matsueda, 1994).

In the area of family violence, sociology has taken a different view from psychology and psychiatry. In contrast to models that view family violence as the result of an aberrant individual, this model notes that family violence is neither a rare event nor is it perpetrated by extremely "different" individuals. Rather than focus on personality disorders or mental illness, sociological theorists often point out that violence is usually perpetrated on a family by an individual who is not "mentally ill" or even noticeably deviant in any other way (Pagelow, 1993). Similarly, contrary to some early psychological expectations, sociological research evidence suggests that female victims are neither pathologically "masochistic" nor mentally ill.

Female Victims and Mental Illness

Some theorists have suggested that battered wives "permit" their husbands to abuse them (Frieze & Browne, 1989). Megargee (1982) noted that other theorists have believed battered women to be secret masochists, allowing the abuse to occur because they enjoy it. Such ideas were probably based on early psychoanalytic theories that held that masochism was normal for women, and that women could be expected to display masochistic tendencies much more frequently than men (J. H. Williams, 1987). However, Pizzy (1974) asserted that such theories were without scientific foundation and that women do not like or desire the abuse that they suffer. Indeed, empirical support for the idea that female victims of abuse are masochistic or in other ways mentally disturbed has lacked consistency (Megargee, 1982), although some studies have found positive correlations between mental illness and being a victim of spouse abuse. Interestingly, Gayford (1983) discovered one possible source of the confusion. Although almost 50% of the battered women in his study had received psychiatric services and almost 75% had been given psychoactive medication, in most cases this intervention occurred after the marital violence had started. This fact makes it unlikely that the women's psychological difficulties could have been a causal factor in the violence. Although it is possible that the battered women had preexisting, causally relevant disorders but simply failed to seek treatment until after the abuse began, this is an improbable scenario to be coincidentally present in so many cases. Neither Gayford (1983) nor other researchers (P. Scott, 1974) have found that masochism was a significant factor in wives' "tolerating" abuse.

Sociological theorists have studied the social factors that keep women in abusive relationships, rather than emphasizing the personality factors that may or may not do so. Several social factors have in fact been identified as key in maintaining the presence of the victim in an abusive relationship. These factors are: financial and social dependence on the spouse; lack of marketable skills; having children in need of support; being burdened by continual childbearing (thus limiting mobility and independence); feeling uncertain about the seriousness of the problem; being fearful of being single, alone, and poor; and lack of knowledge about other options (such as government assistance). (Why women stay in abusive relationships is discussed in more detail in chapter 12.)

The Mental State of Family Offenders

Being an abusive husband and parent has been linked to many personality factors, such as alcohol abuse, inadequacy and poor self-esteem, extreme jealousy, and general immaturity (Bartol, 1991; Gayford, 1983). Abusers frequently do show such characteristics, but attempts to form psychological typologies of abusive males have not been successful; although psychologists may be able to form psychological profiles of individual offenders, it is much more difficult to form a psychological profile that fits all family abusers (Megargee, 1982). Sociological theorists point out that social factors may be more important in predicting *when* a male will become violent (Wilson, 1995); such researchers study factors such as crowding (Bower, 1994; Calhoun, 1961; Evans, 1993; Frankel, 1992; Freedman, Levy, Buchanan, & Price, 1972; Gaes, 1994; Gove, 1979; Ruback & Riad, 1994; Sechrest, 1991), the mass media (Centerwall, 1992; Friedrich & Stein, 1973; Huesmann & Eron, 1986; Huston, Watkins, & Kunkel, 1989; "Reel Violence," 1994; Singer, Singer, & Rapaczynski, 1984), high temperatures (C. Anderson, 1987; C. Anderson & D. Anderson, 1984; C. Anderson, Deuser, & DeNeve, 1995; Rotton, 1993), and their relationships to the onset of violence.

The relationship between crowding and violence has been investigated in both rats and humans. Among rats, crowding seems to lead to a breakdown of normal mating and nesting behaviors and to an increase in aggression and violence. Among humans, "private" space seems more relevant to violent tendencies than "public" space; that is, population density in a neighborhood appears to be relatively less important than density within private living spaces.

High temperatures and violence seem to be strongly related; for example, violence increases during the summer, and is more prevalent in hotter climates. However, this relationship may be complicated by factors such as increased alcohol consumption during hotter summer months. Finally, social factors such as the mass media (particularly television) are clearly related to aggression (although this is a far from simple relationship, and is discussed in much more detail in later chapters).

Family Violence Across Cultures and Societies

The United States has led the virtual explosion in research in the incidence and causes of family violence, and as a result, many assume that family violence is predominately a U.S. problem (Gelles & Pedrick Cornell, 1983).

However, less interest abroad does not mean less violence in the households of other cultures and countries. Leading U.S. researchers have pointed out that there is no evidence to suggest that Americans are particularly violent with their families (Gelles & Pedrick Cornell, 1983).

Furthermore, much important research has been accomplished abroad. However, different countries tend to have different approaches to the problem of family violence. For example, although western Europe and the United States have acknowledged for decades that child abuse is a problem, some other countries (such as China and Russia) appeared to deny—as late as the end of the 1970s—that such abuse even occurs (Tauber, Meda, & Vitro, 1977). Another example may be seen in the area of public policy and childrearing. In contrast to the United States, where the right to use corporal punishment on children often seems to be jealously guarded, more than a decade ago Sweden passed a widely accepted law making corporal punishment of children illegal (Feshbach, 1980). In the United States today, nearly all parents hit their children as a disciplinary measure (Straus, 1983).

Thus, it is clear that despite some pockets of consensus, different cultures take very different approaches to the very idea of family violence. Sociologists make the point that what is criminal violence to an American, or to a westerner, may be perfectly acceptable in other cultures. To date, however, most research on family violence has been conducted by western nations, who share both the financial resources to investigate these problems and the cultural belief that family violence is a problem.

POPULATION DENSITY

Does violence occur more often in rural, relatively unpopulated places, or in highly populated urban cities? There is no doubt that more street violence occurs in major cities; this high-visibility violence has lead most people to assume that population density, or crowding, must be related causally to violence in some way. That assumption aside, what is the evidence that crowding is linked to violence?

In an imaginary world we could subject human beings to crowded and uncrowded conditions and study the effects on their behavior. Obviously, however, this would be unethical and unthinkable. Therefore, much of the research on crowding and violence has been conducted on rats, rather than on human beings. The most interesting studies were conducted in the 1960s by Calhoun (1961), a researcher who found that crowded conditions significantly affect and change the normal lifestyles of rats. For example, male rats in crowded conditions, in comparison to males in uncrowded nests, showed no interest in their offspring and in their mates. They also behaved very aggressively, attacking and destroying other nests. These rats attacked both other males and females, and in general behaved violently and antisocially. On the other hand, studies of crowding in rhesus monkeys found absolutely no increase in aggression—in fact, rhesus monkeys appeared to cope with crowding by increasing their prosocial grooming behaviors, not by attacking each other (Bower, 1994). Thus, although the rat results are interesting, it seems likely that crowding affects different organisms in different ways. At the very least, the relationship is unlikely to be so simple in human beings.

The most straightforward analysis of the crowding–violence question in human beings was conducted as a study of the relationship between U.S.

violent crime rates and population density (Freedman, 1975). Despite the common assumption that violent crime occurs more frequently in urban areas, this study found that when social class (poverty) is controlled for, there are actually fewer crimes of street violence in high-density cities (per capita). Overall, of course, there are more violent street crimes in cities, but it appears that this may be only because there are more people, rather than because the crowding of cities makes people more violent. Of course, this analysis only took into account street violence; it did not really address domestic violence undetected by authorities. In support of this finding, a more recent study (Frankel, 1992) found that suicide rates (albeit a very different form of violence) were highest in states with low population densities, such as Nevada and New Mexico. The lowest suicide rates were in densely populated states, such as Washington, DC, Massachusetts, New Jersey, and New York.

Other recent studies point in a different direction. One study (Rand, 1991) found that between 1985 and 1989 the percentage of urban households victimized by crime rose from 28% to 31%, whereas the percentage of rural households victimized by crime dropped from 20% to 17%. This study is limited because it focuses on crime in general, rather than on violent crime; however, its recent date implies a more accurate accounting of both family and street crime. It is not unusual for different studies to come to different conclusions; before deciding which results are more plausible, let us examine the experimental evidence on human crowding and aggression.

Some researchers have either studied "natural" pseudoexperiments or conducted laboratory experiments wherein they expose groups of individuals to crowded rooms and observe their reactions. Of course, laboratory experiments have limitations: Aggression there cannot be equated with aggression in the home or on the streets, and crowding in a room for a short period of time undoubtedly has less of an effect on human behavior than chronically overcrowded conditions. Nevertheless, there have been interesting results. One typical study (Freedman et al., 1972) found that crowding did make males more aggressive and hostile, although it did not have this effect on females. When males were in uncrowded rooms they did not show this increase in aggression and hostility. On the other hand, pseudoexperiments in prisons (in which rates of violence have been studied in conjunction with increases in crowding) have found no increase in violent behavior among inmates as crowding increases (Gaes, 1994; Sechrest, 1991). Sechrest pointed out that jail populations in the United States grew 10% each year between 1978 and 1987. He studied both inmate-on-inmate assaults and inmate-on-staff assaults in a facility for 1,400 men, and found that the location of the assaults was more important in predicting them than was density or crowding. Of course, studies of prison crowding and violence also may not be representative of street violence, although they do involve "real" violence.

Overall, the evidence that crowding contributes to violence appears to be mixed. Earlier studies of violent crime had suggested no relationship between urban/rural crowding and violence, although domestic violence was probably not taken into account. More recent population studies of crime in general suggest that urban (crowded) areas do experience more victimization, although not necessarily violent victimization. Experimental studies of the crowding of animals and the short-term crowding of humans do suggest an increase in aggression, although the aggressive responses observed cannot be equated with human violence as we see it occurring in the home and on the street. Crowding in prisons, a more natural environment, does not appear to increase the rate of violence in those institutions. Reviewers have noted the marked inconsistency of the data on this relationship (Gaes, 1994). One possible mechanism, and confound, may be differential reactions to crowding. For example, one study compared males and females on their reactions to high density (Ruback & Riad, 1994), and found that although males reacted to high density with more psychological distress, females did not. This study is tangential but suggests that different types of samples may provide different results in the study of crowding and aggression. Undoubtedly, firm conclusions must await more research.

Individual Causes
of Violent Behavior

Violent crimes can be as baffling as they are repelling. In England, two 10-year-old boys lured a 2-year-old away from his mother at a shopping mall; they took him down to the local railroad tracks, where they beat him to death and left his body to be run over by a train. In the United States, a group of teenagers shot and killed a man whose car they were stealing—even though the man had willingly handed over his car keys and was not resisting the theft in any way. In Massachusetts, a group of young teenage schoolgirls planned to murder their English teacher because she was too strict:

> After the final bets were in, Okiki, a 13-year-old honor student, sat stony-faced at her desk in English class, silently preparing to collect a couple of hundred dollars on a dare. She had settled on a simple plan. Just wait for the bell to ring, reach into her book bag, grab the 12-inch fillet knife she had brought from home and stab the teacher in the chest. . . . But there is something that troubles [Sergeant] Cambarere even more [than this plan]: his first glimpse of the girls when they were brought into the police department. "They were giggling." (Hull, 1993, p. 37)

In some social circumstances, it is not so difficult to understand why violence happens. For example, soldiers shoot other soldiers in a battle because failing to do so may mean their own death. Even John Hinckley's assassination attempt on President Ronald Reagan had some purpose behind it: He was attempting to impress Jodie Foster, an actress whom he admired. Other violence, however, seems completely devoid of motive or sense. How could 13-year-old girls possibly plot to kill their teacher "because she 'got in my face' "? How can it be that they were unafraid of repercussions and unconcerned by the idea of committing such a terrible crime? Why would 10-year-old children kill a completely innocent 2-year-old? Why would car thieves risk being charged with murder, when killing their victim was completely unnecessary?

To understand the causes of violence, it is not always enough to understand the external motives that often drive other types of criminal behavior. It is true that violence sometimes results from factors such as an individual's desire for financial gain, or from an individual's repeated exposure to violent behavior in his or her social environments. Sometimes, however, it also happens in an apparently motiveless fashion. Violence is never truly without motive, but its motives may be so complex and elusive that it appears motiveless. In all cases, but particularly in cases of violence that appear to have no motive, internal or individual factors may be critical in understanding the cause of such behavior. A variety of different biological and psychological influences and mechanisms have been considered over the years. I summarize them here and attempt to construct a more comprehensive model of the causes of violent behavior.

BIOLOGICAL PERSPECTIVES

One of the first people to think seriously about why violent people behave the way they do was a man named Cesare Lombroso. Writing in 1876, Lombroso discussed his belief that criminal behavior resulted from a primitive instinct that increased some people's likelihood of behaving in a criminal manner. Lombroso also assumed that people who behave like criminals have biologically different brains. That is, he was interested in the idea that criminals are born destined to behave violently or antisocially, regardless of what their social environment is like. Lombroso was one of the first major figures to publicly advance the theory that violence is primarily, if not completely, due to biological causes.

Types of Biological Influences

There exists a mistaken tendency to use interchangeably the terms *biological* and *genetic*. In fact, genetic influences are only one type of biological influences on behavior. There are (at least) two different types of biological influences: genetic influences and biological environmental influences. *Genetic influences* refer to the blueprints for behavior that are contained in a person's chromosomes. Chromosomes contain deoxyribonucleic acid (DNA), the genetic material a person inherits from his or her biological parents, which is referred to as their *genotype* (Johnson, 1991). An individual's *phenotype* is the outward expression of his or her genotype. For example, DNA certainly predetermines some aspects of an individual's phenotype, such as hair type. Whether, and how strongly, it affects the behavior of an individual is the question many researchers study.

Biological environmental influences, on the other hand, are events that affect a person biologically but are not encoded into the person's DNA. For example, a head injury from a car accident is a biological environmental influence. No genotype determines that someone will have a car accident; however, such an accident, and its accompanying head injury, can still have an important biological effect on the person's behavior.

Lombroso was interested in genetic influences, and considered them the single most important influence in determining criminal behavior. He concluded that people who behaved in violent and antisocial ways were "born criminals." He believed that a life of crime was the inevitable destiny of people who had certain biological features.

The Nature–Nurture Debate

Lombroso's announcement that *biology* was the only important factor in causing crime eventually set off a firestorm of controversy. However, Lombroso was not the only person who believed that biology was the most important factor influencing behavior.

Around the turn of the century, as today, the major discipline examining human behavior was psychology. At that time, most psychologists, like Lombroso, were convinced of the primary importance of genetic influences and did not question the idea that criminal behavior was "inborn" (West, 1988).

> Adler had . . . selected a feature, aggressiveness, common to all instinctual life, and then regarded it as the one and only key to the understanding of all psychological problems. (Jones, 1955, p. 262)

But in 1914, a young, bold psychologist by the name of John Watson (1878–1958) began a revolution. Watson concluded that the genesis of troubled behavior lay in the individual's *psychological environment*, and that it was that environment that exerted the most profound influence on behavior, rather than any biological influences. Rather than examine a patient's physiology or inner mind, Watson proposed to focus simply on overt behavior. He called his new approach *behaviorism* (Reed, 1989). For more established psychologists, these ideas represented a rejection of all their beliefs and work. But these ideas have penetrated criminology, and most criminologists today believe that Lombroso was at least partially wrong about the origins of criminal behavior, and that the *psychological environment* (also called *social learning*) is responsible for crime and violence. This controversy, between those experts who believe that biology is the key to criminality, and those who believe that people learn to be criminals, has been called the *nature–nurture debate.*

Modern Biological Theories

As the 20th century wore on, psychologists continued to make interesting discoveries about learning and violent behavior. However, one finding consistently emerged: Although learning was clearly related to violent behavior, learning theories alone could not fully explain violence in human beings.

As an example, consider the principle of *imitation:* It states that children may learn to be violent by imitating an adult's aggression. According to this principle, one would expect that children who grow up watching violent parents would be violent themselves. As the theory predicts, a higher proportion of children who witness violent parents are violent, in comparison to other children; however, despite their higher risk, many children of violent parents do not, in fact, behave aggressively as adults (Spatz Widom, 1989a).

Does Violence Run in Families?

Most people believe that if a child either witnesses or is the target of violence from a parent, then he or she is destined to become a violent person.

In fact, this isn't really the case. Having a violent parent does increase the risk. However, most children of violent parents do not grow up to become violent themselves.

If you compare children of nonviolent parents to children of violent parents, you would indeed see that proportionately, more children of violent parents were violent themselves. Therefore, it is clear that having violent parents is detrimental, in that it increases the risk of violence in a child. However, having violent parents by no means "dooms" any given child to becoming violent. As stated before, most children of violent parents still won't grow up to become violent.

Some children who are exposed to violent psychosocial environments do become violent; many other children who are similarly exposed do not (Kandel et al., 1988; Spatz Widom, 1989a, 1989b; Werner & Smith, 1982). This fact has led researchers to hypothesize that some children are *vulner-*

able to noxious circumstances, whereas others are *resilient or invincible*—that is, resilient children survive and cope well despite terrible circumstances (Werner & Smith, 1982). For example, consider two siblings—a brother and a sister—who grow up watching their parents fight violently with each other. The brother is ultimately violent with his own family, but the sister never uses violence as an adult. Why did the brother adopt and imitate his parents' violence, whereas the sister remained relatively less vulnerable? Westley Dodd, a notorious serial killer who kidnapped, sexually abused, and brutally murdered several children in the northwest United States, had siblings who evidenced no signs of seriously violent behavior.

What makes one child resilient and another child vulnerable? One possible difference between resilient and vulnerable children is their biology. Perhaps unfortunate genetic influences or biological environmental influences serve to weaken some children—thus making them vulnerable. On the other hand, perhaps positive biological influences strengthen some children—thus making them resilient. The fact that children are differentially vulnerable suggests that biology may be an important difference among violent versus nonviolent people.

Another piece of evidence has emerged that supports the importance of biology as one cause of violence. In the past few decades, researchers have conducted longitudinal studies that track the same group of people over long periods of time, usually years. At least two major longitudinal studies (Farrington, 1978; Olweus, 1979) have found that aggressive behavior is (in some children) a stable characteristic from very early childhood until adulthood. When a behavior begins very early in life, before a child has been exposed to any environment for a lengthy period of time, it is likely that this behavior is strongly influenced by biological factors. Thus, the evidence from longitudinal studies suggests that early biological factors (such as genetic influences) may operate during an individual's entire lifetime to affect their tendency to be violent.

In summary, there are two major pieces of evidence that suggest the importance of biology as well as learning: (a) the early emergence of aggressive behavior as a stable characteristic in some individuals, and (b) individual differences in vulnerability to noxious environmental influences (such as having violent parents). The question that remains is, what type of biological influences are important in making a child more or less vulnerable to poor psychosocial environments?

Physiology and Anatomy

One type of biological factor that might influence the development of violence is *anatomical differences* between the brains of violent individuals and nonviolent individuals—in shape or matter.

One type of anatomical difference that has been studied in relation to violence is the presence of a brain tumor. A brain tumor is an uncontrolled growth mass in the brain. There are two types of brain tumors: those that actively destroy healthy brain tissue, and those that cause problems by compressing brain tissue until it is unable to function normally. Brain tumors, which offer gross (large) insults to brain integrity, undoubtedly cause changes in behavior, including personality changes. A few violent criminals have been found to have brain tumors upon autopsy (Mark & Ervin, 1970). Some testing has also found brain dysfunction in forensic populations (Friedt & Gouvier, 1989). Because of such cases, some excitement was generated in the scientific community; these individuals raised the possibility that extreme, senseless violence may be due, at least in part, to brain tumors that radically affect normal brain function, or that worsen more subtle brain deficits. In reality, however, this is a very unlikely scenario. Most violent offenders do not have brain tumors, and research in this area suggests strongly that brain tumors (and other types of massive brain damage) are not an important factor in the etiology of the majority of violence. To date, the hypothesis that violence is due to massive brain dysfunction appears to have little support, and autopsies of chronically violent offenders usually find no noticeable (i.e., major) brain damage (Goldman, 1977).

However, not all damage to the brain is massive. Damage to the brain ranges from extremely minimal to extremely major. Most cases of brain damage are at the minimal end of the spectrum, although it is the major cases that are the most noticeable.

Minimal Brain Damage. Also called *minimal brain dysfunction*, minimal brain damage does not "look" like major brain damage. A person with minimal brain dysfunction won't have "obvious" brain damage; however, minimal dysfunction may affect behavior, emotions, learning, or memory—that is, the more subtle (or "higher") functions of the brain. For example, although major brain damage might result in severe mental retardation, minor brain dysfunction might result in a learning disability that would not necessarily affect intelligence in any way (e.g., dyslexia). Because we know that minimal brain dysfunction appears to be related to problems such as learning disorders and hyperactivity (Waldrop & Goering, 1971; G. Weiss, 1990), it is logical for scientists to be interested in the possibility that minimal brain dysfunction is related to behavioral problems like violence.

Minor Physical Anomalies. The problem is, how does one measure minimal brain dysfunction? Most neurological tests, including brain scans, only show major damage. Because there are no brain scans for minor damage, we can only measure it indirectly. One indirect way to measure minor brain dysfunction is through external physical markers called *minor physical anomalies*. Minor physical anomalies are minor external malformations of the skin or external features. Examples of minor physical anomalies are having the second toe of your foot be longer than your big toe, or having only one crease on your palm, instead of three.

Such minor malformations are common; almost everyone has one or two minor physical anomalies. However, people who have four or more have an unusually high number. Why would having four or more minor physical anomalies suggest that minor brain dysfunction was present?

During fetal development, the brain develops from a more primitive structure called the *neural tube*. Part of the neural tube is called the *neural crest*. The neural crest is the basis for both the formation of the brain and the formation of other tissues, including skin and bones. This means that pregnancy disturbances that affect the development of the neural crest could result in both minor external malformations and minor brain dysfunction (Geschwind & Galaburda, 1987). Indeed, we know that pregnancy difficulties in rats can result in both minor brain malformations and minor external malformations (Geschwind & Galaburda, 1987).

If minor physical anomalies are an indication of minor brain dysfunction, then individuals with a very high number of anomalies might display violent behavior and other behavioral problems. But has there been any link found between minor physical anomalies and violent behavior?

Interestingly, a series of studies has found a relationship between minor physical anomalies and childhood behaviors related to adult aggression (such as hyperactivity); and criminal violence as an adult. Studies of children with behavior disorders related to delinquency often find that the children have high numbers of minor physical anomalies (Fogel, Mednick, & Michelsen, 1985; Nichols, 1987; Waldrop & Goering, 1971). One longitudinal study found that subjects with high numbers of minor physical anomalies as children were at significantly higher risk of recidivistic, violent criminal activity as adults (Kandel, 1988; Kandel, Brennan, & Mednick, 1989).

Neuropsychological Testing. Minor physical anomalies are only one indirect way of assessing minor brain dysfunction. A second way is *neuropsychological testing*. Neuropsychological tests are verbal or visual tests that measure subtle brain functions such as learning and memory abilities. These tests may reveal subtle brain deficits that go undetected by more conventional neurological testing. Researchers have administered neuropsychological tests to violent criminals, and have found evidence that such individuals often have subtle brain impairments (Elliott, 1978; Friedt & Gouvier, 1989; Krynicki, 1978; Spellacy, 1977, 1978; Yeudall & Fromm-Auch, 1979; Yeudall, Fromm-Auch, & Davies, 1982). One recent study found that a low score on a neuropsychological frontal lobe task predicted aggressiveness among 72 White males (Giancola & Zeichner, 1994). Furthermore, subjects with poor neuropsychological functioning, particularly in the frontal lobe region, are more aggressive when provoked (Lau, Pihl, & Peterson, 1995). Other studies have also linked frontal lobe dysfunction and antisocial behavior (Kandel & Freed, 1989).

Head Injury. A third way of measuring minor brain dysfunction is through studying the medical history of a person to reveal head injuries that did not result in gross brain damage. Head injuries can cause anything from extremely minor to extremely major brain damage. If a head injury seems severe enough to be noticed (e.g., if the patient was knocked unconscious), but the injury did not result in major brain damage, then it is at least possible that it resulted in minor brain damage. Researchers, like Dorothy Otnow Lewis of New York University, have combed the medical histories of some of the most violent people in our society. Lewis and other researchers have found that the medical histories of violent delinquents reveal unusually high levels of head injuries (Busch, Zagar, Hughes, Arbit, & Bussell, 1990; Lewis, Shanok, & Balla, 1979; Rosenbaum & Hoge, 1989).

In summary, although both major and minor brain damage may be important in causing violence, the weight of the evidence suggests that the most important type of brain dysfunction in people who are chronically violent is minimal brain dysfunction. Although it is almost certain that most people with minimal brain dysfunction will never be violent, a noticeably high number of repeat violent offenders show some level of brain dysfunction (usually minimal).

Neurotransmitters

Neurotransmitters, commonly referred to as *brain chemicals*, are chemical messengers that transmit information between neurons in the central nervous system. Because neurons do not physically touch each other, they must send out neurotransmitters to communicate. There are many different types of neurotransmitters, and they tend to specialize in function. How much, or how little, of any particular neurotransmitter chemical is in your brain is an important determinant of many types of behavior. Both biology and psychosocial environment affect the levels of different neurotransmitters, and thus affect behavior. Several psychological disorders, such as schizophrenia (a common form of psychosis or insanity), are at least partially caused by too much or too little of one type of neurotransmitter or another. A logical question, therefore, is whether violent behavior is related (at least in part) to the level of certain neurotransmitters in the brains of violent people.

As stated previously, there are many different types of neurotransmitters in the brain. However, two neurotransmitters have been tentatively linked to increases in aggression: these are called norepinephrine and acetylcholine. Further, a neurotransmitter called serotonin seems to inhibit aggression in humans. Some research has linked low levels of serotonin with violence, particularly with impulsive aggression (Brown, 1990; Virkkunen & Linnoila, 1993). However, despite these tentative links, the relationship does not appear to be simple or strong and controlling the levels of these neurotransmitters does not control violent behavior in humans. The effects of neurotransmitters are complex and are both caused by, and cause, changes in behavior. Thus, although neurotransmitters are an important and even primary causal factor in some behaviors, violence does not appear to be one of them.

Hormones

Hormones are also chemical messengers within the body; they are similar to neurotransmitters, but are also different in several important ways. First, neurotransmitters are very fast messengers, whereas hormones carry messages much more slowly. Second, although neurotransmitters only work within the brain and the spinal cord, hormones are chemical messengers that are distributed throughout the entire body.

The hormones that are of the most interest in causing violence are the male sex hormones, called *androgens*. Both males and females secrete androgens, but males secrete a much greater quantity than do females. Androgens are frequently cited as an important cause of aggressive behavior, particularly intermale aggression. What is the evidence that this is true?

Earlier research certainly suggested a clear relationship between testosterone, one of the androgens, and aggression in both males and females (Goldman, 1977; Moyer, 1971). Of course, males produce more testosterone than females, which may partially explain the difference in levels of violence between males and females. Interestingly, the level of androgens in the body is related to the level of aggressive behavior that a person demonstrates—although this is more true for younger than for older males (Goldman, 1977). During puberty, both the levels of androgens and the probability of intermale violence increase dramatically. Finally, reductions in androgen production in animals (by castration) result in profound reductions of intermale aggression.

Although this evidence seems very strong, research is rarely as clear as it appears at first glance. Most of the evidence on androgens and violence has been gathered on animals, not on human beings. And although the evidence that androgens affect violence is strong in animals, it is much less simple in human beings. For example, one experiment demonstrated that when an individual expects a substance to make them more aggressive, it usually does—even when that substance is a placebo rather than testosterone (Bjorkquist, Nygren, Bjorklund, & Bjorkqvist, 1994). Simple comparisons of violent and nonviolent males have failed to detect significantly different levels of sex hormones (Christiansen & Winkler, 1992), and if testosterone is related to aggression, it is not a simple, linear relationship, at least in adolescent males (Halpern, Udry, Campbell, & Suchindran, 1993). On the other hand, a very interesting study that examined the impact of androgens on female-to-male transsexuals (females who are administered a large dose of male sex hormones as part of a sex change procedure) found that androgens did increase *anger proneness*, but not aggression directly (Van Goozen, Van de Poll, & Frijda, 1994). Other researchers pointed out that it may be *prenatal* exposure to hormones that is critical, rather than merely the level of hormones circulating in the bloodstream (Fishbein, 1992). Fetal exposure to high levels of androgens (male-typical range) may affect the tendency to be violent in two ways. First, prenatal exposure to androgens appears to actually lower the tendency of a person to behave in a prosocial manner (L. Ellis, 1990). Second, levels of prenatal testosterone are theoretically related to levels of MAO, which affects general aggressiveness and feelings of anger and frustration (L. Ellis, 1991). Like androgens administered to transsexuals, androgens administered prenatally may also affect emotions related to aggression.

These studies, in combination with older research and animal studies, suggest that the impact of male sex hormones on human violence is probably significant but indirect. Rather than directly causing humans to be violent, male sex hormones may affect other bodily systems, such as brain development, emotion, or temperament (Kagan, 1988), which in turn may lead to violence. The idea that hormones are indirectly linked to aggression is consistent with the fact that human beings, as stated earlier, are strongly affected both by their biology *and* by their psychological environment.

Genetics

For decades, researchers have searched for the "aggression gene." In one Dutch family with at least 14 men with strong violent tendencies, researchers did find a genetic mutation on the X chromosome (Morell, 1993). Despite such isolated cases, the majority of researchers agree that violence does not appear to be a behavioral tendency that is transmitted genetically (Mednick & Kandel, 1988; Mestel, 1994). At first glance, this may seem incorrect because children with violent parents do have a higher tendency to be violent themselves (Spatz Widom, 1989a, 1989b). In fact, one study that found that adolescent murderers tend to have violent fathers suggested that genetics might be an important cause of the teenagers' aggression (Lewis et al., 1985). The critical distinction, however, appears to be *biological heredity* versus *family psychology*. Parents provide a psychological, as well as a biological, environment for their children. What do parents teach their children, and what do they pass to them through their genes?

Genetics or Environment?

Don was a mean and violent young man, unhappily married, with three children. Although he was frequently absent due to his repeated incarcerations on petty property and violent crimes, when he was home he often beat both his wife and his children. His oldest son, Joe, started to get into trouble as soon as he turned 12; at age 19, he was arrested and convicted of sexual assault with a deadly weapon and attempted murder. He had tried, but failed, to kill his victim. Did Don pass on "violent" genes to his son, or did he "teach" him to be violent by being a violent role model?

In any given case, it may be nearly impossible to tell what factors are most important. However, there is a "natural experiment" through which researchers can identify the separate effects of family psychology and heredity: *Adoption studies* are studies that examine children who have been adopted away into a different family. Adopted children are children who have one set of biological parents, and a different set of psychological parents. By comparing the children's behavior with both their adopted parents and their genetic parents, it is possible to ascertain what behaviors are genetically inherited and what behaviors result from family environments.

Imagine that an adopted boy is having problems with violent or aggressive behavior. If both his biological and his psychological parents are violent people, then there is little we can learn from this case. If neither of his sets of parents are violent, then there is similarly little information.

But what if his biological parents are violent, but his adopted parents are not? If the adopted child is aggressive in the same way as his biological parents, this suggests that violence is primarily inherited genetically, rather than learned. But what if the opposite were true—what if his adopted parents are violent, but his biological parents are not? If the adopted child is aggressive in the same way as his adopted parents, then genetics are probably relatively unimportant in causing violence. In fact, the latter scenario appears to be more true. Several studies have found that adopted-away children are as aggressive as their adopted parents are, rather than as their biological parents are (Mednick, Gabrielli, & Hutchings, 1984).

XYY Syndrome. There is another possibility, however. Apart from heredity, genetic factors affect behavior through *chromosomal anomalies:* that is, mistakes in how the person's DNA copies itself. Because DNA must copy itself millions of times to create a new person, it is almost inevitable that some errors will occur, and these errors may affect behavior. One such error that has been studied in relation to violence is called the XYY syndrome.

The XYY syndrome is an error involving the genes that determine gender. The gender of a developing fetus is determined by the 23rd pair of chromosomes, one of which is inherited from the mother and one of which is inherited from the father. The mother always contributes a gene known as "X." The father contributes either an "X" gene or a "Y" gene. If you are a female, your father contributed an "X" gene, and your gender genotype is XX. If you are a male, your father contributed a "Y" gene, and your gender genotype is XY. Most people have, thus, two genes that determine their gender: one from their mother, and one from their father.

Some males, however, have two Ys contributed to their genotype, rather than the normal one Y. Thus, their genotype is XYY instead of XY. The fact that some notorious criminals have been XYY has raised the question of the role of XYY in determining behavior. If one Y causes you to be a male, does two Ys cause you to be a "super-male"? Would two Ys cause an exaggeration of male qualities, including the higher rate of violence among males? Some scholars have suggested that XYY males are predisposed to aggressive behavior (Horan, 1992). The problem with this theory is that most violent male criminals are not XYY. Although research has indicated that there are some features associated with being XYY (such as unusual height and severe acne), violence does not appear to be one of them (Freyne & O'Connor, 1992).

PSYCHODYNAMIC PERSPECTIVES

Sigmund Freud, a brilliant, stubborn, and opinionated physician who was born in 1856 and who spent most of his life in Vienna, developed original hypotheses about the causes of human behavior. He wrote a great deal about childhood development, although ironically all of his patients were adults. The basis of Freud's hypotheses was his therapy sessions with them.

Interactions with patients led Freud to postulate that a person's behavior, including a tendency to be violent, was the product of unconscious forces in his or her mind. Freud did believe that childhood events were key in determining adult behavior, but he also felt that many of the most important childhood events were innately predetermined (Rizzuto, 1991). Freud called his school of psychology *psychoanalysis*. Modern versions are sometimes called *psychodynamic psychology*.

Unfortunately, he was also a stubborn, headstrong man who had trouble tolerating any serious challenges to his beliefs. Although he attracted a great many talented students and followers, he also broke professional relations with many of them due to his inability to entertain opinions that differed from his own. Since Freud's death in 1939, his school of psychology (and its followers) has developed and changed. Nevertheless, psychoanalysis today still emphasizes the role of the unconscious in shaping behavior.

Psychoanalysis and Violence

Freud believed that aggression was a normal but unconscious impulse that is repressed in well-adjusted people. However, if the aggressive impulsive is particularly strong or repressed to an unusual degree, then some aggression can "leak" out of the unconscious and the person may be aggressive against a random, innocent victim. Freud called this *displaced aggression*, and this theory might explain an attack of "senseless" violence, labeling it as aggression that was too repressed and has broken through to the surface.

Displaced Aggression?

A young boy sits in the front passenger seat of an old Ford as it cruises through his neighborhood. It is a hot summer day and he is uncomfortable and irritated. He is cradling a gun on his lap. As he passes a group of 12- and 13-year-olds playing in the street, he suddenly, and for no apparent reason, points the gun out the car window, aims at one boy, and opens fire. He pulls the trigger three times, each time hitting the child, before the startled driver of the car accelerates sharply.

The most significant criticism of Freud's hypotheses is that they were based on his personal interactions with patients, rather than on any data obtained through experimentation. Despite this, some psychoanalytic theory is widely accepted as valid. For example, the idea that unconscious motives and childhood events are important in understanding adult behavior is a cornerstone of much modern psychological theory. However, other ideas of Freud's are much less widely accepted. For example, the notion that every person has a natural, built-in aggressive impulse that must be repressed does not have scientific support (Adams et al., 1990).

DEVELOPMENTAL PERSPECTIVES

Developmental psychologists have noted that violence does not simply "appear" in previously healthy adults; it is an adult behavioral disorder that is preceded by disturbed behaviors during childhood (Denno, 1990;

Lewis et al., 1985; Rigdon & Tapia, 1977; Robins, 1966, 1978; Weiss, 1990; Weisz, Martin, Walter, & Fernandez, 1991; Zagar, Arbit, Hughes, Busell, & Busch, 1989). Thus, understanding what behaviors precede adult violence may enable society to prevent such violence before it ever happens. Longitudinal research is the tool researchers use to uncover the childhood antecedents of violent behavior. By studying a group of children—both those who behave normally and those who have behavioral disorders—and then subsequently measuring the violence of all these individuals as adults, researchers are able to discover that having behavioral problems as a child increases the risk of adolescent and adult violence.

Developmental psychopathology is a special field that studies behavioral disorders and diseases that arise during development, or disorders that are caused by problems in development. Developmental psychopathologists are most interested in identifying the type of behavior problems during childhood that best predict adult violence and aggression. Their research has revealed a number of behavioral disorders of childhood that noticeably increase the risk of violence during adulthood.

Conduct Disorders

A conduct disorder (CD) is a persistent pattern of behavior in which the child repeatedly violates the basic rights of others or age-appropriate norms of social behavior (Sroufe, Cooper, & DeHart, 1996). The phrase *violating the basic rights of others* refers to behaviors such as stealing from other people, hurting them, or forcing them to do something that they would prefer not doing. Violating "age-appropriate" norms, on the other hand, refers to the child's violation of the behavioral standards that society reasonably expects from a child of that age. For example, no one expects 2-year-olds to sit quietly at desks in a classroom. However, we do expect 10-year-olds to do so. Therefore, sitting quietly at a desk is an age-appropriate norm for a 10-year-old, but not for a 2-year-old. It is not pathological for a 2-year-old to fail to sit quietly; but persistently failing to "act their age" may be a symptom of a CD.

A very important word in this definition is *persistent.* All 10-year-olds, at some time or another, misbehave and fail to sit quietly in class. As any teacher or parent knows, all children do not have CDs. However, a behavioral problem becomes indicative of a CD when it occurs on a persistent, continuing basis.

What causes children to have CDs? Several biological factors have been linked to CDs. For example, one study found that males with CDs had different secretion levels of the hormone testosterone (Dabbs & Morris, 1990), a hormone that has also been associated with violence (see previous discussion). This, and other biological factors, do not appear to single-handedly "cause" the disorder; rather, they increase a child's vulnerability

(Mednick & Hutchings, 1978). Correlational studies suggest that the family environment is important in causing this disorder; negative parenting skills and poor family interactions appear to be relevant factors. One representative study found that children with CD came from families characterized by poor cohesion and higher conflict than children with other psychological difficulties (e.g., anxiety disorders; Haddad, Barocas, & Hollenbeck, 1991). However, it is difficult to tell if the child's disorder has caused the family problems, or if the family problems helped cause the child's disorder, depending on the family, one or both of these scenarios may be true. In any case, family environment is doubtless important in the development of CDs, as evidenced by the success of therapies based on social learning principles in treating the disorder (Miller & Prinz, 1990).

Several studies have found relationships between CD, aggression, and violence later in life (Weisz et al., 1991). One study (Dodge, Price, Bachorowski, & Newman, 1990) examined CDs and their relationship to violence in 128 adolescent boys, ages 14 to 19. These boys were in a maximum security prison for juvenile offenders. The researchers found that factors that were positively related to the number of violent crimes, such as hostile biases in the interpretation of ambiguous events, were also positively related to aggressive CDs. These findings were true even when race, intelligence, and socioeconomic status were accounted for.

Attention Deficit Hyperactivity Disorder

Hyperactivity is a word that has crept into our colloquial speech. As a result of its common usage, most people believe that hyperactivity simply refers to children who are particularly energetic. However, hyperactivity is actually a clinical disorder that, in order to be diagnosed, must meet certain basic criteria. The condition referred to here as hyperactivity is also known as attention deficit hyperactivity disorder (ADHD).

There are three features of ADHD. The first feature of the disorder is the feature that most people are familiar with: a persistent pattern of impulsive and overactive behavior. In everyday life, children might be unable to control their behaviors appropriately; for example, a 7-year old may occasionally have trouble sitting still in a circle of children during storytime. Hyperactive children may try very hard to sit still; but they are simply unable to control their own motor behavior.

The second feature of hyperactivity is a tendency to be very easily distracted and to have significant difficulty concentrating appropriately on a task. This feature is usually labeled *distractibility* or *concentration difficulties*. Children with this symptom are distracted by events that would not typically distract other children. For example, when a teacher is explaining a lesson, a hyperactive child might be distracted by someone walking past the classroom or by the sound of a car driving by. Most individuals are able to "screen out" distracting noise when necessary; for example, you are able to concentrate on this sentence, even if you are reading it in a noisy room. The *target stimulus* is this paragraph, and the *extraneous stimuli* are noise, lights, voices, and other stimulation that you are screening out, rather than concentrating on. Hyperactive children are very sensitive to extraneous stimuli, and may lack the ability to effectively filter them out, thus interfering with their ability to focus on the target stimuli. Their high level of distractibility makes it very difficult for them to concentrate.

The third feature of ADHD is aggression, and this feature is the one that may be most relevant to the discussion here. Hyperactive children have an increased tendency to be aggressive with their playmates. They may be much more likely than other children to become involved in fights with schoolmates and to have playground problems. This is especially true of hyperactive boys (Hubbard & Newcomb, 1991; Pope, Bierman, & Mumma, 1991).

The diagnosis of hyperactivity may be made on any combination of these three features; all three need not be present. Alternatively, all three features may be present in any given hyperactive child.

Hyperactivity is different from many other childhood syndromes. Some behavior disorders of childhood are transient, lasting only a few years and having no long-lasting impact. However, hyperactivity is significantly related to adult outcomes, including violent crime (L. Ellis, 1990; Hughes et al., 1991; G. Weiss, 1990). It appears that hyperactivity affects so many facets of a child's life that permanent repercussions (in an untreated hyperactive child) may result. For example, hyperactive children (again, if left untreated) may have trouble making friends (Pope et al., 1991); they are difficult playmates because of their impulsive, overactive, aggressive behavior and their inability to concentrate on the task at hand. It is not unusual for other children to avoid hyperactive playmates (Hubbard & Newcomb, 1991), or at least to fail to form close friendships with them. The result is that hyperactive children may lack the opportunities other children have to learn how to form close relationships (Pope et al., 1991). Similarly, hyperactive children may not absorb basic skills in their early years of school, because of their inability to concentrate and focus on classroom lessons (Garrison & Earls, 1987). Because all advanced learning is built on basic skills, a lack of these skills can affect school performance for many school years to come.

The causes of hyperactivity are of particular interest to criminologists because hyperactivity has been linked to adolescent and adult crime and violence. One important cause appears to be biological factors (L. Ellis, 1990, 1991; Fogel et al., 1985; Garrison & Earls, 1987; Hughes et al., 1991; Kandel & Mednick, 1989; Sanson, Oberklaid, Pedlow, & Prior, 1991). For example, childhood hyperactivity occurs more frequently in children with poor perinatal health (health problems during pregnancy and delivery; Kandel et al., 1989; Sanson et al., 1991). Minor physical anomalies have also been linked to hyperactivity in a number of studies (Fogel et al., 1985; Waldrop & Goering, 1971).

Interestingly, perinatal problems and minor physical anomalies increase the risk of hyperactivity, and all three factors together (perinatal problems, minor physical anomalies, and hyperactivity) increase the risk of adult violence (Kandel et al., 1989; Sanson et al., 1991). This implies that violence and hyperactivity may share some biological antecedents. In support of the relationship between hyperactivity and violence, hyperactivity is found disproportionately in the histories of violent criminals, although, of course, most hyperactive children still do not become violent as adults (Hughes et al., 1991; Kandel et al., 1989; G. Weiss, 1990; Zagar et al., 1989). Although this body of research implies common biological antecedents for hyperactivity and violence, there is an alternative hypothesis: The interpersonal and social consequences of hyperactivity (rather than the biological bases) may help cause violence (Kandel et al., 1989). Both of these explanations have merit, and both are likely to be partly true.

The family and the other psychosocial factors in a hyperactive child's environment may also be relevant in understanding the causes of this problem, and by association, the causes of violent behavior. Hyperactive children can be found in many different types of families; however, some studies have found links between parenting styles and hyperactivity in children (Jacobvitz & Sroufe, 1987). In contrast to CDs, however, hyperactivity appears to be significantly related to biology and less strongly related to family and social factors.

Treatment of hyperactivity is important because of its potentially far-reaching consequences into the lives of the children it affects. Although it may be tempting to simply wait for children to "outgrow" hyperactivity, its relationship to peer problems, learning problems, and adult outcomes makes this a risky approach. In addition, failing to treat hyperactive children can lead to poor basic academic skills and school failure that persists even after the worst behavioral symptoms are gone; and failing to form significant peer relationships early in life can affect interpersonal skills later on.

Treatment for hyperactivity is controversial because it frequently involves medication—most often the drug methylphenidate (trade name Ritalin), which is a stimulant. Stimulants usually have paradoxical effects on children; although Ritalin would arouse an adult, it calms hyperactive children. It is particularly helpful for concentration problems, and helps hyperactive children succeed in school. Although stimulant use with children is controversial and has been criticized (Divoky, 1989; Kohn, 1989), most evidence suggests that approximately 80% of hyperactive children do respond favorably to stimulants (Fischer & Newby, 1991; Pliszka, 1991). Techniques such as behavior modification are less effective than medication for most children, although they can be the treatment of choice for the remaining 20% (Pliszka, 1991). No one likes administering behavior-altering drugs to children, but the side effects of such medication appear to be less detrimental than the consequences of leaving hyperactivity untreated.

Ideally, psychotherapy should always accompany medication, to help children learn to control their behavior, adjust to having this disorder, and ensure that they maintain positive self-esteem. Parent training and psychotherapy are usually beneficial for any hyperactive child and the child's family (Horn, Ialongo, Greenberg, Packard, & Smith-Winberry, 1990). Like stimulants, therapy can help control the disorder and help alleviate the consequences, but is not a perfect cure.

Learning Disorders

About 100 years ago, physicians started to describe peculiar disorders termed *learning disorders*. Learning disorders are sometimes called *learning disabilities*. This is a label that is attached to children who have problems in one or more of the basic processes that humans use to process understanding of language or numbers (Farnham-Diggory, 1978). Many learning disabled children can process much information normally, but have difficulties in performing particular tasks. These children have normal intelligence, but have reading, writing, drawing, or spelling abilities that are at least 2 years behind those of normal children of the same age (Farnham-Diggory, 1978).

An example of a learning disorder is dyslexia, the inability to read with understanding (Herschel, 1978). Approximately 5% of the population has dyslexia, meaning that they are of normal intelligence but have difficulties reading. A dyslexic child may reverse letters (e.g., the child sees a "b" when a "d" is written). How does one learn to read when the words "read," "doggie," and "hard" appear as "reab," "boggie," and "harb"? In dyslexia, the order of letters may also be affected: Rather than seeing "read," a child may see "erad."

Learning disorders do not affect intelligence per se, but do affect a child's self-esteem and psychological functioning (Moeller, 1994). Obviously, a child who must struggle to read even the most basic words is apt to consider him or herself "dumb" or even "bad" (i.e., uncooperative). Children with undiagnosed learning disorders may be regarded as naughty or stubborn, or as refusing to learn and cooperate with their classes. Because of the possible psychosocial side effects of learning disorders, it is not surprising that violent criminals often have such disorders in their histories. Several researchers have investigated the possibility of a link between learning disorders and crime.

Most studies find that learning disabilities, and their causes, have indeed been linked to an increased risk of delinquency and criminal behavior (L. Ellis, 1991; Geschwind & Galaburda, 1987; Zagar et al., 1989). For example, one study (Zagar et al., 1989) examined almost 2,000 children and adolescents (ages 6–17) who were referred by juvenile court for psychological treatment between 1981 and 1987. Of these children, 70% were either mentally retarded, learning disabled, or hyperactive, suggesting a strong association between delinquency and learning disorders.

Development of Aggression in Normal Children

Again, violence is aggressive behavior with the intent to cause physical or psychological harm. Intent is central to this definition; accidents are not aggression.

Infants do commit physically rough acts; babies like to tug at things, and they may be painfully adept. However, an infant is not a violent being; although an infant may hurt his or her mother by roughly tugging at her hair, the infant has no intention of causing harm.

Like infants, toddlers may engage in rough play, but they are usually surprised when their aggression causes harm. Typical toddlers still lack deliberate intent to harm. However, aggression later in childhood may be related to behavior during the toddler stage of development. The critical process called *socialization* begins during toddlerhood, whereby toddlers begin to acquire the rules and values of their society (Sears, 1961; Sears, Maccoby, & Levin, 1957). Although at first toddlers only obey these rules, after a while they internalize them; that is, they begin to believe that they are correct. This belief, this *internalization* (Grusec & Goodnow, 1994), is the heart of socialization, and socialization is the heart of law-abiding and peaceful behavior.

Preschoolers (in a stage also called *early childhood*; Sroufe et al., 1996) do begin to understand that aggression hurts others, and this understanding results in the ability to form intent, which is the basic underpinning of interpersonal violence (Sears et al., 1957; Vissing, Straus, Gelles, & Harrop, 1991). Other developments during early childhood are also related to aggression. For example, *social competence* emerges. This is an ability seen in a child who plays regularly with peers and is liked by peers, and is related to behavior problems in preschool years (Campbell, 1994). Children with adequate social competence are able to play in a friendly manner with other children, which is important because such play enables them to learn about many different issues—including the acceptability (or unacceptability) of aggression and violence. Children with high social competence are better able than children with poor social competence to absorb peer lessons about prosocial and aggressive behavior (Campbell,

1994; Vaughn, Hogan, Lancelotta, Shapiro, & Walker, 1992). It is during early childhood that both the capacity for prosocial behavior and the capacity for aggression increase dramatically.

What affects a young child's tendency to be aggressive or prosocial? One of the most important events in a child's life (possibly the most important), attachment to a parent or parents, is probably strongly related to the child's tendency to be either prosocial or aggressive. *Attachment* refers to the emotional bond between a child and his or her caregiver. This relationship between the quality of attachment and aggression appears to work in two ways. First, it seems likely that violence in a family—either the presence of spouse or child abuse—interferes in the formation of a strong, positive attachment (Cicchetti & Olson, 1990). Some researchers have reported that being exposed to domestic violence "blunts" a child's emotions, thereby possibly reducing the likelihood of the child becoming attached to caregivers (Schneider-Rosen & Cicchetti, 1984). Second, just as violence may interfere with attachment, lack of attachment may help cause aggression in children. Secure attachment to parents in infancy predicts a high level of prosocial behavior later in life (Troy & Sroufe, 1987), and infant attachment problems seem to lead to hostile-aggressive behavior during the preschool years (Lyons-Ruth, Alpern, & Repacholi, 1993). Attachment is also related to social competence (Cohn, 1990). The findings that violence interferes with attachment, and that a poor attachment may help predict antisocial behavior, might help explain the relationship between parental violence and an increased risk of aggression in the family children (Spatz Widom, 1989b). It is possible to speculate that the resilient children of violent households may form positive attachments to parents despite the domestic aggression they are exposed to, and that it may be this positive attachment that protects them from the noxious influence of domestic violence.

During middle childhood (the school years), developmental changes in peer interaction occur. Generally, most children become more altruistic and kind toward their playmates, and come to understand better that friendship involves caring and understanding, not just mutual play interests. In most children, there is a decrease in *instrumental aggression*; they generally cease to use aggressive behavior merely to get something they want. However, there may be an increase in *hostile aggression* (aggression aimed at hurting the victim; Atkins, Stoff, Osborne, & Brown, 1993). This may be seen especially in the form of verbal aggression between children; and it is during middle childhood that an increase in hostile aggression among children who have witnessed adults deliberately trying to hurt each other emerges.

Interestingly, an examination of peer groups in middle childhood reveals many of the potential bases of adolescent gang activity. First, peer networks during middle childhood are relatively stable clusters of friends.

Second, there are interesting gender differences (Matthys, Cohen-Kettenis, & Berkhout, 1994). Peer groups of boys during this age are generally larger clusters, where the group emphasizes loyalty and activities that members participate in together. As with older boys, peer groups of this age are very interested in competition between members, achievements of peers, and their groups tend to have formal and rigid rules, with some clearly dominating members. Emotional intimacy is not usually present or, if present, is not emphasized.

Girls' peer groups, on the other hand, usually consist of smaller groups and do emphasize emotional intimacy and support of each other. The group activities usually revolve around noncompetitive activities such as playing and talking together, rather than competitive activities such as sports. Girls tend to be significantly more emotionally attached to their peers than are boys (Nada Raja, McGee, & Stanton, 1992). Whereas boys' peer groups tend to emphasize feelings of inclusion, girls' tend to emphasize feelings of intimacy (Vernberg, 1990).

Parenting style during middle childhood and adolescence also has a significant impact on aggressive behavior. Parents who are warm and loving, regardless of their disciplinary practices, usually produce cooperative, prosocial children; however, parents who are highly controlling and feel a strong need to assert power over their children, and who are less warm and loving, tend to produce children who are more aggressive (B. Weiss, Dodge, Bates, & Pettit, 1992). One typical study found that parents who exercised a high degree of physical control had adolescents with significantly more behavior problems (Barber, Olsen, & Shagle, 1994). Of course, this relationship is a two-way street; different types of children provoke different types of parenting. Parents who feel a need to control one child may not feel that need with other children. Doubtless, every child's unique personality provokes a somewhat unique parenting style.

SOCIAL LEARNING PERSPECTIVES

Social learning theory grew out of the behaviorist movement; social learning theorists are thus interested in *overt behavior* (behavior you can actually see and measure), as opposed to inner or unconscious thoughts or conflicts (that cannot be directly seen or measured). This theory stresses that people learn how to behave as a result of the psychosocial environment they live in, both as children and as adults. Early on, social learning theory was used to understand the causes of violent behavior (Sutherland, 1947).

There are two major learning mechanisms that are important to criminologists. The first mechanism is called *observational learning* or *modeling* (Akers, 1985). Modeling refers simply to the imitation of other people.

Do people learn to become aggressive or violent through watching and imitating others who are aggressive? Many criminologists and psychologists believe that they do, and research on the influences of the family and mass media certainly supports this contention (Curtis, 1963).

Learning To Be Violent

In 1992, the newspaper *Education Week* published a story entitled "Children in Boston Exposed Early to Violence." This study reported that 1 in 10 children whose mothers responded to a survey at a Boston health clinic had witnessed a knifing or a shooting by age 6.

The survey involved 115 children whose mothers brought them to Boston City Hospital's primary-care pediatric clinic. The average age of the child was under 3.

Of the children who had witnessed a shooting, half had witnessed that shooting in their own home. Most of the children who had witnessed a knifing had witnessed it in their own home. Twenty-one children also reported having seen shovings, kickings, or punchings; 15 of the 21 had seen these events more than once. (Cohen, 1992)

A classic experiment on modeling and aggression demonstrated just how strong an influence observational learning can be. Bandura, a famous psychologist, decided to conduct an experiment to see if children would behave aggressively after watching aggressive adults (Bandura & Huston, 1961; Bandura, Ross, & Ross, 1963). While a child played in a room, Bandura had an adult enter the room and begin aggressively playing with a large Bobo doll. For approximately 10 minutes the adult kicked and socked the Bobo doll, saying aloud "Kick him!" while the beating went on. Next, after watching the adult, the child was told that he or she would not be allowed to play with a group of very enticing toys. (The goal here was to frustrate the child.) Finally, the child was led into another room where several toys—including a Bobo doll—waited.

The children who had seen the adult assault the Bobo doll were more likely to imitate the adult's aggressive behavior and attack the Bobo doll themselves. Other children, who had also been frustrated but who had not seen the aggressive adult, were much less likely to hit the Bobo doll. Thus, observing an aggressive adult appeared to dramatically increase the likelihood of aggression in the child.

A second principle of behaviorism emphasizes *reward and punishment* as shapers of behavior (Winder & Rau, 1962). Sometimes this principle is called *operant conditioning*. Operant conditioning means simply that behaviors that are rewarded are more likely to occur again, and behaviors that are not rewarded (or are punished) are less likely to recur. A *reward* is any pleasant event or feeling, such as a cookie, pride, parental admiration, or acceptance as a member of a group. *Punishment* is anything that makes it less likely that the behavior will repeat.

According to this principle, violence occurs because the person has been rewarded for being violent, or has seen others rewarded for being violent. Operant conditioning is a very powerful shaper of behavior, and an important step in understanding anyone's violent or criminal behavior is understanding what the rewards of violence or criminality are for them. In real life, however, discerning exactly what these rewards or punishments are is frequently a very difficult task.

An Example: The Rewards of Sexual Assault

Until recently, a general misunderstanding about the rewards of sexual assault led to very poor reporting and conviction rates of this violent crime. Traditionally, sexual assault was assumed to be motivated by sexual desire, and the reward of the assault was obtaining sexual intercourse with the most attractive victim possible.

Believing this, investigators were baffled by offenders who reported assaulting elderly women or children; they were equally baffled by offenders who reported that they did not experience an orgasm or an erection during the assault (a common occurrence). Without these events occurring, they tended to believe that the assault did not even happen.

Today we know that sexual assault is most often motivated and (more importantly) rewarded by a feeling of intense power over the victim; thus, it is a crime that can happen between any two people (even a husband and wife) and need not involve sexual intercourse for the offender to be satisfied. If the victim is rendered powerless, the offender has his reward.

In the case of sexual assault, better understanding of the rewards of the crime has led to dramatically increased detection and conviction rates.

OTHER PSYCHOLOGICAL
AND PSYCHIATRIC PERSPECTIVES

Personality and Violence

Some data point to psychological and personality differences between violent and nonviolent individuals. In their quest to clarify the differences between these two types of individuals, the psychiatric community has created a psychiatric diagnosis called Anti-Social Personality Disorder (ASP). ASP is a *personality disorder*, which is a psychological disorder that exists in a person who is not insane or psychotic, but whose psychological disturbances nevertheless affect their behavior. The behavior of a person with ASP is characterized by constant conflict with society. These individuals are incapable of loyalty to any groups or persons and are grossly selfish, callous, irresponsible, and impulsive. They are marked by a lack of shame or guilt over their behavior; they tend to deny any responsibility for their problems and seem unable to learn from punishment or experience. ASP is diagnosed most frequently in males and in lower class individuals.

The existence of ASP implies that antisocial behavior (such as violent behavior) is the major symptom of an underlying personality disorder. However, a major problem with the psychiatric diagnosis of ASP is that many (if not most) violent individuals do not fit the ASP criteria. The wide range of psychological characteristics in violent individuals defies this attempt to categorize them into one personality type. For example, violent gang members often demonstrate extreme loyalty to their gangs and frequently have a set of ethics that they meticulously follow (although these ethics do not match the values of mainstream society). A wife-beater may be very violent, but may actually feel intense love for his victim. In addition, other predictors of violence have not been associated with ASP (Kandel, 1989). It remains possible, of course, that there is some personality type that is common to all violent individuals, but has yet to be defined. However, given the variety of violent individuals, this does not seem likely.

Serious Mental Illness and Violence

Violence has also been studied in association with more severe mental disorders. *Psychoses* is the medical and psychological term for what laypeople commonly refer to as *insanity*. Individuals are termed *psychotic* when their mental functioning is so badly impaired that they are unable to meet the ordinary demands of life; for example, they may be unable to recognize and interpret reality, and may experience hallucinations (seeing or hearing things that do not exist) or delusions (bizarre beliefs with no basis in reality).

Financial and other pressures have resulted in a widespread policy to treat severely mentally ill individuals in the community whenever possible, rather than treating them in locked hospital facilities. One result of this policy is that mentally ill offenders have become a major safety concern with the public, who perceive them as excessively violent (Hurley, 1994). The consensus of current research, however, is that they are no more likely to be violent than are other members of the general population (Monahan, 1992). The fact that the media tends to focus on violent crimes committed by mentally ill individuals at least partially explains the public's concern. However, some research has suggested that there may be genetic or family environment links between some types of serious mental illness and criminal behavior (Hurley, 1994; Offord, 1971; Silverton, 1985).

Antisocial and violent behavior has been examined in the relatives of psychotic individuals many times, beginning in the 1930s (Bender, 1938). Since then, several studies have noted that the first-degree relatives of psychotic patients are more antisocial than are control subjects (Bleuler, 1972; Robins, 1966). This higher level of antisocial behavior in relatives exists even among those relatives who never become psychotic (Silverton, 1985). One researcher found that adolescent murderers frequently had mothers with a history of psychiatric hospitalization (Lewis et al., 1985). These studies suggest that although mental illness itself may not necessarily cause violence, the genetic or family basis of mental illness may cause psychosis in some members and antisocial or violent behavior in others.

Frustration and Aggression

Several decades ago, psychologists, guided by hypotheses deriving from both psychoanalytic theory and learning theory, began to investigate the possibility that human violence was closely related to, and perhaps preceded by, the emotion that we call *frustration*. Frustration occurs when a person is prevented from reaching a goal; the result is an uncomfortable state of physical arousal that needs to be relieved. Perhaps, this theory stated, violence occurs because it is an attempt to relieve the arousal caused by frustration (Berkowitz, 1962). This theory was called the *frustration–aggression hypothesis*.

Frustration need not be caused only by personal factors, such as not attaining all the material goods that one may want. Frustration may also be caused by factors such as political repression, domination, or a sense of having been unfairly treated. It is not essential that such unfairness be real; it is only necessary that an individual believe that he or she has been unfairly treated for frustration to result. Furthermore, for the aggression to relieve the resulting tension, it need not be aimed at any specific subject; if people feel frustrated because they believe themselves to be victimized and powerless, than any violence that makes them feel powerful will relieve the arousal. Of course, not all frustrated individuals become violent; violence is only expressed in a minority of individuals whose social learning and other individual factors presumably make such an expression possible.

Berkowitz (1983) also demonstrated that violent cues in the environment result in higher levels of aggressive responses to frustration. A commonly examined cue is the presence of guns; for most people, guns are closely associated with violence. Berkowitz and LePage (1967) did indeed demonstrate a heightened aggressive response in frustrated males in the presence of a gun (vs. frustrated males in the presence of a badminton racket). Is it possible, therefore, that an officer carrying a visible weapon might actually elicit more aggression than one who is not carrying such a weapon? This is a controversial issue, especially because in some countries officers do not carry guns, but several studies have yielded mixed results (Berkowitz, 1983; Berkowitz & LePage, 1967; Kang, Magura, & Shapiro, 1994).

More recently, studies have found a general relationship between frustration and aggression but have also noted that this model has a number of possible confounds (Gustafson, 1989). Gustafson found that aggression did correlate with frustration, but that it also correlated with other factors, raising the possibility that frustration and aggression are only correlated because they are both related to some third factor. For example, only marginal differences in aggression were found between subjects who were aroused by frustration and subjects who were aroused by physical exercise. This type of finding suggests that although frustration and aggression may be correlated, in fact it may be the physical arousal of frustration, and not the emotion per se that is responsible for the corresponding rise in aggression (Ahmed & Mapletoft, 1989). In any case, this hypothesis is an interesting, if incomplete, model of violence. Although it is doubtless a factor in at least some violence, the frustration–aggression hypothesis cannot fully explain why some individuals choose violent responses and others do not.

Overcontrolled and Undercontrolled Violence

In the press and in the consciousness of the U.S. public, it is possible that nothing is more fascinating than the prospect of a mild-mannered, introverted, law-abiding citizen who suddenly goes "berserk" and brutally slaughters his or her family or other individuals. Certainly, many people are able to grasp the distinction between habitually violent, uncaring individuals and those rigid, well-behaved individuals who once in a lifetime "break out" and become violent.

That distinction was of particular interest to Megargee (1966), who described these two types of violent offenders as *undercontrolled* and *overcontrolled* individuals. Persons with few or no inhibitions against violence, and thus who used violence frequently as a response, were described as undercontrolled. Such individuals are frequently extroverts. In contrast, overcontrolled individuals have very strict moral codes against misbehavior of all types, including violence. These people are introverted, rigidly self-controlled and oversocialized; they conform to society's standards obsessively. According to Megargee, it is precisely these overcontrolled individuals who will be the most violent, although undercontrolled individuals will be violent much more frequently.

An "Overcontrolled" Offender?

Paul Bernardo was a 30-year-old bookkeeper who "might be Joe Ordinary, from Anytown, Canada" (Nickerson, 1995). A handsome man who had been characterized as domestic and quiet, Bernardo had no criminal record. Apparently, however, he had long harbored fantasies of sexually assaulting young girls and then killing them, fantasies that he allegedly was able to fulfill with the help of his wife. Although Bernardo had no criminal record, he was charged with sexual assaults on women as far back as the early 1980s, leading some to question whether "overcontrolled" offenders truly have no history of violence, or whether they are merely better at hiding their crimes than other offenders. Certainly, Bernardo went to significant lengths to hide the bodies of the girls he had killed: After cutting one body into 10 pieces with a power saw, he allegedly encased the parts in cement and then sank them in a fishing pond (Nickerson, 1995).

Extroversion has, in fact, been linked to habitual violence and aggressiveness (L. Ellis, 1991). In addition, some research has suggested that violent offenders with no previous record of violence are much more likely to show features of the overcontrolled personality than are violent offenders with a history of violence. However, it appears that the overcontrolled versus undercontrolled dichotomy may be more descriptive than useful as etiological information; that is, it may help us understand different types of offenders more than it may help us understand why some people offend and others do not. More recent evidence has pointed out, for example, that many overcontrolled and undercontrolled individuals are also found in the nonviolent population (Henderson, 1983). Why do some overcontrolled individuals break out in extreme violence, whereas others do not? Although the distinction drawn here is very interesting, it may be less significant in understanding what drives violent behavior in general.

Hostile Interpretation of Ambiguous Events

Under certain circumstances, aggression may be a normal and adaptive response. This may particularly be the case when an individual is faced with hostile or threatening forces, and violence is perceived as a necessary response. Given that a hostile environment might provoke an aggressive response in almost anyone, some researchers have investigated the possibility that violent individuals are not people who inappropriately choose violence; rather, they are people who inappropriately perceive hostility where most people would not (Dodge, Bates, & Pettit, 1990; Dodge, Price, et al., 1990). That is, perhaps it is not the response that is skewed, but the perception of the environment.

Dodge studied aggressive and nonaggressive children, and found that aggressive children have two perceptual tendencies that nonaggressive children lack. Aggressive children were more likely to believe that other people had hostile intentions; and they were more likely to evaluate the results of aggression positively.

Dodge and colleagues also studied adolescent offenders in a maximum security prison and found that although these biases were also found in this population, they were only found in undersocialized delinquents. This line of study sheds some light on why it may be so difficult to treat violent offenders. Trying to teach such offenders to be nonviolent may in fact be trying to teach them to react nonviolently to what they perceive to be intensely threatening situations. For example, imagine that you are standing in a field holding a gun, and an elephant is charging toward you at full speed with his tusks aimed right at you. Trying to teach violent offenders to be nonviolent might be like trying to teach them not to shoot that elephant, even though there is every indication that that elephant is deadly.

Other research has noted similar findings. Some of Dodge's later research (e.g., Dodge, 1993) also found that both moderately and severely aggressive children have a number of problems with "social cognition," among them, attributional biases. Other similar studies have found that aggressive children attribute fewer positive intentions to people in problem-solving scenarios (Vitaro, Pelletier, & Coutu, 1989) and that sexually aggressive men use a "suspicious schema" in interpreting women's statements (Malamuth & Brown, 1994). Finally, Downey and Walker (1989) looked more closely at this phenomenon and noted that attributional biases did not appear to mediate the link between high risk and aggression, but rather, appeared to serve as a protective factor against aggression. That is, children who are at high risk for violence—for example, children who have been abused—are not at even higher risk if they also make biased attributions. Rather, those children who do not make biased attributions are at lower risk of becoming aggressive, even if they have been abused. In other words, making accurate rather than biased attributions may be a protective factor that makes children resilient.

> All violent feelings produce in us a falseness in our impressions of external things. (John Ruskin, cited in Cohen & Cohen, 1993)

Recidivism and Violence

One important group of questions concerns *recidivism*, or the probability that a violent offender will commit another violent offense. Do rates of recidivism differ between family- and street-violent offenders? Are some groups of violent offenders more likely to repeat their offenses, once released, then others? Answers to these questions have important implications for public safety; the U.S. public is growing increasingly outraged by the discovery that a violent crime has been perpetrated on an innocent victim, after the offender was released from prison following an earlier violent offense. In Connecticut, a young schoolteacher was shot and killed by her boyfriend—just outside the elementary school where she taught. Even though just 4 months earlier he had put a gun to her head and attempted to kill her, he was free on bail. How likely is it that a murderous young man—or any given offender—will repeat his crime? The answer, not surprisingly, is that it depends on the type of crime perpetrated.

When we examine street-violent crime, a clear pattern emerges. Most street-violent criminals will not, in fact, ever commit more than one violent crime during their careers. This statement may seem erroneous in the face of a great deal of publicity to the contrary, but in fact, it is a few chronically violent offenders who are responsible for the majority of violent crime (Mednick, Harway, Mednick, & Moffitt, 1981; Piper, 1985). Furthermore, some research has suggested that recidivistic violent offenders are much more apt than nonrecidivistic offenders to inflict severe injuries on their victims (Convit, Isay, Otis, & Volavka, 1990). Official records show that only about one third of violent offenders are rearrested within 3 years for a violent crime, with the remaining 67% staying out of trouble (Greenfeld, 1992). In street-violent criminals, furthermore, biological variables are most strongly related to recidivistic violence; in one study, 100% of recidivistic street-violent criminals had strong biological markers for violence—such as highly disturbed prenatal development, high numbers of minor physical anomalies, or high numbers of head injuries (Kandel, 1988; Kandel et al., 1989). All these data suggest the existence of a small but highly recidivistic group of street-violent criminals, with the majority of street violent criminals likely to be only one-time offenders. Is this pattern the same for family violence?

Unfortunately, it appears not. A larger proportion of family-violent offenders appear to offend again—particularly those who victimize children. For example, abused children who are left in formerly abusive households without intervention have a 40% to 70% chance of being reinjured, and a 5% chance of being killed (Jellinek et al., 1992). The first NFVS (Straus & Hotaling, 1980) found that 94% of abused children were abused repeatedly during the year they were studied, suggesting very high recidivism among physical abusers of children. More than half of sexual abusers report that they have committed sexual abuse multiple times (Bernard, 1975). Many sexual abusers of children refuse treatment or fail to cooperate with it, contending that they do not want to be "cured" of their sexual preference for children—an attitude that certainly suggests recidivism (Bernard, 1975; Marshall & Barbaree, 1988).

Similar patterns of recidivism are found in spouse abusers and people who abuse the elderly. Thus, in contrast to street violence, recidivism in family violence appears to be the rule rather than the exception. Why are family-violent offenders so much more likely to repeat their offenses, in comparison to street-violent ones? One major reason is undoubtedly opportunity. A physical abuser's victim is present, in his or her domain, a good deal of the time—there is no need to seek out targets for aggression. One conveniently and repeatedly appears. Similarly, most child sexual abuse is perpetrated by someone who knows the child, and therefore has repeated access to the victim. And a spouse is a "handy" victim; always there, and perhaps too frightened to retaliate. A second reason is impunity, or an offender's lack of fear that he or she will be caught and punished. Physical and sexual abuse occurs in the privacy of the home, with few or no witnesses; any witnesses there are typically have strong motivations to keep silent. Furthermore, police and other authorities are noticeably more reluctant to "interfere" in family violence than in street violence, and tend not to view family-violent individuals as "criminals." In fact, family-violent offenders may not view themselves as criminals.

Perhaps the most important information about the relevance of individual factors in violence comes from recidivism data. Only a small minority of offenders will become chronic recidivists, and these individuals will both commit the majority of criminal acts and show the strongest relationship to internal markers for violence (Convit et al., 1990; Kandel et al., 1989; Kandel & Mednick, 1991; Piper, 1985).

Chapter 5

Television and Violence

One frequently hypothesized cause of contemporary violence is, of course, television, which even less than the other causes we have been discussing, fits into an arbitrary social–individual dichotomy.

TELEVISION VIOLENCE AND AGGRESSION IN CHILDREN

Some groups of experts have long maintained that television is an excessively violent influence on children (Burne, 1993; Centerwall, 1992). Some researchers have even linked television violence to violent crime (Centerwall, 1992), although others have found only weak correlations between television violence and aggressive behavior or other undesirable outcomes (Gortmaker, Salter, Walker, & Dietz, 1990; Harris, 1992; Janokowski, 1985). The same was once said many years ago of radio, which featured shows in which heroes aggressively conquered villains. But recently there has been a major shift in public opinion and mounting concern about a possible link between the epidemic of youth violence and the effects of television violence on children.

The question of whether or not television has a destructive impact on children may be controversial, but there are some facts no one disputes. First, it is clear that U.S. children watch a great deal of television. The average 3- or 4-year-old watches 2 hours each day (Huston, Watkins, & Kunkel, 1989), and older children may watch 40 hours or more every week. In Huston's study (Huston, Wright, Rice, Kerkman, & St. Peters, 1990), young children spent more time watching television than doing any other activity.

In addition, there is no doubt that much of the content of television programs is violent. Some estimates hold that a U.S. child views 3,000 acts of violence every year on television; these acts include murder and robbery, assault, beatings, and torture (Pierce, 1984; Strasburger, 1985). Whereas 85% of prime-time shows were nonviolent during the 1950s, only 20% to 30% are nonviolent in the mid-1990s ("Reel Violence," 1994). The reality is that television is a business, not a public service (for the most part), and is run by individuals who are trying to sell commercial airtime. In order to succeed, sponsors must entice people to watch as much television as possible: and violence has dramatic appeal.

Interestingly, however, it is not the shows aimed at adults that are most violent, but the shows aimed at children. Prime-time (or "family-oriented") shows include, on the average, 6 violent acts per hour; children's Saturday and Sunday shows (e.g., cartoons), in contrast, about 26 violent acts per hour (Gerbner, 1990). Before the average U.S. child even reaches high school, he or she has seen about 100,000 acts of violence on television, 8,000 of which are murders (Radecki, 1989; "Reel Violence," 1994). When asked, many children protest that they know the difference between television "fake" violence and "real" violence; in fact, this may be true for most, if not for all (Atkin, 1983). Nevertheless, it remains possible that even "fake" violence has an impact. The only way to test this hypothesis is to review the research on exposure to television violence and the development of violent behavior. If it appears that amounts of exposure are related to levels of violence, then there must be an effect. If no such relationship exists, then perhaps children are able to distinguish between fantasy and reality, and the issue is as simple as that.

Two types of studies have been conducted: correlational studies and experimental studies. A *correlational* study addresses the question of whether behavior becomes more violent as a child watches more violent television; that is, whether the two factors vary together? If they do, than a child who watches 1 hour of violent television might (theoretically) be mildly aggressive in his or her play, whereas a child who watches 3 hours might be more aggressive, and a child who watches 5 hours might be extremely aggressive. Such a pattern, in which one measure increases as a second measure increases, is called a *positive correlation*. In fact, a positive correlation between violent television watching and aggressive behavior has been reported in several studies (Eron, 1987; Huesmann & Eron, 1986; Turner, Hesse, & Peterson-Lewis, 1986). Other studies have found that violent television watching only increases aggressive behavior in children who already tend toward aggressive behavior (Friedrich & Stein, 1973). Do these studies prove that violent television watching causes an increase in violent behavior (at least in some children)? Unfortunately, they do not. Correlations are highly suggestive but do not prove the direction of influence. In this case, the positive correlation could equally suggest one of three interpretations:

1. Violent television watching causes violent behavior to increase.
2. Children who are violent choose to, and prefer to, watch violent television more than their nonviolent counterparts.
3. Some third factor—for instance, lack of parental involvement—is responsible for both the increase in violent television watching and the increase in violent behavior.

Because correlational studies cannot tell us which of these three interpretations is the correct one, experimental studies have been conducted in an attempt to sift them apart. An *experimental* study is one in which the researcher controls one factor (such as television watching) while measuring changes in a second factor (such as aggressive behavior). The dilemma is how a researcher, in a society in which almost everyone has a television at home, might completely control a child's exposure to television violence. The truth is that total control is impossible. A child may agree to watch only certain programs, or at certain times, but may be exposed to television violence in other settings—for example, at a playmate's house, or home alone without parents to control television viewing. Therefore, investigators have been limited to attempting to see whether aggressive responses rise immediately after exposure to violent television. A typical experimental study might proceed according to this scenario:

1. The investigator randomly separates the subjects into two groups: Group A and Group B.
2. Group A is exposed to 1 hour of violent television.
3. Group B is exposed to 1 hour of nonviolent television.
4. Then both Groups A and B are given some task that frustrates them.
5. The investigator watches both groups closely: Are the members of Group A more likely to react aggressively than the members of Group B?

Suppose Group A does react more violently. There are several possibilities: Perhaps Group A members tended to watch more violent television before the experiment ever began. Alternatively, perhaps Group A just happens to contain individuals who tended to be more aggressive before the experiment ever began. In a well-designed study, where the subjects

An Insider's View: One Response From the Television Industry
by Stephen Kandel

I am a writer; mostly television, some films (6), some books (2), some stories, some journalism, some radio, some theater.

During that Mostly Television period, as a writer/producer, I dealt primarily in melodrama (e.g., violence); ergo I have concluded that one of the most enduring problems of commercial television is a *shortage* of real sex and violence. Instead, commercial simulacra have been substituted, and the result is a gaudy fantasy, suitable for political punditry, but with at best a limited causal connection to *real* violence. Television violence lacks consequence; after a savage beating, the hero strolls away, unharmed. After one punch, the villain collapses, unconscious. After a fusillade of machine gun bullets Rambo is untouched; when Rambo hurls one spear, it skewers a hapless brace of faceless enemies. This is the trivialization of violence.

Ergo my thesis: we need *truer* violence. Not *Die Hard With a Vengeance* but *Schindler's List*; violence with painful, felt aftereffects; violence that derives from human rage, or fear or brutal power—violence that hurts, maims, leaves real marks and real victims.

If TV violence provokes a rise in viewer acting-out, violently, it is not because of violence—it is because of *untruthful* violence. Children watch the *Mighty Morphin Power Rangers*—and learn that one can become invulnerable, dealing out risk-free damage to the clearly deserving. But in drama, the uses of violence begin with ambiguity: The victim may not be altogether innocent; the attacker may be corrupted by the attack. Most important: The attack has painful consequences for *both* assailant and target. Attention *is* paid.

To place TV violence in another cultural context, consider Japanese television, especially made-for-cable "dramas" double-dipped in gore and extremely brutal sex. In such productions as UROTSUKIDOJI I and II, the heroine is anally raped by a demon; a succubus takes human female form, seduces a man and at the moment of graphic coition slaughters him by tearing out his throat with "her" fangs. Despite this extreme violence, crime rates in Japanese cities are remarkably low, by U.S. standards; police frequently operate without the use of firearms; children spend their afterschool hours in study rather than random urban wilding.

I suggest, therefore, that television violence is a minor element in a range of influences urging violence as a solution in the United States. We live in a visual/aural world of desensitization. If humans did not employ violence, it would scarcely be necessary to invent it; as we do employ violence—consistently and painfully—the only responsible role mass communication media can play is to ground that violence in reality; to present it as ugly, painful, sometimes necessary, rarely pleasurable, never without a context.

are picked for the study randomly, the two groups should be equal and these two possibilities can be ruled out.

In fact, in well-designed research adults do appear to react more violently after they have been exposed to violent television compared to adults who have been exposed to nonviolent television. This suggests that television violence may have the immediate effect of causing an increase in violence (Huston et al., 1989). But what about long-term effects? Do years of television violence "build up" in children and cause them to be violent as adolescents and adults? That is the question that remains unanswered. What we can conclude is that correlational studies suggest that television violence may be related to violent behavior as an adult, and that television violence appears to provoke more aggressive behavior in the short term.

"I Watched Violent Television as a Kid, and I'm Okay"

This is perhaps the most common argument presented in favor of dismissing the impact of violent television on behavior. On the surface, it makes sense. How can violent television be destructive if everyone watches it, and most people are never violent? The answer lies in an understanding of risk factors and behavior. Violence never has one single cause; there are a multitude of important influences, including biological predisposition, temperament, and family experience. Sometimes a universal influence, something experienced by everyone, can contribute to violent behavior, but only in people who have other risk factors (such as a violent family life) as well. In these at-risk individuals, television violence may in fact be a very important influence. This observation is consistent with the findings of some of the research previously reviewed, which have also suggested that violent television has its most destructive impact on children already at risk for violence.

By what mechanisms might exposure to television violence lead to more aggressive behavior? There are three major theories:

- Learning and Imitation. According to this theory, television may model violent behavior that some children (and adults) will imitate (Sutherland, 1947). The assumption is that television teaches people how to be violent.

- Trigger Mechanism. According to this theory, television violence may "trigger" violent behavior in those few people who already tend to behave violently (Wood, Wong, & Chachere, 1991). In this view, television violence may be the "final straw," not the only or even the most important influence, but the influence that finally leads the already at-risk individual toward violent behavior.

• Desensitization. According to this theory, television violence may so accustom people to violence that they do not notice it anymore (Linz, Donnerstein, & Adams, 1989). It occurs when people encounter something shocking so often that after a while it fails to provoke any emotional response at all. One example of desensitization is the response of most people in major U.S. cities to homeless individuals. Many years ago, the sight of someone living on the street was shocking and upsetting to most Americans. Today, however, most New Yorkers can walk past a homeless person and feel virtually nothing because they see homeless individuals so frequently. Some research has suggested that the same principle may operate in the case of television violence (Linz et al., 1989). Perhaps watching hundreds of thousands of violent acts on television desensitizes us to violence so much that we consider "real" violence to be ordinary and unavoidable.

All of these theories contribute to a possible explanation of the relationship between television violence and aggression in television watchers. However, because all three theories postulate a causal relationship, they must at this point be viewed as speculative.

Chapter 6

The Biosocial Model

INADEQUACY OF SINGLE-FACTOR EXPLANATIONS

Most investigators examine the causes of violence as they relate to only one factor. For example, one study might examine the association between television and violence, whereas a separate study might focus on the relation between a biological factor and aggression. Although this is an effective method for expanding our knowledge, it distorts our perspective. Individual factors can be shown to be related to violence, but no single-factor model has been effective in fully explaining why some individuals are violent and others are not. For example, as we saw in chapter 5, exposure to television may be linked with violent behavior in children; but almost all U.S. children watch television, so the question of why it affects some children strongly and not others remains.

A more accurate approach to the explanation of violent behavior is an epidemiological approach. Epidemiology seeks to understand what factors increase the risk of disorders, rather than attempting to find the "cause" of a problem disease or behavior. *Risk factors* are any factors that increase the risk of getting a disorder or a disease. For example, driving without a seat belt increases the risk of injury in an accident. Driving without a seat belt is not a cause of an injury, but wearing no seat belt is associated with higher levels of injury. *Protective factors*, on the other hand, are factors that promote health. Wearing a seat belt is a protective factor against auto injury. Although wearing a seat belt does not guarantee no injury, it is associated with lower levels of injury.

Similarly, having four or more minor physical anomalies (MPA) is associated with higher rates of recidivistic violence. Watching violent television is associated with higher rates of childhood aggression. This is not to say that MPAs and television single-handedly cause violence; rather, these are risk factors that increase the probability of violence. No one risk factor alone is enough to cause the behavioral disorder we call *violence*; rather, multiple risk factors must be present.

Just as there are risk factors, there are protective factors against violence. Living in a family that clearly rewards prosocial behavior and punishes aggression and violence is one protective factor; although such a family cannot guarantee that no child in it will grow up to be violent, the risk of such a disorder is clearly lower.

Conceptualizing the causes of violence as a risk and protective factor equation can clarify the role that all of the factors discussed in chapters 3, 4, and 5 must play. Furthermore, it helps explain why some factors seem relevant in some violent offenders, although they seem clearly irrelevant in other violent offenders. Rather than emphasizing any given theoretical approach (e.g., theorizing that individuals learn to be violent), epidemiology seeks only to identify factors that clearly affect the risk that an individual will demonstrate a disorder. Accordingly, the biosocial model can account for the potential contribution of both biological and psychosocial factors. It seems clear that neither set of factors alone can explain the existence of human violence.

In addition, several important risk factors associated with violent behavior are clearly influenced both by an individual's internal makeup and by his or her external conditions. These risk factors, being among the most important in predicting violent behavior, clearly demonstrate the importance of both types of influences.

GENDER AND VIOLENCE

One of the most intriguing aspects of violence is how gender-based it is. In other words, males and females differ in their rates of violent behavior to a greater extent than they differ in their patterns of most human behaviors. We have seen the increased vulnerability of males to childhood disorders related to violence, and the importance of androgens in the etiology of violence (L. Ellis, 1990, 1991).

But how large is the male–female difference? Is it really true, as we frequently assume, that males are responsible for most violence? Although some researchers have argued that gender differences in aggression are exaggerated, particularly if different types of aggression are accounted for (Bjorkqvist, 1994), most studies would certainly suggest that such an assumption is warranted. In 1958, Wolfgang studied the police records for all homicides occurring in Philadelphia between 1948 and 1952, and found that 82% of the perpetrators were male. That study, considered a classic, is nevertheless several decades old; do more modern statistics continue to follow this pattern? They seem to. The UCR (1989), compiled each year by the FBI, also finds that about 9 out of every 10 murderers are male. Similarly, perpetrators of assault and rape are primarily (if not exclusively) male, when official statistics are examined; in fact, the gender difference is presumed to be so marked that many researchers do not even bother to include women as subjects in their studies of violence (Cervi, 1991; Huesmann, Eron, Lefkowitz, & Walder, 1984; Olweus, 1979; Rosenbaum & Hoge, 1989; Spellacy, 1978).

Once again, however, we see an important distinction between family violence and street violence, and between official and self-report statistics. Most official statistics, as we know, reflect street crime and do not accurately reflect domestic violence. However, as we have seen, most violence in the United States appears to occur in the domestic domain, rather than in the community (Hotaling et al., 1989; Kandel-Englander, 1992). Therefore, as we attempt to understand the male to female ratio, it is very important to examine both self-report research and research on family violence. When we do so, the picture changes somewhat. For example, both men and women engage in child abuse; in fact, the 1975 NFVS found that 71% of mothers and 58% of fathers reported some violence against their children (Straus et al., 1980). Does this study suggest that, given the appropriate victim, a woman is just as likely to be violent as a man? Not really. Although women abused children at least as often as men in this study, the men used significantly more severe violence. In addition, the comparison is probably not a fair one; after all, women have much more opportunity to abuse children than do men because they are typically the primary caretakers. A truly informative study that sought to compare rates of male- versus female-perpetrated child abuse would have to compare men who are primary caregivers with women who are primary caregivers. Unfortunately, no such study has as yet been conducted.

The data on spouse abuse present another interesting challenge to the notion that violence is primarily male. Although the government, via the NCS, has estimated that the husband is the perpetrator in 70% of violent assaults between spouses (Langan & Innes, 1986), self-report surveys suggest otherwise. In the 1975 NFVS, approximately 12% of both men and women admitted using some form of violence against their spouse (Straus et al., 1980). More recent surveys, including the 1985 NFVS, also suggest approximately equal rates of male- and female-perpetrated spousal violence (O'Leary et al., 1989; Straus & Gelles, 1986). However, as with child abuse, the type of violence and the motive for the violence may still differ dramatically between the sexes. For example, men are more likely to use severe violence (e.g., punching and kicking), whereas women are more likely to use minor violence (such as throwing things or slapping; Straus & Gelles, 1990; Straus et al., 1980). In addition, men use violence against their wives in order to establish control or to get them to do something, whereas women use violence against their husbands in self-defense or retaliation, or to reduce their own tension or in an attempt to convince their husbands to talk (Adler, 1991; Straus & Gelles, 1990).

In summary, therefore, men perpetrate street violence in numbers overwhelmingly larger than women. In contrast, women seem to perpetrate family violence as often as men do, although their aggression is generally significantly less severe, is much less often fatal, and is more likely to result from self-defense.

There are two major approaches to explaining these differences—one via biological factors, and one via sociopsychological ones.

Biological Explanations

Biological explanations emphasize the role of male biology in the gender gap in aggressive behavior. Although the presence of the "Y" gene on the 23rd pair of chromosomes is known to make males more vulnerable to many physical disorders (e.g., heart disease), genetic influences do not appear to be critical in the etiology of violence (Mednick et al., 1984; see chapter 2). However, several biological markers of violence are found more often in men than women. For example, minimal brain dysfunction has been found to occur more frequently in men (Nichols, 1987); similarly, perinatal complications are more common in them (Kandel, 1989; Pasamanick, Rodgers, & Lilienfield, 1956).

A fruitful area of research, explored in chapter 4, is the role of androgens in violence. Recall that androgens are male sex hormones, secreted by both males and females, but much more abundant in males. Androgens have certainly been linked to criminal violence (L. Ellis, 1990), as well as to other sex-typed "male" behaviors (Berenbaum & Hines, 1992). One study of girls with congenital adrenal hyperplasia, a disorder in which they are exposed to high levels of androgens in utero, found a marked preference for boys' toys (Berenbaum & Hines, 1992). Although androgens probably only play an indirect role in aggression, it seems likely that the fact that males are exposed to more androgens in utero is one reason why males are more prone to behave violently.

Another biological factor that has been linked both to males and to violence is MAO (monoamine oxidase, an enzyme). Blood levels of MAO have been related to a number of behavioral patterns, including level of motor activity and infant fussiness (L. Ellis, 1991). Low levels of MAO in the blood of infants is associated with problems such as nail-biting and enuresis (bedwetting; L. Ellis, 1991). Statistically, men have lower MAO levels than women. They drop especially low during a person's 20s and 30s (coincidentally, when aggressive behavior peaks). Lower MAO levels are associated with aggressiveness in general, sudden feelings of anger and frustration, and especially to impulsiveness (L. Ellis, 1991). MAO levels vary with levels of testosterone, one of the androgens (L. Ellis, 1990). One case study of a family with a high number of aggressive men found a defect on the chromosome that regulates MAO (Morell, 1993). All in all, MAO seems to constitute one more piece of the gender discrepancy puzzle.

Sociopsychological Explanations

Biology aside, there are clearly important differences in the manner in which boys and girls are socialized that are relevant to the gender gap in violence. Girls are much more likely to be taught to be expressive caregivers in preparation for their role as the central parent of children and the spouse who is the emotional watchdog in marital relationships. Individuals who are socialized in this way are undoubtedly less likely to be violent and assaultive. Male socialization, by contrast, typically involves emphasis on the role of competition with others and the importance of being dominant and powerful; much adult violence is in fact in pursuit of these goals. Parents treat boys and girls differently; boys are generally encouraged to be independent, exploratory, assertive, and sometimes even openly aggressive; girls, to be dependent on their families and nurturing of others. After the preschool years, parents are much more likely to use physical punishment with boys than with girls (J. Anderson, 1972). The different ways that parents and society raise boys and girls undoubtedly result in different behavioral styles and tendencies.

Apart from the way in which they are treated, some differences in childhood behavior between boys and girls undoubtedly lead into different emotional landscapes. Developmentally, boys are more prone to more behavioral disorders, including those that are linked to aggression and violence. For example, hyperactivity is more common in boys, as are CDs (G. Weiss, 1990; Zagar et al., 1989). Because we know that developmentally a child who is hyperactive or conduct disordered is at greater risk of becoming violent, the fact that boys have higher rates of these childhood disorders makes them one more part of the causal equation explaining the male–female discrepancy in violent behavior.

Even a child's reaction to violent victimization may depend, at least to some extent, on his or her gender. Faced with psychological trauma in general, girls are more apt to withdraw, whereas boys are more apt to act out aggressively. When girls and boys who had been violently abused were compared, one study found that although girls had significant adolescent problems, it was the boys who were violently abused as children who were more likely to commit crimes (Rivera & Spatz Widom, 1990). In general, men are freer to react aggressively to stressors because society forgives violence more readily in men and even applauds it at times.

EDUCATION AND VIOLENCE

A person's educational achievement is strongly affected by both external and internal factors, including the quality of the school they attend, the family's attitude toward education, social investment in education, and the child's inherent abilities that can make school success easier or more difficult. The evidence regarding school achievement and violent and criminal behavior is monotonous in its uniformly positive findings of an important relationship between school success and antisocial behavior.

A number of studies have examined school performance and its relationship to criminality or delinquency in general. G. Weiss (1990) found that hyperactivity (a risk factor for criminality) was associated with lowered educational achievement, and that recovery from mild to moderate perinatal complications (a risk factor for violence) seems to depend (at least in part) on the quality of a child's educational experiences. L. Ellis (1990) also found that school achievement is important in combination with other factors in leading to criminality. Kirkegaard-Sorenson and Mednick (1977) noted that school behavior in general is a good predictor of criminality, and Denno's (1990) study of Philadelphia delinquents found that language achievement and maternal educational levels were good discriminators between delinquents and nondelinquents. Finally, one study found that children who are at high risk for delinquency but do not become delinquent may be protected by factors, such as high IQ, that make it easy for them to succeed in school (Kandel, 1987; Kandel et al., 1988).

Other research has examined school achievement in relation to violent behavior, rather than criminal behavior in general. One report focused on family violence specifically, and noted that most studies reviewed found evidence for an inverse (opposite) relationship between a man's educational achievement and his risk of being violently abusive toward his wife (Hotaling & Sugarman, 1986). Similarly, a 1986 study of adults on death row for capital crimes found a clear and consistent pattern of childhood and adolescent educational and intellectual difficulties (Lewis, Pincus, Feldman, Jackson, & Bard, 1986). Other research has focused on juveniles, particularly on juveniles who are among the most violent: those convicted of murder. Busch et al. (1990) studied adolescents who had killed both family and nonfamily victims, and compared them to other delinquent teenagers. He found that severe educational difficulties were common in the backgrounds of the homicidal adolescents; he also noted that although intelligence discriminated between adolescent murderers and nonmurderers, it did so to a lesser degree than other factors such as having a violent family member, gang membership, and alcohol abuse. Other research on homicidal adolescents has found essentially the same results: Individuals who kill as adolescents are inevitably marked by "insurmountable" and "severe" educational difficulties (Bender, 1959; Lewis et al., 1988; Zagar, Arbit, Sylvies, Busch, & Hughes, 1990).

The evidence points strongly to an association between school achievement, criminality, and criminal violence. But how does school achievement relate to different types of criminal violence? Does the level of education an individual achieves have an impact on his or her tendency to be violent, either across the board, with family members, or on the street? In other words, do different types of violent offenders show different relationships to education? One approach to this question is to compare the number of years of school completed by violent and nonviolent men. In my 1992 study (Kandel-Englander, 1992), I compared educational patterns among different groups of subjects. Violent and nonviolent White subjects, it turned out, did not differ much in years of schooling completed. Violent and nonviolent non-White men did. Education, therefore, may be a more important contributor to violence among non-White, than among White, men.

As we have seen, there are real differences between those men who are street- and pan-violent, and those who are violent only with their families. These differences were correlated with differences in education. Overall, family violent men stayed in school as long, or longer, than nonviolent men. The pan- and street-violent attained, on the average, much less education. When only White men are considered, however, education appeared not to differ between the family-, pan- and street-violent males. (Note that this analysis only considers the years in school, not the quality of school experiences.) A very different pattern characterized non-White violent men. The family violent and nonviolent had completed a similar number of years in school; the street- and pan-violent had completed significantly fewer years.

To summarize, the number of years a child goes to school may be important in determining whether or not that child will become violent, but if this is the case, it is less true for White men than for non-White men. Among Whites, there were no differences among street-, pan-, family-violent, and nonviolent offenders. Among non-Whites, family-violent and nonviolent offenders were similarly highly educated, whereas pan-violent and street-violent offenders were less educated.

It is interesting to note that although non-White subjects in the study achieved less education than White subjects, they were similar to the U.S.

population as a whole. For example, 12% of the U.S. population drops out of school before high school; this is in comparison to 14% of the non-White study sample, and only 5% of the White study sample. Thus, non-White subjects were not characterized by extremely low educational achievement; rather, White subjects were characterized by higher educational achievement. Other research has suggested that longer stays in school may actually protect otherwise high-risk children from developing antisocial behavior (Kandel et al., 1988).

Why would family-violent offenders be as highly educated as nonviolent men? One possibility is that violent men who are as highly educated as nonviolent men may be "protected" from involvement in street violence by their investment in their status. Thus, if they stayed in school, they choose only family victims because doing so is less risky than choosing outside victims. This interpretation rests on the social truism, well-documented, that violence against the family is less often regarded as a "crime" than is violence in the streets. It certainly seems very likely that battering is seen as more socially acceptable (and thus is less socially controlled) than street violence (Straus, 1976). Because of such cultural beliefs, men may perceive that street violence carries much more risk of official detection and punishment than does the commission of family violence. Those men who have managed to stay in school and achieve a higher social class may not wish to jeopardize their gains by assaulting outsiders, when they feel able to assault family members more easily and with relatively greater impunity.

More generally, how might educational achievement help protect children against delinquency and violence? High achievement in school seems to increase children's self-esteem, which may protect them against becoming involved in delinquent or aggressive activities (Moeller, 1994). Students who achieve in school rate their own competence and abilities highly; their parents have similarly high expectations for them (Sink, Barnett, & Pool, 1993). High educational achievement is also associated with higher social class, which in turns helps prevent aggressivenss in boys (Moss, Mezzick, Yao, Gavaler, & Martin, 1995). One study found that low educational achievement—but not low IQ—during the early school years predicted later delinquency in both boys and girls (Fergusson & Horwood, 1995). Although low IQ does not predict well to delinquency, high IQ seems to protect children who are at high risk for violent and delinquent behavior—probably because high IQ makes school achievement relatively easy (Kandel, 1987; Kandel et al., 1988). School achievement helps children develop an internal locus of control and a belief in their own power to influence their environment (Ferrari & Parker, 1992). Finally, high achievement during school years is one of the best predictors of college attendance, which undoubtedly rewards children for maintaining good behavior (Wesley, 1994). Thus, school achievement is itself predictive of prosocial behavior, and is related to other variables, such as financial success, high self-esteem, and internal locus of control, which by themselves appear to help protect vulnerable children.

UNDERSTANDING BIOSOCIAL CAUSES
OF EXTREME VIOLENCE

Instead of studying all violent offenders, some researchers focus on only the most violent individuals in our society: those sentenced to execution and thus on death row. Although these individuals, who are highly violent and highly recidivistic, are relatively rare, their propensity for aggression clearly sets them apart. Thus, their characteristics may tell us something about what the most critical determinants of risk for violence are. These determinants seem to be medical history (an internal factor), family history (their external environment), and record of school achievement (an internal factor).

Dorothy Otnow Lewis is a psychiatrist and physician at New York University. With several colleagues, she has studied several groups of inmates on death row for violent offenses. It is her work that gives us most of our knowledge of the psychological functioning of these criminals.

In 1986, Lewis and her colleagues studied 15 condemned adult men (13) and women (2) in five states. Medically, Lewis noted several important points. For example, every single inmate studied had a history of significant head injury. The injuries were severe enough in all cases to lead to possible brain dysfunction. In addition to head injury, 12 of the 15 (80%) inmates had other neurologically abnormal symptoms, such as paralysis, seizures, and blackouts. Intellectually, all but one of the inmates tested in the "average" range on psychoeducational intelligence tests. However, despite their total average scores, subjects generally showed intellectual problems in specific areas. This suggests that although educationally the inmates may not have suffered from global intelligence impairment, they may have had specific learning problems (e.g., an inmate as a child may have had adequate intelligence overall, but great difficulty learning to read). In general, the evidence of medical and neurological problems was somewhat stronger than the evidence of intellectual problems, although the two are typically related and intelligence problems appeared likely in all inmates. Psychologically, 6 (40%) of the inmates were found to be psychotic—so seriously mentally ill that they were out of contact with reality. The presence of these disorders indicates both a probable biological propensity and, often, a disturbed family environment. (Lay people tend to think of *psychotic* as synonymous with *insane*, although the two terms are not necessarily identical technically and legally.) Nine (60%) of the inmates had suffered symptoms of mental disturbance during childhood that were severe enough to require medical attention or to make it impossible for the child to attend school in a normal classroom (Lewis et al., 1986).

Having completed her study of adult condemned inmates, Lewis and her colleagues then began to study juveniles who had committed such serious violent crimes that they had been condemned to death. All 14 boys studied had committed capital offenses before they reached the age of 18, and had been sentenced to death in one of four states that permitted the execution of minors.

Of the adults previously studied, all had had histories of significant head injuries. Of these 14 juveniles, 8 (57%) had a history of head injuries that were severe enough that hospitalization was required, or that a permanent skull indentation resulted. In addition, 9 (64%) of the juveniles had "serious neurological abnormalities," which could be documented a history of seizures or abnormal EEG findings, suggesting that the difference in rates of neurological abnormalities between the adults and the children could have occurred by chance alone; after all, only 15 and 14 cases were examined in each study, respectively. Another possibility is that the juveniles had less time to acquire neurological abnormalities, relative to the adult offenders (e.g., a juvenile offender may have had only 15 years to injure his head prior to incarceration, whereas an adult offender may have had 25 years to do so). In any case, it seems clear that abnormalities in the way the brain functions are more common than not among the most violent offenders.

Psychologically, 7 of the 14 juvenile inmates were psychotic at the time of the study, or had been diagnosed as psychotic earlier in their lives. Four others (for a total of 11 juveniles, or 79%) had evidence of severe mood disorders, which can be as severe as psychosis but involve very extreme mood swings rather than impairments of cognition. Psychologically, therefore, it was even more common for the violent juveniles than for the violent adults to have severe psychological disorders.

Although almost all adult violent death row inmates had normal intelligence, 12 (86%) of the juvenile inmates had IQs below the "average" range, and almost all of them failed to read at their appropriate grade level.

The researchers took a family history of each juvenile, and paid particular attention to any episode of physical or sexual abuse. Not surprisingly, 12 (86%) of the juveniles had been "brutally" physically abused, and 5 (36%) had been sexually abused (sodomized) by an adult male relative during their childhood. In addition, again not surprisingly, the families of these very violent juveniles showed very high rates of a multitude of serious problems, such as alcoholism and drug abuse and histories of psychiatric treatment and hospitalization (Lewis et al., 1988).

Clearly, very violent and recidivistic individuals frequently have a multitude of handicaps, including neurological and medical disorders, profound psychological disorders, and intellectual and familial dysfunction. Noting these, we realize just how important it is to intervene in their lives early on, to minimize the incidence of the kind of predatory and relentless violence committed by most death row inmates.[1]

The causes of violence can be controversial and disturbing to study. It is difficult and painful to contemplate the ways in which we may be damaging, or damaged by, our children. But scientists seek not what is pleasant to know, but what is true.

It is easy to confuse the study of very violent criminals with a desire to treat them leniently. The first priority of every psychocriminologist is public safety and preservation of the basic rights of all not to be victimized. However, unless we learn the truth about what makes very violent people "tick," prevention is an impossible goal.

---

[1]The understanding that extremely violent people frequently have problems that predispose them to aggressive behavior does not necessarily imply any political stand on how they should be treated (e.g., support for or criticism of the death penalty or "three-strikes" laws).

Part II

SPECIAL ISSUES

Chapter 7

Substance Abuse
and Violent Behavior

Personality, biology, and socioenvironmental variables may generally predispose individuals to violence, but other, more immediate influences can
place a particular individual at a particular point in time at high risk. Why
might a man be violent today, and not yesterday? One frequently cited
reason and a focus of public concern is the relationship between substance
abuse and aggressive behavior (Bakan, 1971; Busch, Zagar, Hughes, Arbit,
& Bussell, 1990; Jackson, 1958; Rosenbaum & Hoge, 1989; Snell, 1992;
Stephens, 1994; Taylor & Sears, 1988; U.S. Department of Justice, 1990;
Zagar et al., 1990). Can intoxication cause an otherwise nonaggressive
individual to become violent? Do different types of substances cause different degrees of behavioral change?

SUBSTANCE ABUSE (DRUGS AND ALCOHOL)
AND VIOLENCE

The proliferation of drug abuse grabbed the spotlight during the 1980s
in the United States. The number of persons arrested, convicted, and
imprisoned for drug offenses has skyrocketed in the last decade. For example, the fastest growing group of female prison inmates are those convicted of a drug offense (Snell, 1992). One of the most compelling
arguments in favor of strict enforcement of drug laws is the presumed
association between substance abuse and violence.

Background

The U.S. Department of Justice conducted a comprehensive survey in 1990 of drugs and crime. The results were as expected. By 1989, 38% of Americans who responded to the Gallup Poll indicated that drug abuse was the most serious problem facing our country. This was in comparison to 2% in January 1985. In addition, 58% of these Americans felt that drugs were the factor most responsible for crime in the United States (vs. 13% in 1981). In 1992, President George Bush called for a renewed effort to fight drugs and crime (Dillingham, 1992). How bad was (and is) the problem? Only 9% of public school students stated that it was "impossible" to obtain drugs at their schools (Bastian & Taylor, 1991).

When victims of violent crimes were surveyed in a recent study, the results were equally compelling. Victims reported that they believed their assailants were under the influence of drugs or alcohol in about 36% of the incidents of rape, robbery, and assault, taken together (U.S. Department of Justice, 1990). In 43% of the violent incidents, victims did not know if their assailants were under the influence of a substance. In only 20% did they feel certain that the offender was not under the influence.

Another part of the same study surveyed criminals themselves. Nearly two thirds (64%) of state prison inmates serving time for a violent offense reported that either they or their victims (or both) were under the influence of drugs or alcohol at the time of the offense. Fifty-four percent reported that they themselves were using drugs or alcohol, whereas nearly 30% of the victims were perceived by the perpetrator to be using drugs or alcohol at the time of the assault.

Interestingly, drug use appeared to be highest among violent offenders who victimized strangers (as opposed to family). Manslaughter was the crime that most often involved drug or alcohol use by the offender, victim, or both (76% of manslaughter convictions involved such use). Sexual assault other than rape was, relatively speaking, the least likely to involve drug or alcohol use, although 50% of such assaults still involved substance abuse.

Substances can have a variety of effects on human behavior. These include either stimulation or depression of the central nervous system (CNS) and alteration of basic thought processes. The effect a drug has on any given person depends both on the drug chosen and the dose taken as well as on psychological and emotional factors. A drug can worsen psychological symptoms in already disturbed individuals; for example, slightly paranoid individuals may become extremely paranoid when they ingest alcohol, and thus may commit crime in the belief that they are defending themselves against imaginary evil. Individuals' expectations about how the drug will affect them also have profound effects; people can, for example, even become "drunk" on flavored water when they believe it is alcohol!

There are three mechanisms whereby a substance might increase a person's tendency to be violent. First, drugs might change a person's behavior from nonviolent to violent—for example, cause extreme paranoia in a person who, when sober, was only mildly paranoid. Second, a person might commit a violent crime in order to obtain drugs (or money for drugs), especially if he or she was addicted, although it is true that most violent crime is not committed strictly for material or financial gain (Vince, 1989). Finally, substance abuse and violence might be linked through a third factor: for example, alcohol abuse is associated with a high level of head injury from accidents (Rosenbaum & Hoge, 1989). Head injury is associated in turn with violence (Lewis et al., 1979). At least in some cases, the drugs-and-violence link may have more to do with brain dysfunction than with the effects of drugs per se.

"Addiction" to drugs, also called *dependency*, can be either physical or psychological. Physical dependency is more acute and painful, because it involves a physical need for the drug. Not having the substance results in real physical pain, which can be a powerful motive for committing instrumental violence. Psychological dependency is generally less serious although it may also be a motivation for crime because a person who is psychologically dependent on a substance generally believes that he or she must have that substance in order to function. Not having the substance, the psychological addict believes, could lead to devastating consequences. Such a belief might be motive enough to do anything necessary to obtain a "fix."

Alcohol and Violence

What drugs are most likely to increase the possibility of violence? Alcohol is one drug that has certainly been linked to aggressive behavior. Because it is legal, widely available, and socially acceptable (even desirable), alcohol is the drug most commonly used and abused in the United States. It is consumed "socially" (i.e., in at least occasional small quantities) by a majority of Americans (Bassuk, Schoonover, & Gelenberg, 1983). About one third of all U.S. families include at least one person who has, or has had, a problem with alcohol, on a continuum from heavy drinking without addiction to full-blown alcoholism (Peele, 1984). In addition to high levels of consumption, Americans tend to have different consumption patterns than members of other Western societies. They tend to drink heavily during short periods of time, whereas others tend to spread out their drinking throughout the day (Bartol, 1991). For example, a French individual may have several glasses of wine with both lunch and dinner, whereas an American is more likely to consume his or her daily alcohol in stronger liquor or in a compressed period of time (e.g., during a "happy hour" after work).

Alcohol certainly has some strong effects. Its most marked effect is on the brain (Bassuk et al., 1983), where it impairs nearly every aspect of information processing (National Institute on Alcohol Abuse and Alcoholism, 1994). Perhaps most notably, it is the third leading cause of death in the United States, and is responsible for more deaths than all other drugs combined (Bartol, 1991). Forty percent of all deaths from traffic accidents are alcohol-related—and traffic accidents are the leading cause of death in the United States (Zobeck, Stinson, Grant, & Bertolucci, 1993). People can become dependent (or addicted) to alcohol, both psychologically and physically. Whether alcohol causes an increase in violence is a less simple question. As stated previously, some research has suggested that alcohol was involved in the crimes of about half of the violent inmates in prisons. Alcohol seems to have the strongest impact on violence when both offender and victim are not sober; possibly a sober potential victim is more able than an intoxicated one to defend him or herself or otherwise avoid victimization. Laboratory studies have found that subjects who are given alcohol are consistently more willing to be aggressive than sober subjects (Taylor & Sears, 1988). Among college students, alcohol was one of the factors related to sexual aggression on campus (Koss & Gaines, 1993). In the case of family violence, treatment programs for abusive husbands have noted that alcohol use after treatment helps to predict violent recidivism (Hamberger & Hastings, 1990).

This evidence seems overwhelming. However, some caveats are in order. As hypothesized earlier, alcohol may be related to violence through a third factor. A study showing an association between accidental head injury and high levels of alcohol use has already been cited (Rosenbaum & Hoge, 1989), and head injury is one of the biological markers of a predisposition to violence in at least some cases (see chapter 4). Thus, alcohol may not always directly increase aggression. In some men, high levels of alcohol use may be related to high-risk activities (such as fast driving or dangerous sports), which in turn increase their risk of head injury and violence.

Furthermore, in low doses, alcohol may actually inhibit violent behavior. There seems to be a direct relationship between the amount of alcohol ingested and the tendency to be aggressive (Taylor & Sears, 1988). Lower doses of alcohol do not seem to have the same effect as higher doses; studies comparing individuals who had ingested low versus higher amounts of alcohol found that it was only the higher amounts that increased the subject's tendency to be aggressive (Taylor, Schmutte, Leonard, & Cranston, 1979).

Finally, social expectations may be critical in mediating the alcohol–aggression relationship. People expect to become "drunk" when they drink, and drinking is an at least marginally socially acceptable excuse for what might otherwise be inexcusable behavior. Many researchers now believe that individuals' expectations strongly influence the effects of alcohol on their behavior in general and their aggressive behavior in particular (Koss & Gaines, 1993). In addition, subjects in one study given alcohol appeared to become more aggressive at least in part because they were frustrated or provoked while intoxicated (Taylor et al., 1979). Thus, it has been suggested that alcohol must be combined with provoking or inciting experiences in order to produce an increase in violence or aggression (Bartol, 1991).

CNS Stimulants and Violence

The CNS stimulants most commonly associated with violence are cocaine and crack cocaine. Toward the end of the 1970s, cocaine and crack cocaine use in the United States sharply increased. Cocaine has been used in the United States since the 19th century, and was once legal; it was not criminalized until the early years of the 20th century, when social policymakers became concerned about the epidemic of individuals addicted to cocaine-laced "tonics" and "medicines." As the popularity of illegal cocaine rose in the 1970s, massive amounts of the drug began to be smuggled into the United States from South America, where the drug grows as a shrub. Crack cocaine has been so named because of the "crackling" sound it gives off when smoked. It is not really purified cocaine but a product made of cocaine, baking soda, water, and various other products. Crack cocaine results in euphoric "highs" and "crashes"; addicts continually crave more and more crack, and will go to any lengths to obtain it. Crack may be the most addictive drug currently available (Bartol, 1991). The rise in violent crime during the same decade as the rise in cocaine and crack cocaine use has suggested to many that the two are related (Fagan & Chin, 1989; "The Wages of Crack," 1994). Some research has found an association between crack cocaine use and number of arrests, as well as other multiple risk factors, such as a history of sexual molestation (Kang, Magura, & Shapiro, 1994). However, such research is limited because cocaine use is typically only one of many risk factors found in crime-prone individuals, leaving open the possibility that other risk factors are more important (Kang et al., 1994). In addition, the impact of cocaine on antisocial behavior may depend on how the drug is used (e.g., sniffed vs. injected; Giannini, Miller, Loiselle, & Turner, 1993) or on the gender of the user (Goldstein, Bellucci, Spunt, & Miller, 1991). In fact, a substantial body of research suggests that there is no simple, direct relationship between cocaine use and an increase in violent crime. One study of 427 New York City male adolescents found that although cocaine or crack use and rates of crime were similarly high, use of cocaine or crack was not related to any particular type of crime, including violent crime (Kang et al., 1994). Another study in Miami found that crack use was related primarily to the crime of drug sales (Inciardi & Pottieger, 1994). Even parental use of crack, while placing children at higher risk of behavioral problems, did not predict the number of child's arrests before age 18 (Caudill, Hoffman, Hubbard, Flynn, & Luckey, 1994). Thus, despite the widespread belief that crack directly causes violence, there is no definitive evidence that cocaine causes a general increase in violent crime, although in high doses, via certain routes of administration, and when given to people who already tend to be aggressive, it may increase levels of aggression.

Chapter 8

Gangs

Adolescent criminal "gang" activity has become a significant threat to public safety, both in the United States and abroad. Although the United States has seen gang activity of one form or another since World War II, western Europe has begun to see gang formation in response to an increased drug trade (Kroeker & Haut, 1995). What currently alarms communities is not the existence of gangs, but rather disturbing trends toward increasingly violent behavior (Gaustad, 1990). Previously unheard-of gang behavior, such as drive-by shootings, now occurs across many different types of communities and studies suggest that violent gang behavior has increased dramatically in recent years (R. Davis, 1995). Once confined to inner cities, gangs are now seen even on Native American reservations (Mydans, 1995). President Bill Clinton declared September 12th to September 16th, 1994, "National Gang Violence Prevention Week." He expressed concern about the rise in gang-related violence and especially about the increasing involvement of preadolescent children in gangs (Clinton, 1994). In Chicago, an 11-year-old child (Robert Sandifer), already a member of the "Black Disciples" gang, fired a gun that hit and killed a 14-year-old boy. He was later executed by other gang members (Grace, 1994). The average age of gang members is dropping; in 1984 it was 15, but by 1987 it was only 13½ (McKinney, 1988). Despite this trend, the composition of what we call *gangs* varies enormously, both in membership and in activities. Gangs can have a few members or a few hundred. They are usually male, but some gangs are female (Moore, Vigil, & Levy, 1995). They may belong to one race or be interracial, and come together for the express purpose of behaving violently or criminally—or just to socialize (Spergel, 1986). Members typically advertise membership through distinctive dress, behaviors, or the guarding of territory ("turf"; Gaustad, 1990). Gangs that do have territory will frequently mark it as theirs with graffiti and meaningful symbols.

There is no doubt that during the 1980s and 1990s violent gang activity increased; gang-related homicides have risen in Los Angeles County alone by 250% since the mid-1980s (Brantley & DiRosa, 1994). Despite media portrayals, however, all juvenile offenders are not violent gang members. What proportion of violent youths commit their crimes while in a gang?

In May 1995, the Office of Juvenile Justice and Delinquency Prevention released a summary of juvenile involvement in violent crime (Snyder & Sickmund, 1995). That report noted several important facts about juvenile gang behavior. In 1991, 6% of all serious violent crimes were committed by juvenile groups; another 8% were committed by a group of offenders that included at least one juvenile and one adult. Adults are less likely to commit crimes in groups; of all the serious violent crime committed by juveniles, fully one half involved a group of offenders (Snyder & Sickmund, 1995). Most serious violent crime involves assaults; when one examines homicide alone, the picture presented is different. Although a great deal of juvenile assault may be committed in gangs, most juvenile homicide is not (contrary to popular belief). In fact, most juvenile murderers commit homicide alone. Furthermore, the percentages of murders committed decreases as the number of involved offenders increases. For example, 14% of juvenile homicides involved two offenders, 6% involved three offenders, and only 3% involved four or more offenders. Gang murders, when they do happen, occur as often as not during the commission of other felonies (e.g., armed robbery, forcible rape). Almost all group offenders are male (92%) and about half are Black (52%). By 1990, criminally oriented groups or "gangs" were located in almost every state throughout the United States (Spergel, 1989).

One interesting difference between group homicides and individual homicides is the crossing of racial lines. Individual homicides are committed intraracially when the offender is White; 95% of White juveniles choose White victims. When the single offender is Black, the choice of victim is mixed: 57% were White and 37% were Black (Snyder & Sickmund, 1995). Overall, only 11% of single-offender killings by juveniles were interracial, compared with 25% of group killings. Group killings are predominately Black offenders killing White victims (71%), usually during the commission of a robbery (60%).

Developmental predecessors of adolescent gang formation can be seen in preadolescent "friendship networks," as reviewed in chapter 4 (see the section on the "Developmental Model"). Certainly, male preadolescent friendship groups tend to display many of the hallmarks of later adolescent gangs, including an emphasis on competition, loyalty, and a rigid status hierarchy. They also de-emphasize emotional intimacy and emphasize shared activities instead. Rules are clearly laid out and rigidly enforced (*Los Solidos Nation,* 1995). Despite these similarities, gangs are not always mere social networks. For example, some gangs specialize in a particular type of crime, and surveys of incarcerated teenage boys who claim to belong to gangs reveal that at least some gangs form particular friendship networks specifically to commit crimes (Sheley, Zhang, Brody, & Wright, 1995). Nor is all criminal behavior by gangs local or relatively unimportant. One gang, before being stopped by federal authorities, had a cocaine distribution network that stretched across five states (Bonfante, 1995). Others are similar to organized crime groups, gleaning large profits from larceny, robbery, and burglary (Sccente, 1993).

However, most boys who engage in preadolescent networks do not become involved in criminal behavior as a part of an adolescent gang. How do such criminal networks develop? Many years ago, Tuckman (1965) suggested that gangs are groups that establish roles and relationships and focus on achievements and tasks, and reward productivity. Indeed, although many might not consider criminal activities to be "achievements," this description might fit some modern gang involvement. Certainly not all teenage gangs engage in criminal behavior (Clay & Aquila, 1994); the purpose of such a group might be shared activities, socializing, or merely demographic convenience (e.g., living close together). Teenage gangs that do specialize in criminal behavior might do so actively or only sporadically (Clay & Aquila, 1994). Some researchers have suggested that the increase in gang involvement among U.S. youth is due primarily to the lucrative nature of the narcotics trade (Sccente, 1993), but others dismiss this explanation and point out that many children join gangs for protection from increasingly dangerous neighborhoods ("The Wages of Crack," 1994). Indeed, one study of gangs in Milwaukee found that the more hierarchical a gang is, the less likely it is to be involved in selling drugs, suggesting that larger, more complexly organized gangs are not joined primarily for the potential profits from narcotics trade (Hagedorn, 1994). Another study found that most gang members were engaged in the drug trade only sporadically, moving in and out of the conventional labor market (Hagedorn, 1994).

If the drug trade is not always the motive for joining a gang, what other motives are feasible? Some answers emerge from research on the differences between adolescents who join gangs and those who do not. One study compared 36 high school students who were in gangs with 65 students who were not. The two groups similarly held negative racial stereotypes, but gang members had much lower self-esteem and were significantly less likely to name a parent or teacher as a role model. This study suggested that an absence of parental or teacher role models may result in lower self-esteem, which in turn may help explain why some high school students join gangs (Wang, 1994). Other research has suggested that adolescents become gang members because they need a family structure and are already familiar with violence (J. W. Williams, 1992). Poorer communities, which have higher rates of both family breakdown and street violence, may thus provide fertile ground for the formation of gangs. Gangs may offer kids a boost in their status and self-esteem, which may be particularly important if they believe they are worthless and powerless (Stover, 1986). Although the drug trade may not be the most important reason for joining a gang for all children, at least for some prospective members the lure of financial gain must be very tempting, especially for youths with no education and no hope of lucrative employment. There certainly are vast sums of money available through the drug trade, although most gang members do not become vastly rich; perhaps psychologically the mere possibility of money is enough to lure youngsters with no other prospects into gang membership (McKinney, 1988).

As previously stated, gang-committed homicides usually involve Black perpetrators, predominately young and male. The young Black male in North America today faces a multitude of difficulties that increase his vulnerability to joining a gang (Ascher, 1991). African-American young males suffer from too few prosocial adult male models; on the other hand, they are bombarded with negative images of Black men. Similarly, their self-esteem in general may suffer from pervasive negative images of African Americans, and inner-city ghettos typically lack the resources necessary to sustain academic achievement (which could protect such at-risk boys from joining gangs). Single-parent, low-income homes make enormous demands on stressed parents who may be unable to control their adolescent offspring, and fatherless households may make the transition to manhood particularly difficult. These boys are exposed to violent communities, given little supervision by adults who are struggling to make ends meet, and placed in schools that are chronically underfunded and that unfortunately lack Black male teachers who could serve as positive role models (Ascher, 1991). Given the situation in many U.S. inner cities today, it is hardly surprising that many young African-American males choose to increase their status and prospects by rejecting the mainstream culture and joining gangs.

Although the mass media popularly depicts gang violence as occurring primarily in the streets, schools often become the focus of gangs. Although some types of school crime and violence have remained level or even diminished, violence in the schools—particularly between gangs—has been increasing since the early 1970s (Gaustad, 1991). The U.S. Department of Education reported in 1989 that assaults and weapon possession in schools increased by 16% and 28%, respectively, between 1985 and 1989. In addition, the National School Safety Center estimated that in 1987, 135,000 boys carried guns to school daily. Many of these weapons and these assaults occurred between children who were members of gangs.

Why has the rate of school crime and violence increased so dramatically so quickly? Increased gang membership and gang violence is one reason. Battles between gangs often occur on school grounds and during school hours (Gaustad, 1991). Gangs even increase violence in schools among students who do not belong to their groups; non-gang members often carry weapons to school because they fear being targeted by gangs or becoming involved in a fight with a gang member, and even gang members themselves note that if a student has a weapon, when challenged he or she is extremely likely to use it (Barrett, 1991). Availability of weapons is no longer a problem in the United States; the Center to Prevent Handgun Violence noted that every household in the United States has, on the average, two guns owned by private citizens, and in major U.S. cities guns can even be "rented" for temporary use (Barrett, 1991). The problem of gang violence in schools is complicated by the fact that other students may not want to "tattle" on their peers and that school personnel may erroneously see gang activity as a stage "all kids go through" (Gaustad, 1991). Admitting to gang activity is also humiliating for many schools that may like to pride themselves on being better achieving schools. Despite this, many schools have openly admitted that they are struggling with gang violence and have begun programs designed to combat the problem. School administrators have noted that teenage gang members often need to be taught not simply to be nonviolent, but also what alternative prosocial behaviors exist to resolve disputes. Several states are experimenting with programs designed to teach high school students how to identify emotions and resolve conflictual situations. The Bureau of Alcohol, Tobacco, and Firearms has even initiated programs with seventh graders, entitled Gang Resistance Education and Training (GREAT; Magaw, 1995). What impact such programs can have, in the face of such significant social catalysts to gang violence, remains to be seen.

Sexual Assault

Few researchers disagree with the characterization of sexual assault as a violent crime (Roberts, 1995), both in a legal and a psychological sense. As such, perpetrators of sexual assault frequently suffer from the same general causes of violence as perpetrators of other violent crimes (see chapters 3 and 4). However, there are other causes that have been specifically associated with the crime of sexual assault, both against domestic partners and against strangers. Although sexual assault is frequently studied as a street crime, it also occurs domestically (Finkelhor & Yllo, 1985). Like other interpersonal violent crimes, sexual assault involves a perpetrator, a victim, and a set of circumstances. All three of these variables must be considered in the search for the causes of rape.

PERPETRATOR CHARACTERISTICS

Anger and violence are clearly associated with some incidents of sexual assault, whereas others are committed with a minimum of violence and injury (Groth, 1979; Finkelhor & Yllo, 1985). Several writers, in forming typologies of rapists, suggest that the distinction between violent and nonviolent rape is an important one. Groth is a psychologist who bases his types of rapists on his interviews with convicted felons. Like Finkelhor and Yllo (1985), he characterized the angry or violent rapist as an offender who uses sexual assault as an expression of hostility and rage. This perpetrator typically does not confine his violence to the sexual assault, and beats his victim brutally, usually causing significant injury. Such an offender consciously experiences "bad" feelings and frequently knows that he is attacking because he is angry, enraged, and/or depressed. As Groth described it, this offender uses sexual assault in addition to physical assault because he believes that rape is especially hurtful to his victim. Sexuality is secondary to this offender, and he will typically not find the attack "sexy" or arousing; in fact, he may have difficulty achieving an erection or ejaculating.

Violent and brutal rape also occurs between spouses or partners. Finkelhor and Yllo (1985) describe the case of Gretchen, whose husband frequently raped her after beating her. He went so far as to beat and rape her 2 days before she was expecting a child, and again 2 days after the baby was born. He ripped her vagina with his hand and liked to "play rape" (p. 32). Although this case occurred between spouses, it is no less violent than angry rape that occurs between strangers. A case described by Groth (1979), which occurred between strangers, portrays a rapist who randomly victimizes a woman who has driven up in a car; the offender beats her and rapes her brutally, never even sure why he did it (pp. 15–16). Finkelhor found that when violent rapes occurred between spouses, it was not because of sexual difficulties in the marriage but rather as a way for the husband to punish, dominate, and humiliate his wife. Groth pointed out that such offenders are typically very conflicted and perpetually angry and displace their anger onto anyone available—either a partner or a stranger.

In contrast to violent rape, both Groth and Finkelhor described a second type of sexual assault called *power rape*, which involves only enough force to complete the offense. Power rapes are not characterized by excessive violence and typically do not involve brutal beatings or other physical injury. Finkelhor and Yllo (1985) found that power rapes between spouses were more typically committed by middle-class, relatively educated offenders whose conflicts with their wives often revolved around sexual difficulties. A husband who committed power rape did so to demonstrate his dominance over his wife and to show her that he held ultimate power over when they had intercourse. Among strangers, Groth pointed to underlying feelings of inadequacy as the motive for power rape. Like violent rape, power rape can occur either between an established couple (as a demonstration of the man's power in the sexual relationship) or between strangers (as a reassurance to the perpetrator of his own power). The assault may not live up to the man's sexual fantasies, but it succeeds in the sense that it establishes that he is powerful and, in the case of marital rape, that he is in charge of the relationship—or at least in charge of the sexual relationship.

Apart from the distinction between power and anger rape, there are other characteristics that sexual offenders tend to have in common. One of these is a lack of empathy (*empathy* is the ability to feel for another person, to place oneself in another person's shoes, so to speak, and feel what they feel). Most research has noted that sexual arousal is frequently inhibited in men when they are presented with descriptions of violence during a sexual encounter (i.e., rape; Malamuth, 1992). However, men who commit sexual assault may differ in this respect from other men. One study examined this issue directly by hypothesizing that although a nonrapist male would feel empathy for a rape victim, and thus not feel sexually aroused by her rape, a rapist might not experience such empathy. In fact, when presented with an account of a rape with the victim suffering, 14 nonrapists displayed significantly more empathy for the victim in comparison to 14 heterosexual rapists (Rice, Chaplin, Harris, & Coutts, 1994). The rapists' lack of empathy, particularly in association with victim distress and violence during rape, appears to increase their sexual arousal in response to the accounts of rape.

Although lack of empathy is an emotional issue, cognitive issues have also been examined in rapists (and in other samples). One of the most important cognitive factors associated with sexual assault is the belief in, and acceptance of, rape myths (Lonsway & Fitzgerald, 1994). Examples of rape myths include those that justify sexual violence ("She asked for it"; "He got drunk or carried away and couldn't help himself"), those that deny the existence of sexual violence ("Rape is a crime that only occurs between strangers"; "No woman can be raped against her will"; "All women secretly want to be raped and enjoy rape"), and those that deny the importance of sexual assault ("She's making a big fuss over nothing"; "Rape doesn't really hurt women"). This body of research has been criticized for its lack of precise definitions (Lonsway & Fitzgerald, 1994), but it nevertheless reveals the breadth and depth of the myths about sexual violence that our society holds. Belief in rape myths has been found in both males and females as young as eighth-grade students (Boxley, Lawrance, & Gruchow, 1995). Although most children in this study did not believe in rape myths, 10% of the girls and fully 30% of the boys did tend to accept such myths. Another study conducted on 315 male and female college students at a midwestern university found similarly that men were more likely to accept rape myths than were women (Struckman-Johnson & Struckman-Johnson, 1992). Both studies found that despite a substantial minority of subjects who accepted rape myths, most subjects tended to reject such myths (Boxley et al., 1995; Struckman-Johnson & Struckman-Johnson, 1992). However, in the minority of subjects who do tend to believe in such myths, how might such beliefs be related to tolerance of, or even perpetration of, sexual assault?

A tendency to believe in rape myths has been associated with a variety of risk factors for sexual assault, including: (a) the sex-role stereotyping of women (associated in turn with tolerance of sexual violence; Boxley et al., 1995); (b) the heightened perception that female *targets* of sexual assault behave sexually (Abbey & Harnish, 1995); (c) a weak association with viewing nonviolent pornography, and a stronger association with the viewing of violent pornography (Allen, Emmers, & Giery, 1995); (d) the use of

pornography for sexual enhancement, versus its use for sexual release
(Perse, 1994); (e) the belief that forced, nonconsensual sexual intercourse
with an acquaintance does not constitute rape (Kahn, Mathie, & Torgler,
1994); and (f) a history of violent sexual victimization (Kalof, 1993).

Apart from personality types, emotional factors, and cognitive factors,
Thornhill and Thornhill (1992) proposed that rape may have evolved in
much the same way that other human characteristics have evolved. That
is, they hypothesized that rape has evolved because males who commit
rape have been more successful at passing on their genes. The result is
that men may respond positively to rape (be sexually aroused by it) or
commit rape because they are descended from males who have successfully
committed sexual assault in the past. Needless to say, the response to the
Thornhills' proposed theory has been vocal and adamant. Most of the
criticism has centered on two counterarguments: first, that human sexual
behavior is much more complex than a simplistic evolutionary analysis
suggests, as it always occurs in the context of complex social interactions
(Akins & Windham, 1992; Futterman & Zirkel, 1992), and second, that
most studies find that men are more sexually aroused by willing females
than by rape victims, which directly contradicts the Thornhills' theory
(Allgeier & Wiederman, 1992; Malamuth, 1992). Despite the validity of
these criticisms, research has not ruled out the possibility that a tendency
to behave in a sexually coercive or violent manner may be at least partly
inherited or adaptive. At present, it remains an intriguing but largely un-
substantiated theory.

VICTIM CHARACTERISTICS

As with any interpersonal violence, certain individuals are at higher risk
than others of being vulnerable to sexual victimization. Which factors
determine an individual's vulnerability? A number of recent studies have
suggested that prior sexual victimization may increase vulnerability to future victimization. Prospective research, following 857 college women,
found that earlier victimization experiences were a risk factor for later
victimization (Gidycz, Coble, Latham, & Layman, 1993), possibly because
earlier victimization experiences change a woman's cognitive and emotional resources and thus limit her ability to protect herself. A follow-up
of this study also found that the severity of prior sexual victimization was
related to the likelihood of current sexual victimization; the more severe
the earlier victimization, the greater the chance of current victimization
(Gidycz, Hanson, & Layman, 1995). Another study found a statistical relationship between childhood sexual victimization and sexual victimization
with dating partners (Himelein, Vogel, & Wachowiak, 1994). One re-

searcher who compared sorority to nonsorority women, found that sorority women were more likely to have been both violently sexually victimized and to have rape-supportive attitudes (Kalof, 1993). Finally, a prior history of rape or incest was found to be a risk factor for sexual assault in a study that examined a wide variety of ethnic groups of women (C. Scott, Lefley, & Hicks, 1993).

Apart from personal history, some studies suggest that certain groups of women are more vulnerable than other groups. For example, two studies have found particularly low rates of sexual victimization among Hispanic women (C. Scott et al., 1993; Sorenson & Siegel, 1992), although this may be partly due to less willingness to report. Women with psychiatric or developmental difficulties appear to be at particular risk of sexual victimization (C. Scott et al., 1993; Sorenson & Siegel, 1992), as do women who are tourists and thus unfamiliar with their surroundings (C. Scott et al., 1993). Homeless women are of course at higher risk for all sorts of victimization, including sexual assault (C. Scott et al., 1993).

SOCIAL CONDITIONS

Apart from factors related to the perpetrator and to the vulnerability of some potential victims, situational factors can contribute to sexual assault. One such factor that appears to be very important is alcohol. Several studies have found that alcohol use affects both the incidence and the severity of sexual assault; in fact, one study found that alcohol was the "most significant predictor of the level of sexual aggression" (Koss & Gaines, 1993). Furthermore, alcohol appears to be even more potent when consumed by both perpetrator and victim; in that case, it affects not only in the likelihood of assault, but also others' perception of sexual suggestiveness of both perpetrator and victim (Abbey & Harnish, 1995). Groth (1979) found that more than 40% of the rapists he interviewed had a history of problem drinking, and half of their sexual offenses were committed after having used some substance, usually alcohol. Groth reasoned that although alcohol appears to reduce the offender's inhibitions, reasoning, and judgment, by itself it cannot fully account for the assault. Nevertheless, as with all violent crime, alcohol and other drugs appear to substantially contribute to the crime of sexual assault, particularly when used by both the perpetrator and the victim (see chapter 7).

Although a great deal of research has pointed to victim and perpetrator behavior and other factors as important causes of sexual assault, several researchers have suggested that such an approach misses a critical point in understanding why and how sexual assault occurs. It is possible that although individual factors contribute to sexual assault, the most critical variables may be larger social circumstances, such as poverty, racism, and sexism (Sorenson & White, 1992). It appears probable that there is some evidence of racism in how the criminal justice system handles sexual assault: One study of 206 convicted sex offenders found that a disproportionate number of rapists were Black, and other studies have noted that African-American males are more likely to be targets of arrest and conviction than are White males (J. West & Templer, 1994). Thus, racism may account for some of the arrests and convictions for sexual assault. Other researchers have pointed to sexism as the social evil responsible for rape. Several researchers have suggested that the link between pornography and sexual assault implies that the root cause of sexual assault is sexism; however, one intriguing study found that all pornography use is not equal (Perse, 1994). That is, Perse found that individuals who used pornography for sexual enhancement did indeed demonstrate a link between sexism and accept-ance of rape myths, whereas individuals who used pornography for sexual release did not. Thus, for some individuals pornographic environments do seem to encourage sexism, which in turn is linked to acceptance of rape myths. Sexism may also be important in the commission of sexual assault via the subordinate position of women in the economic and social systems (Peterson & Baily, 1992). The income differential between males and females is statistically linked to sexual assault rates, although occupa-tional status does not appear to be a contributor (Peterson & Baily, 1992). Such an analysis points out the importance of controlling for economic factors in trying to assess any individual's vulnerability to sexual assault.

Chapter 10

Spouse Homicide

One of the most common questions regarding domestic violence is: "How frequently does it occur?" Another, equally important, is: "How serious is it when it does happen?" This chapter looks at the severity of spousal violence in general, and considers in detail one of the most severe types of partner violence—the homicide or murder of one partner.

It is not rare, in the United States, for couples to be violent. In both 1975 and 1985, the NFVS was conducted. The 1985 NFVS found that approximately 16% of U.S. couples—one out of every six—experienced at least one incident over the past year in which one spouse physically assaulted the other spouse (Straus & Gelles, 1988). Most of the incidents were "minor" (i.e., they only involved one partner pushing, slapping, shoving, or throwing things at the other partner). However, approximately 40% were potentially injury causing (e.g., ones in which the violent partner kicked, punched, or stabbed the victim partner). Furthermore, one quarter of the homicides in the United States are perpetrated against domestic victims (Straus, 1992b).

Most individuals think of spousal violence as husband-on-wife attacks. Indeed, husband-on-wife attacks tend to draw much more attention than wife-on-husband attacks, both because men's relatively larger physical sizes imply a much greater potential for injury (Straus & Gelles, 1988), and because men tend to use violence to dominate and control, whereas women tend to use violence in self-defense or as retaliation after a beating (Adler, 1991). Additionally, men tend to be perceived as more violent and aggressive in general, probably because they are so much more violent in the streets and outside the home, and account for an overwhelming number of arrests for violent offenses (Stephan & Jankowski, 1991).

116

The perception of the seriousness of husband-on-wife violence is not a mistaken one. However, serious violence is also sometimes perpetrated on husbands by wives. One purpose of this chapter is to compare spousal homicides committed by husbands with spousal homicides committed by wives. Women commit almost as many spousal murders as men do, albeit for very different reasons (Straus & Gelles, 1988). What are the differences between men and women who kill their spouses? In addition, how can we identify and characterize women who kill abusive spouses from more "typical" female murderers?

RATES OF SEVERE VIOLENCE BY HUSBANDS AND WIVES

How frequently are men extremely violent with their wives? The results of studies vary, but most suggest that approximately 5% of U.S. men resort to severe violence against their wives. Interestingly, although the NCS estimates that the husband is the perpetrator in 70% of spousal attacks (Langan & Innes, 1986), other surveys and longitudinal studies find that husbands and wives aggress almost equally (O'Leary et al., 1989; Straus & Gelles, 1988). However, it should be noted that men appear to underreport their own severe violence in surveys, whereas women do not (Stets & Straus, 1990a).

How frequently are women extremely violent with their husbands? Again, the results of studies vary, but most suggest that approximately 5% to 6% of U.S. women resort to severe violence against their husbands at some point (Makepeace, 1981; Meredith, Abbott, & Adams, 1986; Straus et al., 1980). Furthermore, when the 1985 NFVS asked who had initiated or started the hitting during those conflicts, it appeared that men and women report about equal rates of hitting first (Straus & Gelles, 1988). In other words, when only the conflicts in which women hit are examined, about half the time men hit first and then women hit; in the other half, women initiate the violence. What this survey did not examine, however, was how often women hit first when they use severe violence. Other research, discussed later, examines that question. In all such research, however, it should be remembered that, as stated previously, women are less likely to underreport their own use of severe violence (Stets & Straus, 1990a).

MALE- VERSUS FEMALE-PERPETRATED DOMESTIC HOMICIDE

Some research has compared male- and female-perpetrated domestic homicide. Cazenave and Zahn (1992) conducted an unique study in which some of the differences in spouse homicides by men and women in 1985 in the cities of Philadelphia and Chicago were described. Cazenave and Zahn examined 83 cases of homicide: 42 cases involved husbands who had killed their wives; 41 cases involved wives who had killed their husbands.

Several differences between male and female perpetrators of domestic homicide were immediately apparent. First, female killers picked only victims with whom they were living; male killers were much more likely to kill estranged spouses from whom they were separated. Once out of the relationship, potential male victims were safe; however, potential female victims remained at risk regardless of whether or not they had left the relationship.

In addition, men and women showed very different "styles" of killing. Men were much more likely to use guns, to kill their spouses by beating them to death, or to strangle them. Women tended to use knives or other kitchen implements. Part of the reason is undoubtedly a matter of opportunity (e.g., men typically have more access to guns than do women), although part of it is probably also related to the fact that men tended to kill more violently in general. Although other research (Straus & Gelles, 1988) concluded that when women are ultimately violent in a relationship, men and women initiate violence equally, Cazenave and Zahn (1992) found that when domestic homicide occurs, the man was the initiator of violence more than 90% of the time. This was true regardless of whether the man was ultimately the victim or the killer. Therefore, there appears to be a substantial difference between couples who are violent with each other and couples who kill each other. When couples are "only" violent with each other, either partner may have initiated the violence; when couples kill each other, however, the male initiates the violence 90% of the time. This is in accord with Browne's (1987) findings that when battered women kill their abusive spouses they are typically too terrified of them to initiate violence.

An examination of the type of killing also supported Cazenave and Zahn's finding that men are more violent when they kill their spouses. In 18 of the 42 male-perpetrated homicides (43%), the killing involved multiple blows to the wife. In many cases, the husbands inflicted more blows than were needed to kill their wives. In contrast, only 5 of the 41 female-perpetrated homicides (12%) involved multiple blows to the husband-victim.

MOTIVE IN MALE- VERSUS FEMALE-PERPETRATED DOMESTIC HOMICIDE

Men and women also tended to differ in the reasons why they killed their spouses. These differences tended to mirror differences in the reasons why women and men use violence in the first place—specifically, that women tend to use violence in self-defense and men tend to use it to control and dominate their partners (Adler, 1991). Cazenave and Zahn (1992) found similar distinctions between male and female homicide. In their study, the largest class of female killers were those who had used lethal violence against their spouses in self-defense. In contrast, the largest class of male killers were those who killed their wives in response to the victim's attempt to leave the relationship.

Eighteen of their 83 cases involved killing in self-defense—all of men by women. In two thirds of these cases, it was confirmed that the female killer had been beaten by the victim prior to the killing. Furthermore, alcohol was found to be used by either the victim or the killer in 39% of these cases.

There were 14 cases of homicide because the women was trying to leave the relationship—12 of women being killed by men. In contrast to the self-defense killings, these killings did not occur immediately after a beating had taken place. Apparently, women may kill their husbands when they fear a beating is becoming so dangerous that they may be killed themselves, but when a husband decides to kill his wife for attempting to leave the relationship, he does not beat her first; he simply kills her.

Another difference between self-defense killings and attempts-to-terminate-the-relationship killings is the use of alcohol. As was just mentioned, alcohol seems to be frequently inolved in self-defense killings, but it was involved in none of the killings of wives who wanted to leave the relationship by husbands. As Cazenave and Zahn noted, in contrast to the self-defense killings, these killings appear to be much more carefully planned and not a spontaneous reaction to ongoing violence.

Although the two largest categories of murder by far were self-defense and killing in response to an attempt to leave, other motives were noted. The next most common motive (a distant third) was jealousy. These killings typically involved the man's jealousy about the woman's seeing or expressing a desire to see other men. Most jealousy killings (83%) involved men killing their spouses; there were no cases in which a woman killed a man because she was jealous of the possibility that he was seeing other women, although in one case a woman killed her husband after he had initiated an argument over her seeing other men.

These studies have noted important differences between men and women who are involved in the most severe form of domestic violence: domestic homicide. The definitive study on women who kill domestically, however, was conducted in 1987 by Browne, in her groundbreaking study of women who killed abusive spouses.

BATTERED WOMEN WHO KILL ABUSIVE SPOUSES

What are homicidally violent couples like? What are their marriages like? Browne set out to discover this in her research, conducted on and comparing couples who abused, couples who did not abuse, and couples whose abuse had led to the killing of the husband by the wife. Browne's study included 42 couples in which the wife had killed or seriously wounded the husband and had subsequently been charged with a crime. Almost all were charged with murder, although a handful were charged with conspiracy to commit murder or attempted murder. The average age of these women was 36 years; they had an average of two children each. More than 50% were White; the remaining 33% were Black and Hispanic. Of these women, 46% were from working-class homes, 25% were middle-class, and 25% were from lower class backgrounds. Only 1 in 5 had attended college, but more than 66% had finished high school. Approximately 50% of the women were employed. One point that is evident from this description of Browne's sample is that the problem of severe abuse, and domestic homicide, cuts across social and ethnic lines and affects nearly every group of Americans. Although poor and minority women were more likely to receive jail terms for their killings (Browne, 1987), they were by no means the only domestic killers.

A conclusion that became apparent early on in the study is that the nature of violence was fundamentally different in couples in which the husband was eventually killed. It is not merely that these wives were battered, but that they were extremely severely battered, in prolonged sessions of physical torture and sexual assault that culminated in serious injuries. Browne described wife-beating sessions in which the victim was dragged through the house by her hair, kicked and punched; had her eyes blackened, her ribs broken; her hair hacked off, and her eyes severely gouged with her broken eyeglasses; and was anally raped. Clearly, the degree to which many of these women are abused is almost unthinkable.

A second conclusion is that the dynamics of the violence were also different. Several researchers found that some domestic violence between spouses is mutual; that is, that although wives are beaten, a substantial number tend to hit their husbands back (typically in self-defense; Adler, 1991; Straus & Gelles, 1990). Browne noted, however, that this pattern does not hold in couples in which the severely abusing husband is eventually killed by the wife. In such couples, wives appear too terrified of the potential violence of their husbands to hit back, even in self-defense. Their goal is survival, and rather than risk escalating the already severe violence to lethal levels, they take the extreme abuse and hope to live through it.

Although many of the homicidal women experienced physical and sexual abuse as children, it is interesting to note that they did not differ from nonhomicidal abuse victims in this respect: In both groups, approximately 75% of the women experienced physical abuse and more than 50% were victims of sexual abuse (attempted or completed). Thus, it appears that a history of abusive victimization as a child may be important in determining whether one becomes a victim of spouse abuse—but less, if at all, important in determining whether one kills one's spouse.

One factor that does appear to stand out in the background of domestically homicidal female abuse victims is the behavior of the abuser before the wife abuse began. Specifically: "Women noted that these men were, in the first weeks and months they knew them, the most romantic and attentive lovers they'd ever had" (Browne, 1987, p. 40). This attention appeared, in retrospect, to have an obsessive quality, but during a short courtship it may have been very pleasant. Because violence between couples typically does not develop until the couple is seriously involved, living together, or married (Makepeace, 1981), early stages of these relationships might entail extreme attentiveness without beatings. Eventually, however, it was common for Browne to find that this attentiveness had developed into a paranoid obsession. In several cases, these severely abusive husbands were so obsessed with their wives that they controlled and restricted their movements to an extreme degree; for example, they might remove the telephones, forbid their wives to leave the house without permission, and/or force their wives to sever all relations with their families and friends. Many beatings, in addition, were initiated on the paranoid suspicion that the wives were unfaithful or treasonous—even in the total absence of any justification or evidence.

As in the case of other battered women, the beatings in these severely violent relationships did not begin until after the couple had made some major commitment to each other. Occasionally, one of the women who killed reported some minor isolated incident of violence before marriage, but such incidents were unusual and when they did occur, the violence was less extreme.

Apart from being unusually severe, the wife-beatings in these domestically homicidal couples also appeared to have no precipitating event: that is, the wives reported that they were unable to predict when a beating might occur and thus they were equally unable to anticipate and avoid the violence. Furthermore, after the initial beatings began, most of the severely abused women did not immediately seek help, probably as the result of shock, disbelief, and a general pattern of passive acceptance that came to characterize their behavior and that permitted them to survive living with such an intensely violent husband. Typically, later repeated attempts to get help (from police or other authorities) failed to stop the violence.

Eventually, some patterns in the extremely severe beatings did emerge. For example, many of the beatings seemed to stem from jealousy on the part of the husband, or from his inability to tolerate any hint of his wife's independence (e.g., her being employed or simply talking to other people, even a neighbor over a fence). Any threat or suggestion that the wife might leave the relationship was extremely dangerous for her; in fact, leaving or attempting to leave the relationship provoked a great deal of potentially lethal violence on the part of the husband.

Another pattern that emerged was a steady decrease in contrition. During the early years of the relationship, husbands would often beg forgiveness, cry or sob, and express extreme remorse over their violence. As the relationship progressed, however, and the wives remained despite the beatings, the expressions of remorse generally ceased and the severity of the beatings gradually increased. In the case of the homicidal wives, the severity of the beatings they underwent increased to a very extreme degree. In addition to physically and sexually assaulting, these extremely abusive men commonly threatened to kill their wives, themselves, and/or other people. The frequency of the battering episodes also increased over time; almost half of the women in the homicide group reported that by the end of the relationship, they were being beaten by their husbands more than once a week.

It is in the dynamics of these relationships, in the severity of the abuse, and in the personality adopted by these battered women that the key to their lethal behavior lies. Why did these women kill their abusive husbands? It is simplest to conceptualize the killings in terms of self-defense. These women typically perceived that they were completely in the power of their abusers. In the relationship, they were watched constantly and beaten viciously, with no possibility of defense. They all lacked family or friends who were able or willing to come to their defense effectively. In leaving the relationship, they faced even greater peril. The abuser typically understood his victim's desire to leave the relationship and reminded her frequently that if she did so he would hunt her down and kill her and/or kill their children. When and if she did attempt to leave, these men tended to be as good as their word: Several of Browne's cases involved women who had left the marriage but who were stalked constantly by their ex-husbands, whose homes were repeatedly broken into, and whose lives were continually disrupted by violence, which they were not able to escape. The killing incident, therefore, occurred in this context: a victim of abuse who feels totally powerless to escape her abuser, and who knows her abuser to be capable of extreme violence.

Although these batterers had typically threatened to kill before, most of the lethal episodes in which they were killed occurred because they had escalated the threat to some new level; for example, threatened to kill a child for the first time, or given some sign of readiness to act on the past threats of killing the woman. It is this new level of threat that Browne noticed in the histories of women who kill their batterers; although the batterer may have threatened to kill before, for some reason, this time she believed him and decided to kill him first. Even if the danger was not acute (e.g., if the husband was asleep), the wife perceived it as present, ongoing, and real, believed escape impossible, and knew the extreme violence of which the victim was capable. Hence, the characterization of the killings as self-defense.

All battered women face the question, "Why don't you just leave?" It may seem particularly perplexing in the case of a woman who is so severely abused that she feels obligated to kill to defend herself and her children. The answer is that she failed to leave the relationship because she was seeking to survive the violence. A woman in a severely abusive relationship often knows clearly that leaving the relationship puts her in even more danger; the batterer might beat her if she stays, but he might very well kill her if she leaves. The desire to survive aside, there are also practical considerations that limit the ability of any battered woman to leave a relationship (discussed in more detail in later chapters). These include financial dependency on the batterer, fear of poverty and homelessness, the belief that the children benefit from having a father in the home, and the belief that marriage is a permanent never-to-be-abandoned relationship within which all problems should be solved.

Finally, how are battered women who kill different from female murderers who do not kill abusive spouses? Perhaps the most noticeable difference is in past behavior. For example, battered women who kill are typically women with no previous criminal record of any kind. In contrast, female murderers who choose other victims tend to have criminal records, and often records of violent crime. In addition, they may have a history of antisocial behavior in work, relationships, and school. The battered woman who kills is very different. Rather than a history of antisocial behavior, she tends to have a history of prosocial behavior: She loves and cares for her children to the best of her ability and is driven to try to keep her family together despite tremendous odds.

These two types of female killers also differ markedly in their personality styles. Battered women who kill tend, by the time of the homicide, to have developed an extremely passive, obedient personality style. In their attempts to forestall the beatings they receive, they live their lives attempting to please and placate their abusers. They do not pursue their own needs and goals; rather, they hope that by completely subsuming their own needs to those of their abusers' they may end the abuse. This strategy is successful in that the victim survives. On the other hand, it ultimately fails to change the abuser's behavior and it leaves a strong passive streak in the battered woman's psyche. This hypothesis should not be confused with other outmoded theories that battered women actually masochistically enjoy the abuse (Pizzy, 1974); rather, it is clear that in cases of extremely severe abuse, the victim becomes passive not out of enjoyment but out of survival instinct.[1] In this sense, victims of very severe chronic battering have been likened to survivors of other major catastrophes, employing the same type of coping mechanisms (Browne, 1987).

---

[1]For a discussion of why women "tolerate" abuse and the theories of female masochism, see chapter 12.

Chapter 11

Child Abuse and Physical Punishment

CHILD ABUSE

In any interpersonal conflict, there are always three relevant factors: the victim (in this case the child), the perpetrator (in this case the abuser), and environmental factors that increase the probability of the crime occurring.

Of course, in some cases the motive for child abuse may seem obvious. Stanley Kidd, a 28-year-old father in Alabama, asphyxiated his 14-month-old twin daughters—apparently because a child support payment of $806 had been deducted from his paycheck. Astonishingly, the jury rejected the charge of capital murder (Associated Press, 1995b). In most cases of child abuse, however, there is not an obvious monetary motive. So what factors do predict to child abuse?

Factors Associated With the Child

Earlier in this century and historically, it was not unusual for experts to conclude that child abuse occurred because a parent lost control with an exceptionally difficult child. This perspective assumed a "normal" parent and a "deviant" child who was largely to blame. Although we now know that abused children can be either "difficult" or "easy," it does seem true that children with profound health and behavior problems, especially during infancy, are at greater risk of being abused (Berkow, 1987). For example, studies of hearing-impaired children find a higher rate of physical and sexual victimization, relative to the general population of children

(Porter, Yuille, & Bent, 1995). Another recent study by the National Center on Child Abuse and Neglect found that handicapped children were significantly more likely than able-bodied children to become victims of parental abuse (Sargeant, 1994). A child's gender even affects his or her level of risk: Boys are at more risk of abuse than girls, and when boys are abused, their parents are more likely to be particularly aggressive (Hegar, Zuravin, & Orme, 1994; Jouriles & Norwood, 1995). It is important to keep in mind that none of these findings are intended to imply that the child is responsible for his or her own abuse. Rather, these findings suggest an increase in parental stress that may sap emotional, financial, and social resources, and thus contribute to abuse (Berkow, 1987; Burrell, 1990; Sargeant, 1994). Just as it is important not to blame children for their victimization, it is equally important to understand the dynamics of the parent–child relationship that lead violent adults to victimize their own children.

Factors Associated With the Parent and the Situation

Psychologists have long sought evidence that abusive parents suffer from a particular mental illness or personality disorder (Francis, Hughes, & Hitz, 1992; Yanagida & Ching, 1993). However, in one typical study, Minnesota Multiphasic Personality Inventory (MMPI) profiles that were taken on 183 abusive adults found no major abnormalities or consistent personality types (Yanagida & Ching, 1993). Other research has noted similar findings, and no one personality type nor major mental illness seems to characterize the child abuser. Of course, it remains possible that there are several different types of child abusers (Francis et al., 1992), but using such information predictively seems unlikely.

Despite this, there are some factors that frequently characterize abusers and that are often associated with their behavior. For example, a good deal of research has been conducted on the association between substance abuse and child abuse. This association is not, as reviewed earlier, unique to child abuse but could theoretically contribute to it, nevertheless. One study found that 40% of child abusers also abused substances (Kellcher, Chaffin, Hollenberg, & Fischer, 1994). This, and similar studies, have led to a general acceptance of the hypothesis that substance abuse and child abuse are linked (Sheridan, 1995). However, the relationship is not presumed to be so simple. Perhaps it is not substance abuse per se causing child abuse, but rather, other problems in family functioning that lead to both substance abuse and child abuse. For example, one study found that the quality of family functioning and criminal offending were inexorably linked to both substance abuse and child abuse, at least among incarcerated individuals (Sheridan, 1995). Mothers who use drugs also experience higher levels of stress, both of which could affect rates of child abuse (Kelley, 1992). On the other hand, research has shown that a relationship between child abuse and substance abuse remains even when confounding factors are controlled for statistically (Kelleher et al., 1994). In summary, the research suggests that substance abuse probably affects the probability of child abuse both directly and via other, related factors.

Adolescent mothers have received special attention in the child abuse literature and are perceived as being at relatively higher risk of child abuse than adult mothers. Generally, teenage mothers may be more rigid in their parenting attitudes and are more likely to have inappropriate expectations for their children (Haskett, Johnson, & Miller, 1994). Thus, although most mothers may believe that a toddler cries because he or she is hurt, a parent with inappropriate expectations may believe that a 2-year-old is crying deliberately to annoy his or her parents. If this inappropriate perception is rigid, it may result in extreme anger or a parent's perception that the child is crying "to get me mad." Haskett and her colleagues (1994) also pointed out that teenage mothers are generally less happy than older women and readily accept the notion of hitting children as a form of discipline. Although Haskett's conclusions are common, other researchers have pointed out that a teenage mother's likelihood of being abusive may not be due to being an adolescent per se, but rather, may be due to the level of stressors she encounters and the financial and social resources she has (Buchholz & Korn-Bursztyn, 1993). Thus, teenage mothers may only be at risk for increased child abuse because they frequently lack the resources that older parents enjoy. It is possible to conceptualize all of the adolescent parent's increased risk of child abuse as being the result of fewer resources: fewer financial and social supports, of course, but inadequate emotional and cognitive resources, as well.

Similar to research noting stable perceptual biases in some violent individuals (see chapter 4), some studies have found cognitive biases in abusive parents specifically. For example, mothers who are at low risk for child abuse typically display a great deal of empathy when shown a picture of a crying or distressed infant. However, mothers at high risk failed to show empathy when shown the same pictures (D. Jones, 1995; Milner, Halsey, & Fultz, 1995). Such findings suggest that abusive parents, in common with other violent individuals, may perceive the world differently in ways that predispose them to behave aggressively.

> Speak roughly to your little boy
> And beat him when he sneezes;
> He only does it to annoy
> Because he knows it teases.
> —Lewis Carroll (*Alice In Wonderland*)

PHYSICAL PUNISHMENT: DOMESTIC VIOLENCE OR RESPONSIBLE CHILDREARING?

Parental aggression to children is commonly conceptualized on a continuum (as shown below), ranging from the use of mild corporal or physical punishment to very severe child abuse.

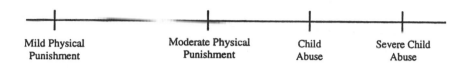

| Mild Physical Punishment | Moderate Physical Punishment | Child Abuse | Severe Child Abuse |

The use of physical punishment or spanking by parents is enormously controversial among researchers who study the causes of violence. Some experts are opposed to any parental physical punishment (Maurer, 1974). Their concern is that it will lead to aggressive behavior in children (Straus, 1983). The potential harmfulness of physical punishment has even been acknowledged by the American Psychological Association, which announced its opposition to corporal punishment in schools in 1975 (K. Anderson & D. Anderson, 1976).

On the other hand, some experts believe that spanking can be an effective and useful socialization tool (K. Anderson & D. Anderson, 1976; Leviton, 1976; Lowenstein, 1977; Maurer, 1974). Although other experts worry that physical punishment could cause aggression in children, these professionals point out that even abusive parental violence does not always lead to an increase in children's aggression (Spatz Widom, 1989b). In addition, recent surveys have suggested that almost all U.S. parents resort to physical punishment at one point or another (see frequency data reviewed later). Despite the psychological controversy, many, if not most, Americans appear to regard physical punishment as an appropriate childrearing technique, at least under certain circumstances.

Apart from the controversy over whether any relationship exists between physical punishment and aggression, the nature of this relationship has been questioned. Briefly, there are three types of relationships that could (theoretically) exist between physical punishment and aggression. First, perhaps any parental aggression (even spanking) causes the child who receives it to become more violent (Maurer, 1974; Steinmetz, 1979). On the other hand, perhaps a lack of physical punishment causes the child, unchecked, to become more violent (DiLalla, Mitchell, Arthur, & Pagliocca, 1988). Finally, perhaps the most violent children are reared not by parents who spank, but by parents who spank either too much or too little (Gelles, 1974; Lefkowitz, Eron, Walder, & Huesmann, 1977).

How much research has actually been done on physical punishment? Not a great deal. Typically, more severe forms of parental violence (e.g., child abuse) are examined and are the subject of comprehensive reviews (Spatz Widom, 1989b). Many studies have strongly suggested that being exposed to abusive parental violence constitutes a significant risk factor for the development of violent behavior (Parke & Slaby, 1983; Spatz Widom, 1989b). Given this justifiable emphasis on extreme forms of parental aggression, fewer researchers have examined the consequences of the most common type of physical aggression by parents—physical punishment. Physical punishment differs significantly from abusive parental violence in many ways, including (but not limited to) the degree of aggression used, the potential for injury, the deviance (atypicality) of the behavior, and the intention of the parent. Because they are so different, the research that examines child abuse cannot really address the issue of physical punishment. The goal of this chapter is to clarify the relation, if any, between physical punishment and child aggression.

To understand the impact of any variable on any outcome it is important to understand base rates of the studied phenomenon: In other words, before we can examine the possible link between physical punishment and violence, we need to know how common physical punishment is in our society (Spatz Widom, 1989a).

Frequency of Physical Punishment

Frequency estimates range greatly, depending on how people are questioned. When parents of school-age and adolescent children are questioned about their use of physical punishment over short periods (e.g., over the previous month or year), the percentage of parents who admit using such discipline varies between 17% (DiLalla et al., 1988), 57% (Lefkowitz, Walder, & Eron, 1963), and 71% (Gelles, 1978). But when adults are asked about their own exposure to physical punishment over their entire childhood, much higher percentages are reported: For example, Deley (1988) found that 89% of his subjects reported that they had experienced physical punishment; similarly, 95% of Bryan and Freed's (1982) subjects recalled experiencing such punishment. Furthermore, studies of very young children almost always show that more than 90% of parents use physical punishment (Sears, Maccoby, & Levin, 1957; Straus & Gelles, 1990). Thus, it seems very likely that the vast majority of Americans are subjected to corporal punishment at one point or another during their lifetime.

The almost "universal" nature of physical punishment is similar to the almost universal exposure to television violence. As in the case of television violence, the near-universal nature of physical punishment seems to convince people of the safety of its use (Killory, 1974; Leviton, 1976; Lowenstein, 1977; Straus, 1983). However, as in the case of media violence, this fact does not, by itself, mean that we should simply dismiss physical punishment as a potentially important cause of violence and domestic violence.

To appreciate the potential contribution of near-universal variables such as physical punishment, it is important to remember that there are many universal or nearly universal events that are necessary conditions for the development of rare events. For example, although sexual intercourse is an almost universal behavior, it is associated with a rare event: cervical cancer. Intercourse alone does not "cause" cervical cancer in any simple sense, but cervical cancer almost never develops in people who do not have sexual intercourse (Skrabanek, 1988). A universal event (intercourse) alone does not cause this rare cancer, but it is a necessary condition for the cancer to develop. Just as not all people who have intercourse will get cancer, perhaps not all people who are physically punished will become too aggressive.

It is not preposterous to hypothesize that physical punishment could be a "mere" contributing factor to the development of violence, rather than its sole cause. In fact, it seems highly unlikely that any parental aggression could single-handedly cause the development of deviant violence (Curtis, 1963; Spatz Widom, 1989a). There is no doubt that childhood violence experiences interact with other important factors in causing aggression and violence (Miller & Challas, 1981). In fact, this was precisely what Spatz Widom (1989a) found in the case of child abuse and aggression. However, just because it is theoretically possible for physical punishment to be related to violence does not make it so. What is the evidence for a relationship between physical punishment and the development of violence or domestic violence?

Retrospective Research

In six studies individuals were asked to remember their experiences of physical punishment during childhood. In a nationwide survey of 1,176 adult respondents, Owens and Straus (1975) found that the frequency of physical punishment received as a child was related to adult approval of the use of violence. Owens and Straus asked individuals to remember both spanking and more abusive violence (e.g., punching, choking). They then related these childhood experiences to adult attitudes to violence, rather than to adult violent behavior. In other words, they gave adults scenarios that measured their approval of violence in a variety of settings, rather than measuring violent behavior directly.

In the remaining five studies, people were asked to remember their experiences of physical punishment and to judge themselves on how violent they were. Bryan and Freed (1982) questioned 170 community college students about their history of physical punishment and their self-reported "problems with aggression." They found that students who had received a "high" amount of corporal punishment also reported more problems with aggression (among other difficulties). Parke and Collmer (1975) found that child abusers often had memories of "physically punitive childhood experiences" (the remembered violence was usually severe and more similar to abuse than to physical punishment). In 1977, Carroll studied 96 adults and found that 37% of those who had rated their childhood experiences as having "high" physical punishment were violent, compared to only 15% of those who reported experiencing "low" physical punishment.

In a similar study, Caesar (1988) found that a sample of 26 wife batterers recalled more parental use of physical punishment than a sample of 18 nonviolent men (58% vs. 31%). Finally, Gelles (1974) found that respondents who recalled being hit by their parents frequently (six or more times per year) were far more likely to physically fight with their spouses than were respondents who recalled being infrequently hit.

Cross-Sectional Research

Cross-sectional research studies examine children directly and try to find a link between a child's current exposure to physical punishment and aggression in that child. For example, Straus (1983) found, in a nationally representative sample of children, that 15% of children who were not physically punished "repeatedly and severely attacked a sibling," compared to 40% of children who were physically punished and 76% of children who were repeatedly abused. Because children change so rapidly as they grow, however, and because children of different ages have different tendencies to be aggressive, it is most useful to separate these studies by the age of the child.

Preschool-Age Children. This age group includes children who are less than 6 years old. Several studies have found that the more often a small child is spanked, the more often that child is aggressive toward his or her siblings and parents, as judged by parents, teachers, and researchers (Larzelere, 1986; Sears et al., 1957; Sears, Whiting, Nowlis, & Sears, 1953). Predictably, however, this relation between frequency of spanking in small children and frequency of aggression appears to be stronger for boys than for girls (Becker, Peterson, Luria, Shoemaker, & Hellmer, 1962; Sears et al., 1953). Although the results of these studies seems clear, other research has found very different results. For example, Yarrow, Campbell, and Burton (1968) found no relation between parental use of physical punishment and the child's aggression. Other research has agreed that the data do not strongly support any relation between physical punishment and aggression in small children (Schuck, 1974). What conclusions can be drawn when studies differ so much in their findings? The relation between spanking and aggression in preschool-age children is a good example of "mixed results"—an area in which more research is needed before any specific conclusions can be drawn.

School-Age Children. For children old enough to be in school but not yet adolescents (typically 6- to 12-year-olds), the research is more consistent. Several studies agree that in children this age, the level of aggressive behavior rises in conjunction with the frequency with which they are spanked (Eron, 1982; Larzelere, 1986; Lefkowitz et al., 1963; Straus, 1983).

Adolescent Children. Two studies examined the coexistence of physical punishment and aggression in adolescents, and both found a relation between physical punishment and aggression. Larzelere (1986) looked at a representative sample of 13- to 17-year-olds (i.e., adolescents from every social class, ethnic background, etc.) and found a positive relation between the use of physical punishment and aggression toward siblings and parents. Welsh (1976) studied 77 aggressive delinquents and found that 97% reported they had undergone either severe physical punishment (e.g., being hit with a belt) or abuse.

To summarize, retrospective studies have all found that violent and aggressive adults recall receiving more physical punishment than nonaggressive adults. When children are examined for the coexistence of spanking and aggressive behavior, the data consistently suggest that in children 6 years and older, there is a significant link between physical punishment and aggression. However, in younger children, the evidence is mixed, and it is less clear that physical punishment is related to aggressive behavior.

Despite the suggestiveness of the research just discussed, a serious problem exists: Retrospective and cross-sectional research cannot tell us causal direction. In other words, studies tell us there is a link between physical punishment and aggression, but leave open three equally possible interpretations:

1. Children who are physically punished become aggressive following the punishment.
2. Children who are aggressive for other reasons provoke more frequent physical punishment (Bell, 1979).
3. Some third variable (e.g., poor parenting skills) is responsible for both an increase in a child's aggression and an increase in his or her parents' use of physical punishment (meaning that the correlation between physical punishment and aggression does not, in fact, mean that one variable causes another).

That is, it may be that the spanking increases aggression, or it may be that aggressive ("naughty") children are spanked more because they are aggressive.

There are other problems with the designs of the studies described. For example, cross-sectional research can only focus on childhood aggression, which is clearly not the same thing as adult violence. Retrospective designs are able to assess adult violence, but rely on the adult's memory of childhood spanking, which might be inaccurate (Eron, 1982).

Because of these problems, a few studies have sought to prospectively examine the association between physical punishment and the later development of aggressive or violent behavior. Prospective studies are longitudinal: Researchers look at a child's experience of physical punishment and then wait until the child grows before examining his or her aggressive behavior. Longitudinal research does not rely on human memory and is not limited to the study of childhood behavior. In addition, because the physical punishment is measured first and the adult aggression is measured years later, we know that the aggression cannot have caused the physical punishment.[1]

Prospective Research

Seven studies have examined parental use of physical punishment and the later development of aggressive or violent behavior. Two of these studies focused on samples of children who were under the care of a physician or psychiatrist for behavior problems such as aggression; they both found that "harsh" physical punishment was common in the clinical histories of violent patients (Nagaraja, 1984; Rigdon & Tapia, 1977). It is interesting to examine the backgrounds of psychiatric patients and to try to uncover the reasons for their violent behavior, but the reports of studies such as these are of limited use because they tend to use vague language (e.g., what does "harsh" mean?) and the researchers do not conduct controlled, systematic analyses.

More important and useful prospective studies have also been conducted, ranging in length from 3 to more than 20 years. Singer et al. (1984) followed 55 children for 3 years and found a relation between the parents' use of childrearing techniques that emphasized "control and physical punishment" at age 6, and aggression when children were 9 years old, as measured by teacher reports. Lefkowitz et al. (1977) followed 427 chil-

---

[1]One possible confound is that the children in the study may demonstrate adult aggression merely because they were aggressive as children, and not because they were physically punished. However, most longitudinal research included in the sample children who are not initially aggressive in an effort to preclude this possibility.

dren between the ages of 8 and 18, over a 10-year period. They questioned parents about any use of "spanking" or "slapping" as a punishment when the children were 8 years old. Ten years later Lefkowitz and his colleagues found that physical punishment at age 8 was positively related to aggression at age 18, but only for boys. However, this study did not find that the more frequent the spanking, the more frequent the violence; rather, the relation was more complicated. The results suggested that parents who used no punishment, and parents who used very harsh physical punishment, had the most aggressive boys by age 18; the parents who used physical punishment moderately had the least aggressive boys by age 18.

Finally, McCord (1979) followed 253 boys over a 20-year span. At the beginning of the study, parents were classified as "aggressive" or "nonaggressive" with their children. Twenty years later, McCord gathered official correctional records (prison and conviction records) on the men and found that parental aggression 20 years before predicted to so-called "personal" crimes (violent crimes such as rape and murder).

The results of all prospective studies discussed thus far imply that physical punishment during childhood, probably in larger amounts, may contribute to violence and aggression later in life. However, other prospective research has failed to find any relation between physical punishment and later aggression. Sears (1961) followed 160 children over a 7-year period but failed to find any significant relation between physical punishment at age 5 and attitudes toward aggression at age 12. Similarly, Johannesson (1974) studied 212 children and found that nonaggressive children were "smacked" by their parents just as often as children who were rated as "aggressive" by their teachers.

In summary, then, five of the seven prospective studies found a relation between earlier use of physical punishment and later aggressive and violent behavior. Of these five, three were high-quality prospective research designs. Two other high-quality designs, however (Johannesson, 1974; Sears, 1961), found no evidence for any relation between physical punishment and aggression.

Again, we are faced with mixed results. However, a close examination of the studies does reveal some consistent trends. For example, different studies examined children at different ages. Johannesson (1974) and Sears (1961) found no link, but only studied the physical punishment of younger children (aged 9 months to 5 years), whereas Lefkowitz et al. (1977); Singer et al. (1984); and McCord (1979) studied older children and did find a link between spanking and aggression years later. Spanking or slapping older children is certainly more unusual and more deviant (Straus, 1983); this may explain why studies that focused on the physical punishment of school-age and older children found a relation between it and later aggressive behavior. In addition, parents who are unusual enough to spank or slap older children may have other unusual parenting practices that could affect the child's tendency to become aggressive or violent. The "mixed" results, thus, do have a consistent thread when they are examined closely. Physical punishment may be linked to violence, but only in children who are school-aged and older.

SUMMARY OF RESEARCH FINDINGS

Most, but not all, of the cross-sectional and retrospective research reviewed here found a positive relation between physical punishment and aggressive behavior. Correlations between physical punishment and aggression in the best designed studies suggest a moderate relation, with a stronger relation for males. Prospective research examined how well this association is maintained longitudinally, and suggested that when physically aggressive behavior is directly measured in older children (over 5 years old), corporal punishment may be included in the group of variables that potentially contribute to aggressive behavior.

The Relation Between Low Physical Punishment and Aggression

Let us examine more closely different types of physical punishment and their relations to aggressive behavior. One important issue is the relation between low (or no) use of physical punishment and aggression in children. For example, are children who are rarely or never spanked the least aggressive of all? Perhaps, in contrast, children who are rarely or never spanked are among the most aggressive.

Most studies agreed that severely punished children were among the most aggressive (Bryan & Freed, 1982; Eron, 1982; Gelles, 1974; Larzelere, 1986; Lefkowitz et al., 1977; Lefkowitz et al., 1963; Sears, 1961; Straus, 1983). However, some studies found that "low" physical punishment was associated with higher aggression (Gelles, 1974; Lefkowitz et al., 1977; Sears, 1961), whereas in other studies, "low" physical punishment was associated with lower aggression (Bryan & Freed, 1982; Eron, 1982; Larzelere, 1986; Lefkowitz et al., 1963; Straus, 1983). Why would studies reveal such mixed results?

One problem is the way the different researchers defined *low punishment*. In some studies, the low punishment condition consisted of parents who literally used no physical punishment (Straus, 1983), whereas in other studies, the low punishment condition included parents who used some physical punishment (usually to an imprecise extent; Bryan & Freed, 1982). Other studies do not report what the criteria was (Eron, 1982; Sears, 1961), and Lefkowitz et al. (1963) based their comparison groups on the number of types of physical punishments used, rather than on their frequency. Another difficulty in studying the impact of low or no physical punishment is accuracy. Given that almost the entire population uses physical punishment to some degree, the possibility of any researcher locating a group of parents who literally utilize no physical punishment at all seems low. It is very plausible that parents often use mild physical punishment that they later fail to remember (e.g., slapping the hand of a toddler). Because of these problems, it is very difficult to draw any conclusions about "low" or "no" use of physical punishment, and whether it is harmful or helpful to a child's development.

Child Abuse and Physical Punishment

As we noted earlier, parental aggression may be thought of as occurring on a continuum from abusive violence to very mild physical punishment. One of the greatest difficulties in studying physical punishment is the "teasing apart" of the effects of abusive violence versus the effects of more common and mild aggressive responses to a child's behavior.

It is difficult to separate these two parental behaviors because they may be related to one another. Parents who regularly use physical punishment are also more likely to abuse (Kosky, 1983; Maurer, 1974), although the two do not necessarily go together. Because of this relation between physical punishment and child abuse, Sweden passed a 1979 civil law that forbids parental use of physical punishment (Feshbach, 1980), in an attempt to lower the frequency of child abuse.

Because child abuse and physical punishment are related, and because any large, representative sample of Americans is bound to include some child abusers (Straus & Gelles, 1990), it is probable that child abusers were included among the parents studied by the investigators of the effects of physical punishment. We know that abuse is causally related to aggression (Spatz Widom, 1989a), so the parents who are abusers (rather than the parents who are only spankers) may be responsible for the relations with aggression previously noted. Thus, one important factor to control for, in the study of physical punishment and aggression, is child abuse. The critical question is this: When the presence of child abuse is controlled for, does the association between physical punishment and aggression remain? Does parental violence have to be extreme (i.e., abusive) before it is associated with the development of violence in the child?

Unfortunately, only two studies directly address this issue by controlling for child abuse. In one study of a clinical sample comparing wife batterers to nonbatterers, Caesar (1988) questioned subjects about their exposure to parental violence in their families of origin. They rated the batterers' and nonbatterers' parents as being aggressive at three levels: "spanking"; "use of a switch, belt, razor strap, paddle, etc."; and "beating." Batterers, in comparison to nonbatterers, had experienced more parental use of a switch, belt, razor strap, paddle, and so forth. Importantly, however, batterers and nonbatterers were no different in their exposure to spanking. Whether or not one considers use of a razor strap or belt abusive, the important point is that spanking alone was not associated with wife-battering specifically.

The different effects of child abuse and physical punishment have also been investigated in a nationally representative sample (Straus, 1983). Straus studied a group of several thousand children and interviewed their parents, asking both about the parents' use of physical punishment (e.g., slapping) and child abuse (e.g., hitting with a closed fist). He then compared how aggressive two groups of children were: those whose parents had only used physical punishment, versus those children whose parents had used physical punishment and abusive violence. The study found that aggression was much more common in abused children, when compared to only physically punished children. Although physically punished children were not as aggressive as abused children, they were more aggressive than children whose parents used neither physical punishment nor abusive violence. This second study is stronger because it uses a nationally representative sample, rather than a sample from a clinical setting. However, it does assess childhood aggression, which is not the same thing as adult violence.

Another way of examining the impact of child abuse is to ask whether only moderate physical punishment increases aggression. If the answer is no, then it remains possible that abuse accounts for the relation between physical punishment and aggression. If the answer is yes, then it is more likely that physical punishment may be related to aggression independently of abuse.

Lefkowitz et al. (1963) separated children into "none," "once a year," and "more than once a year" recipients of physical punishment. He found that the crucial distinction in aggression lay between the "no-spanking" children and the other children, implying that any (even very infrequent) use of physical punishment serves to increase aggression in children. Another study also found that even moderate use of physical punishment increased aggression in children (Eron, 1982). As we have come to expect, however, other studies have found the opposite: namely, that moderate punishment does not serve to increase aggression in children. In fact, a number of studies have found that children of parents who use physical punishment moderately were the least aggressive (Gelles, 1974; Lefkowitz et al., 1977; Sears, 1961). Others noted that children exposed to "low" and "moderate" physical punishment were similarly low in aggression (Bryan & Freed, 1982; Larzelere, 1986).

In summary, then, nine studies address the issue of moderate or low use of physical punishment versus child abuse by accounting for severity and/or frequency of use of parental physical punishment. Of these nine, six found that moderate use of spanking produced either the least aggressive children or children who were no more aggressive than the children of low physical punishment parents. The other three studies (Eron, 1982; Lefkowitz et al., 1963; Straus, 1983) found that moderate use of spanking did increase aggression in children (over low/no physical punishment). These results are clearly mixed but lean in favor of the hypothesis that low and moderate use of physical punishment does not result in increased aggression and violence in children.[2]

Males Versus Females

Here, results are consistent. Five studies compared male–female differences in correlations between experience of physical punishment and aggressive behavior; four of these found that the correlations for male subjects were stronger (Becker et al., 1962; Eron, 1982; Lefkowitz et al., 1977; Owens & Straus, 1975). It appears that the relation between severe physical punishment and increased aggression is much stronger for male than for female children.

Physical Punishment and Other Parenting Behaviors

Another issue that is important in evaluating the strength of the connection between physical punishment and the development of aggression is raised by Parke and Slaby (1983), who noted that parents who use physical punishment (especially severe physical punishment) may also have other detrimental parenting behaviors. Perhaps it is these other parenting behaviors that are responsible for the increase in aggression (rather than the use of spanking per se).

For example, some studies have suggested that people who choose to spank children may be different from people who prefer other methods of punishment. One of these found that "close-mindedness" and "neuroticism" were highly related to the use of corporal punishment by public school teachers (Rust & Kinnard, 1983). Another study found that parental anger-proneness was related to the use of "harsh" parental punishment (Engfer & Schneewind, 1982). Becker et al. (1962) found that "hostile" parents tended to use more physical punishment than less hostile parents.

---

[2]One possible interpretation of this is that moderate physical punishment may tend to be logically related to a child's behavior, whereas more severe punishment may seem irrational from the child's perspective and may be more related to the parents' needs than the child's misbehaviors.

Family factors have also been tentatively related to the use of spanking; such factors include socioeconomic status (Magmer & Ipfling, 1973), cultural values (Escovar & Escovar, 1985), size of family (Wagner et al., 1985), a high degree of family conflict (Engfer & Schneewind, 1982), and marital satisfaction (Kemper & Reichler, 1976).

Physical Punishment and Other Parenting Factors

The relation between personality and parenting styles and parental choice of punishment method must be very complex; these few studies can only be suggestive. Before we can definitively tease apart the impact of physical punishment from the impact of other parental and family factors, we must have a much clearer idea of what factors are most strongly associated with the use of physical punishment. Very little research has actually been conducted on other differences in parenting styles between parents who choose to spank and those who choose not to spank. Nevertheless, a few studies have been completed.

One retrospective study (Carroll, 1977) investigated the relation between parental "warmth," use of physical punishment, and the development of aggression. Interestingly, Carroll found that when parental warmth was accounted for, physical punishment was not related to the level of aggression in the children. This finding implies that it is parental warmth, and not the use of spanking per se, that is related to the child's aggressiveness. Larzelere (1986) also found that when parents frequently talked things over with their children, no relation remained between physical punishment and aggression. He did note, however, in preadolescents and adolescents, a particular increase in aggression among those children whose parents used both frequent spanking and minimal discussion.

Finally, Eron and his colleagues noted that physical punishment increased aggression only in boys who lacked close identification with their fathers. When boys were closely identified with their fathers, spanking appeared actually to decrease aggression (Eron, 1982). Lefkowitz et al. (1977) noted the same result. These few studies, although only suggestive, imply that such factors as the warmth and intimacy of the relationship between children and their punishers may be very important when considering the impact of physical punishment on children's aggressive (or lack of aggressive) behavior. In the context of affectionate and effective parenting, physical punishment may not increase a child's risk of aggressive behavior.

CONCLUSION

Whether or not to spank children is one of the most controversial issues in child psychology today. The claim is frequently made that physical punishment, or spanking, increases the likelihood that a child will grow up to be aggressive or violent (Caesar, 1988; Deley, 1988; Maurer, 1974; McCord, 1979; Straus, 1983). However, as we have seen, it is very difficult to make such a simple claim.

First, many studies only examine children and childhood aggression, or they rely on the memory of adults. Second, it seems very possible that different degrees of physical punishment have different effects. Harsh and frequent use of hitting and spanking in older children does seem to increase their aggression, although whether they remain aggressive through adulthood is uncertain. Low and/or moderate use of physical punishment does not appear to increase a younger child's aggression, although the evidence is clearly mixed. Finally, a few studies tentatively suggest that for a child who has a warm, close relationship with parents who frequently discuss as well as punish, spanking or other types of physical punishment may have no deleterious effects at all.

Chapter 12

Victims: The Consequences
of Family Violence

Thus far, we have discussed several important issues: the definition of violence in general and family violence in particular, the frequency of violence, the types of behaviors that may or may not be called *violent*, and finally, the characteristics of perpetrators of violence and the possible causes of their violence. In this chapter, the focus shifts to the victims, and I consider the effects and consequences of either witnessing or being the target of violence in the home.

Researchers have studied the impact of two different types of domestic violence: *ordinary* family violence, such as "minor" spouse abuse or physical punishment; and *deviant* family violence, such as severe spouse abuse, intimate rape, and child abuse. I begin with the first.

ORDINARY FAMILY VIOLENCE
AND ITS CONSEQUENCES

Physical Punishment

In chapter 11, I discussed the possibility that one consequence of corporal punishment of children may be an increase in the child's tendency to behave aggressively or violently. Apart from this tendency, does ordinary physical punishment result in any negative psychological consequences for its recipient? Certainly we are justified in calling physical punishment, or spanking, *ordinary*; as we have seen, it is used by nearly all U.S. parents (Straus, 1991).

140

One possible side effect of being spanked as a child may be an increased risk of becoming a child or spouse abuser as an adult. Straus found that the more parents believe in the use of corporal punishment and the more extensively they were physically punished themselves as children, the more likely they were to abuse either their spouses or their children.

A second possible consequence of physical punishment that has been studied is depression. Greven (1991) theorized that being hit or hurt by a loved and trusted adult causes intense childhood anger, which does not simply "go away," but rather is transformed into adult depression. Straus (1992a) tested Greven's theory on a study of representative U.S. families who physically punish their adolescent children. Straus and his colleagues interviewed more than 6,000 U.S. families for the 1985 NFVS (Straus & Gelles, 1990). Physically punishing teenagers is common in the United States, but still much less frequent than physically punishing younger children. Straus studied the effects of physical punishment by mothers and by fathers separately. He found that when mothers physically punish teenage boys, depressive symptoms seem to increase as the frequency of the physical punishment increases. For example, boys who were spanked once a year by their mothers had an average depression score of 46, whereas boys who were spanked 11 to 20 times a year by their mothers had an average depression score of approximately 52.

Girls who were spanked by their mothers may also tend to be more depressed than girls who were not spanked, although ironically the girls in the study who were spanked the most often (11–20 or more times per year) had lower depression scores than those who were spanked a moderate amount (3–10 times per year). Nevertheless, the lowest depression scores were among those girls whose mothers never spanked them. The relation between the father's use of physical punishment and depression was similar to the relation between the mother's use of physical punishment and depression.

Furthermore, it was true that both boys and girls had more suicidal thoughts if their parents had used physical punishment while they were teenagers (Straus, 1992a). These findings suggest that depression as an adult may be related to physical punishment as a teenager. Unfortunately, they do not give us information about the relation (if any) between physical punishment as a younger child and depression as an adult. Also, the study did not control for confounding factors: Because spanking teenagers is not near universal (the way spanking small children is), perhaps the parents who spanked their adolescents were deficient in other ways and it was these deficiencies that led to increased depression in their children.

Finally, McCord (1988) studied the general personality differences between people who were physically punished as children and those who were not. What she found was that children whose parents were "generally aggressive" became aggressive adults. In contrast, those who had been reared by generally nonaggressive parents who nevertheless used physical punishment tended to be "self-centered"; that is, they took pride in their own accomplishments and were unlikely to volunteer their services to other people.

In summary, some research has suggested that physical punishment does have a negative psychological effect on children. In general, however, the evidence is too weak for definitive conclusions and no research on any possible positive effects has been conducted.

Minor Spouse Abuse

Although marital violence occurs between more than 16% of U.S. couples, most incidents are relatively minor; that is, they involve pushing, slapping, shoving, or throwing things, rather than kicking, punching, biting, or assault with a weapon. Almost two thirds of the violent couples (10% of the married population) report engaging in minor spouse assaults only (Straus & Gelles, 1990). Slightly more than 8% of U.S. couples experienced minor husband-on-wife assaults; nearly 8% minor wife-on-husband assaults. It is clear that minor violence between spouses is much more normative and acceptable than severe violence; nevertheless, it seems probable that there are consequences. What are they?

Psychological injury resulting from minor spousal violence seems to be similar to, although less severe than, psychological injury resulting from severe spousal violence. In nonviolent marriages, 27% of women and 16% of men reported experiencing a "high" level of psychosomatic illness at one point or another. In contrast, in marriages characterized by minor violence, 33% of women and 22% of men experienced high levels of psychosomatic illness (Stets & Straus, 1990b). Minor violence also appears to exacerbate the level of stress a respondent reports feeling; the percentage of women in minor-violence marriages who reported feeling a "high" level of stress was almost 13% higher than that of women in nonviolent marriages. Similarly, the male rate of self-reported high stress doubled from 15% to 30% when men in nonviolent marriages were compared to those in minor-violence marriages (Stets & Straus, 1990b). Finally, the rate of depression in married couples also appeared to be affected by even minor violence. Slightly more than one third of women and 30% of men in minor-violence marriages reported a high level of depression, versus only 21% of women and 14% of men in nonviolent marriages.

What these data make clear is that marital violence does worsen psychological distress, even when it is minor. Severe violence results in even more psychological distress, but minor violence by itself does have an impact on the psychological health of the persons involved.

DEVIANT FAMILY VIOLENCE
AND ITS CONSEQUENCES

Child Sexual Abuse

Sexual abuse puts a child's psychological well-being at serious risk, and thus has potentially major mental health effects. Much more specific information is needed, however, if we are to understand its impact precisely. For example, what symptoms do victims of child sexual abuse demonstrate? Are there common symptoms, or do individual victims tend to have different patterns? In general, studies seem to indicate that children who are sexually abused show at least certain symptoms more frequently than children who are not sexually abused (Kendall-Tackett, Williams, & Finkelhor, 1993). Individual symptoms include fears, nightmares, withdrawn behavior, cruelty, delinquency, sexually inappropriate behaviors, regressive behaviors (reverting to an earlier stage of development), running away, self-injury, and poor self-esteem. In addition, such children are more often clinically diagnosed with posttraumatic stress disorder (PTSD), neuroses, and a variety of general behavior problems. This is clearly a long and varied list and no one symptom is manifested by all, or even the majority of, sexually abused children. Researchers have reported that "only" about 20% to 30% of sexually abused children exhibited any given symptom. However, they were different from nonabused children in that their total number of symptoms was significantly greater.

Another difficulty in studying the effects of child sexual abuse is that many of the symptoms listed here can have a wide variety of causes. Are there any symptoms that seem to occur in children who are sexually abused, but not in children with other psychological problems? In fact, one study suggests that PTSD and sexualized behaviors seem to be more frequently associated with prior sexual abuse than with other difficulties in a child's life (Kendall-Tackett et al., 1993). Other symptoms may be caused by sexual abuse, but they may also be caused by other factors in a child's life. Nevertheless, it is important to reiterate that sexually abused children do show all of the symptoms listed more frequently than nonsexually abused children.

When studying the impact of any event on children, it is important to remember that children of different ages are apt to react very differently. That is, the symptoms a younger child shows are likely to be different from those an older child shows, although some symptoms seem to appear across all age groups. For example, depression in reaction to sexual abuse has been noted across a wide variety of age groups (Beitchman, Zucker, Hood, DaCosta, & Akman, 1991). In addition, Kendall-Tackett and her colleagues (1993) pointed out that difficulties in school are also common among childhood sexual abuse victims of all ages.

In contrast, anxiety appears to be a symptom that is much more common in the preschool years and becomes less common as older children are studied. Nightmares, sexualized behavior, hyperactivity, and regression similarly appear to be dominant in preschool- and school-aged children, but are less commonly found in adolescents (Kendall-Tackett et al., 1993). In contrast, sexually abused adolescents are more likely than their younger counterparts to display poor self-esteem, or to be withdrawn or suicidal as a result of the abuse. They also may be more likely to engage in self-destructive behavior, run away, or get into trouble with the law.

Interestingly, a substantial proportion of children who are sexually abused apparently have no psychological symptoms after the abuse. The percentage who are symptom-free ranges from about 20% (Conte & Schuerman, 1987), to 33% (Mannarino & Cohen, 1986; Tong, Oates, & McDowell, 1987), to about 50% (Caffaro-Rouget, Lang, & vanSanten, 1989), depending on the study. It has been pointed out that the children who seem to be symptom-free may in fact have symptoms that they are not asked about or that may manifest themselves later (Kendall-Tackett et al., 1993). Alternatively, it is also possible that some children are resilient: that is, traumatic as the abuse is, it may not (in a minority of children) lead to significant psychological distress.

Some types of sexual abuse seem to place children at higher risk of developing symptoms than other types. For example, molestation by a perpetrator who is close to the child may result in more trauma. Similarly, if the abuse is chronic and ongoing (not a one-time event), a child is more likely to be affected. If the perpetrator uses force (rather than manipulation) or if the perpetrator attempts or succeeds in physically penetrating the child (engaging in some type of intercourse), the psychological damage may be greater. In any case, however, many symptoms of child sexual abuse abate, or lessen, as time goes on. In 50% to 70% of sexually abused children, symptoms will lessen within 18 months of the child's disclosing the attack. However, in a minority of children (10%–24%), symptoms will actually worsen. Whether a child's symptoms abate or worsen is related to the supportiveness of the child's family. As with many childhood traumas, the more loving and supportive the child's family is, the better the sexually abused child will recover.

Child Physical Abuse

Apart from the physical damage caused by physical abuse, what are the psychological consequences? Certainly children who are physically abused tend to have low self-esteem (Coster, Gersten, Beeghly, & Cicchetti, 1989). They may even blame themselves for the abuse because young children tend to believe that they are responsible for all events in their lives, both positive and negative (Sroufe, Cooper, & DeHart, 1992). Physical abuse can disrupt a child's ability to form relationships (Cicchetti & Olson, 1990), and may blunt general feelings and expressions of emotions (Schneider-Rosen & Cicchetti, 1984). Additionally, abused children may see themselves as capable of handling interpersonal relationships only in violent and abusive ways (Gardner & Timmons-Mitchell, 1990). Because children are unable to control the abuse and may be unable to predict when it will happen, learned helplessness may also result: In other words, children may learn that attempts to avoid distress or pain have no impact on how they are ultimately treated (A. Goldstein, Keller, & Erne, 1985). Not surprisingly, children who are physically abused tend to be more aggressive than other children; it may be that living in an abusive family teaches these children that violence is a normal part of relationships with other people, especially relationships with other family members (Gardner & Timmons-Mitchell, 1990). Like sexual abuse, therefore, physical abuse is likely to leave children with one or several of a myriad of possible psychological symptoms.

Well-intentioned adults are sometimes frustrated by children who do not defend themselves against parental abuse and furthermore, do not report the abuse to parties who might be willing to protect them (e.g., police, teachers). Why would children resist the help of adults who are concerned by their victimization? Clearly, children cannot defend themselves against an abusive adult, but why would they choose to remain abused when they are offered a chance to escape their families?

Some researchers have pointed out that children in abusive families lack the experience of normality, and thus tend to assume that abuse is a typical state of affairs (Bakan, 1971). After all, children know only the families in which they have lived; therefore, it is logical that they may assume that there are no situations in which they would not be abused. As a child grows, or possibly experiences other families (such as in foster care), this assumption becomes less plausible; however, in a younger child, it may be a strong incentive to remain with parents.

A second reason may be apparent to anyone. Children are completely dependent on their caregivers, abusive or loving. That dependency is both financial and deeply emotional. Children may clearly see that turning in a parent to authorities is a betrayal that will rob them of their only perceived resource for survival. Abusive parents may even remind a child that if anyone knows about the "secret" (i.e., the abuse), the child will be homeless and will have to live on the street. A child's profound fear of losing parents may make it impossible for him or her to reveal abuse or to support an investigation of abuse.

Third, it is not unusual for abused children to blame themselves for the abuse (Ney, 1992). Developmentally, it is appropriate for young children to believe themselves responsible for most of what happens to them—good or bad (Sroufe et al., 1992). Furthermore, abusive parents frequently assure their victimized children that the abuse is a punishment for their "badness." Given these circumstances, it is not unusual for children to hold themselves responsible for their parents' violence and to seek the answers to that violence in their own behavior.

Finally, abused children, like abused spouses, may be fearful of punishment or retribution. Their chronic poor self-esteem may lead them to believe that they are apt to be punished for reporting, or the abuser him- or herself may emphasize that the child will be punished if the abuse is discovered. Children may fear that the abuser will "come back to get them" and that any respite from the abuse will only be temporary. It is certainly true that abused children, like other victims of domestic violence, may be threatened with retribution and assured by the abuser that he or she will not be imprisoned long, if at all.

Intimate Sexual Assault

What are the effects of sexual assault on the victim when the perpetrator is someone the victim is intimately acquainted with, such as a husband or boyfriend? In general, female rape victims tend to demonstrate a cluster of symptoms. Fears and anxiety following the assault are probably most commonly noted (Resick, 1993); researchers have found that they are much more common among victims of sexual assault than they are among nonvictims. However, when victims of sexual assault are compared with victims of robbery, the only difference is that the former have more sexual fears (Resick, Jordan, Girelli, Hutter, & Marhoefer-Dvorak, 1988). PTSD appears to be almost universal among rape victims immediately following the assault, and may persist in those victims who report the most severe distress immediately following the attack (Rothbaum, Foa, Murdock, Riggs, & Walsh, 1992). Depression is not universal, but is still quite common among rape victims (Resick et al., 1988; Rothbaum et al., 1992). Problems adjusting to work may often surface following a sexual assault, although marital and family adjustment problems were not necessarily noted (Resick, Calhoun, Atkeson, & Ellis, 1981). Finally, sexual problems are among the longest lasting of the symptoms following the rape; one study (E. Ellis, Calhoun, & Atkeson, 1980) found that almost two thirds of the victims had reduced or eliminated sexual activity at 2 weeks following the rape and almost half were still not sexually active a month after the assault. For women with a regular sexual partner, sexual activity had returned to normal levels within 1 year postassault.

Given that these are all common reactions to the trauma of sexual assault, are there differences in recovery between women who are raped by an intimate and women who are raped by strangers? It is commonly believed that rape by a stranger is much more traumatic than rape by an intimate. However, several researchers have noted that there is little or no difference in symptoms between women who are raped by strangers and those who are raped by intimates (Resick, 1993). Other researchers have actually found that victims of intimate rape suffer significantly more than victims of stranger rape, particularly in the areas of self-esteem and general maladjustment (Hassell, 1981; McCahill, Meyer, & Fishman, 1979). Thus, contrary to common beliefs, rape by an intimate is at least as traumatic as stranger rape, and in fact may be even more traumatic.

Severe Spouse Abuse

Severe spouse abuse (kicking, punching, using weapons, etc.) is less common than minor spouse abuse, but still far too common in the United States. The rates of reported severe spouse abuse tend to differ, depending on whether men or women are questioned. Men report that they severely abuse their wives in 1.3% of marriages, whereas women report that they are the victims of severe abuse by their husbands in approximately 5% of marriages.[1] Both men and women report that women severely abuse their husbands in approximately 5% of U.S. marriages. What are the effects of severe marital violence (Stets & Straus, 1990a)?

Physical injury is a very real danger in severe spouse abuse. Of those women reporting severe spouse abuse, 7% needed to see a doctor for their injuries. Probably because of their typically larger size and strength, men were much less likely to sustain injuries severe enough to require medical attention: Only 1% of male victims of severe spouse abuse needed to see a doctor (Stets & Straus, 1990a).

Sometimes injuries prevent victims from going to work. In fact, this problem was very common: 19% of female victims and 10% of male victims of severe spouse assault reported that they needed to take time off from their jobs (Stets & Straus, 1990a). In keeping with this trend, female victims are more likely to need a day in bed to recover from their injuries than are male victims of severe spouse assault: 23% of women versus 14% of men reported needed time in bed.

Physical injury aside, there are serious psychological costs to severe spouse abuse as well. Levels of psychosomatic illness, stress, and depression all rise precipitously when individuals are involved in severely violent marriages. For example, whereas only 21% of women in nonviolent marriages and 33% of women in minor-violent marriages report problems with depression, almost 60% of women in severely violent marriages have depressive difficulties. Similarly, approximately 60% of women in severely violent

---

[1]As discussed in chapter 6, research suggests that men may underreport their rates of abusive behavior, which may account for the discrepancy between men's and women's reported rates of severe husband-on-wife abuse.

marriages report problems with stress, with about 33% of men in severely violent marriages reporting high levels of stress and depression (Stets & Straus, 1990a).

Why Does She Stay? To outsiders, to those who have never known domestic abuse, and even to some victims, perhaps the most confusing aspect of family violence is the senselessness of the crime and the apparent futility of the relationships. Why on earth would any woman choose to live with a man who beats her? If such behavior appears "crazy" to laypeople, it has seemed that way to experts as well.

In the past, psychologists have suggested that women who "willingly" endured an abusive relationship did so because they had a masochistic personality disorder. *Masochism,* which is defined as excessively self-defeating behavior, has been associated with women in the psychiatric and psychological literature. Masochists are thought of as those who are excessively self-sacrificing and are too willing to please others, and masochistic women have been characterized as likely to choose cold and unloving mates (Glickauf-Hughes & Wells, 1991). Masochistic personality disorder is a clinical disorder in which women might remain in an abusive relationship because they enjoyed the abuse or because it met some psychological need or desire (Pizzy, 1974). Many psychologists have protested the association of masochistic personality disorder and being a battered woman (Ritchie, 1989), and research does not support that hypothesis; it is now known that abused women are no more likely to be masochistic than any other segment of the population (Pizzy, 1974; Skodol, Oldham, Gallaher, & Bezirganian, 1994).

Of course, this does not mean that there are not women who choose to stay with men who are abusive. More recent research has provided explanations of why abused women tend to stay in abusive relationships, and sometimes even defend their mate and their relationship when it is threatened by agencies seeking to protect the woman (such as the police). One reason that "women stay" is that they may believe that their husbands or boyfriends have the right to beat them because they "belong" to their mates (Straus, 1976). As pointed out in chapter 1, husbands did indeed have that right until relatively recently.

Poor self-esteem frequently characterizes women who endure abusive relationships. The sense that one is worthless and unlovable makes abuse seem more logical and less a violation of rights. Believing that you deserve to be treated badly facilitates deciding to tolerate bad treatment. One typical study, which examined violence in dating relationships, found that low self-esteem predicted sustained abuse, particularly sexual abuse (Pirog-Good, 1992). In fact, this study found that a small decrease in a subject's self-esteem score disporportionately increased her chance of multiple victimizations. Other studies have also noted low self-esteem in abused women

(Follingstad, 1980), but all these studies have found that it is difficult to know whether the low self-esteem anteceded the abuse or resulted from it. If women with poor self-esteem tend to become entangled in abusive relationships that they choose to endure, then poor self-esteem may be a central risk factor for victimization. If, conversely, women begin to suffer from poor self-esteem following the onset of abuse, then poor self-esteem may not be a preexisting risk factor but a consequence of which the abuser takes advantage to keep the woman in the relationship.

Other cognitive characteristics may increase the chance that a victim remains in an abusive relationship. Beliefs and thought patterns and habits may operate to keep women from leaving abusive partners. One study of college students found that some students in violent relationships consider the violence to be an indication of love (Cate, Henton, Koval, Christopher, & Lloyd, 1982). This attitude was more prevalent in couples who remained together even after the violent episodes had begun. Earlier researchers have pointed out that the beliefs of an abused woman may be part of the reason she accepts the violence and stays in the relationship (Gelles, 1985; Walker, 1979). For example, Owens and Straus (1975) found that witnessing physical abuse during one's childhood may predispose some women to believe that it is tolerable in adulthood. Forsstrom-Cohen and Rosenbaum (1985) found that women who witnessed parental abuse as children tend to be more depressed, which may put them at greater risk for tolerating abuse. L. Davis and Carlson (1987) noted specifically that such women tended to react passively to their parents' violence, which may teach them that a passive response is the best. Finally, Adler (1991) found that 54% of women in persistently abusive relationships had witnessed parental abuse. Although these studies indicate that a woman's cognitive and psychological development may be affected by parental abuse in such a way as to place her at increased risk of victimization, they do not point to what may be the most important reason why women stay: their attempt to promote their own safety.

For many women, the ultimate reason why they cannot leave an abusive relationship is fear. It is common for abusive husbands to warn wives against entertaining any ideas of leaving, and to insist that if they attempt to flee they will be tracked down and beaten or killed (Browne, 1987). The threat of retaliation, made by an individual who clearly has the capacity to be violent, can be serious enough to deter even the most severely beaten wife from attempting to leave an abuser. Certainly it deters many women from pressing assault or other charges against their abusers because many believe that any jail time would be temporary and the subsequent consequences even worse.

All these factors make it logical, rather than illogical, that most women choose to stay in abusive relationships. Staying may mean abuse and violence, but leaving may mean death. A bureaucracy may promise safety, but cannot ensure it. For many battered women, this is a risk they cannot take.

Effects on the Children. Serious spouse abuse has effects beyond those on the participants, however. Although women in severely violent marriages are usually the most seriously injured victims, their children suffer as well (Forsstrom-Cohen & Rosenbaum, 1985). It is often difficult to tease apart the effects of witnessing parental violence from the effects of having been abused oneself as a child. However, some research has excluded all abused individuals and subsequently compared individuals who had witnessed parental violence with those whose parents had nonviolent discord and those whose parents were satisfactorily married (Forsstrom-Cohen et al., 1985). The results indicated clearly that having witnessed severe spouse abuse has a psychological impact on the children involved; specifically, children who witnessed violence between their parents were much more likely, as young adults, to have difficulties with anxiety, depression, and aggression. Other studies have noted similarly that spouse abuse tends to cause depression and anxiety in the witnessing children (Levine, 1975).

*   *   *

In summary, even when it is not severe, domestic violence appears to have a detrimental effect on both the victim and the family. The more severe the violence is, the more serious the psychological symptoms that result. Some victims appear resilient but many have serious difficulties.

Among those who work to help victims of abuse, perhaps the most frustrating aspect of an abusive situation is a victim's refusal to press criminal charges against the violent abuser. This refusal may, and almost certainly will, hurt the victim; it also tends to feed the public's perception that domestic abuse is not a serious criminal offense. If abuse were serious, the reasoning goes, victims would be eager to press charges and would not repeatedly return to the abuser.

Although in some cases the minimal nature of the violence may be the reason that victims of abuse refuse to press charges, in the majority of cases it is not. Victims may in fact abhor the abuse, may see it correctly as very violent, and may even fear for their lives. If despite all this, they refuse to press charges, it is simply because doing so appears even more dangerous to their welfare than remaining with the abuser. Victims may believe that while their abusers may kill them if they stay, they will certainly kill them if they leave and press charges. The victim's lack of faith in the protection offered by the criminal justice system may compel him or her to accept what appears to be the lesser of two evils. This lack of faith in the criminal justice system, moreover, may not be mistaken; most experts in that system agree that if an estranged spouse is determined to wreak revenge, he (or, less often, she) will probably do so despite restraining orders and other legal niceties.

Furthermore, family members may or may not be happy at the prospect of punishment or incarceration for the perpetrator of the abuse. Although they may desire immediate safety from the violence, they may fear the effect of punishment on the abuser, and lifetime imprisonment is generally not a possibility. Furthermore, victims of abuse may undergo a process similar to that undergone by drug and alcohol abusers, in which they need to "hit bottom" before they are really ready to release their desire to have both an intact family and no abuse. Generally, these two goals are incompatible, but victims of abuse must accept that if they are to escape their abusers they may have to relinquish their dream of a happy, intact family. Because hope springs eternal, and victims of abuse (like other people) would generally prefer to solve problems rather than escape them, it can be difficult for a victim who has not hit bottom to accept that escape is the only logical alternative.

Victims of abuse require support to escape the abuser (Sullivan et al., 1991). This support must assure them of physical safety and help them meet basic needs, including emotional needs. If the support is inadequate on either of these counts, which it generally is, it is not surprising that abuse may be seen as the lesser of two evils, for which the victim must settle.

Chapter 13

Epilogue: Preventing and Controlling Violence

Investigations of the causes of violence may be very interesting intellectually, but what can the results do for us today? How can we apply our knowledge to increase our safety and sense of security? How can we reduce violence in our society?

These are more complicated questions than they appear to be. Reading newspapers or listening to Congressional debates, I do not get a clear message that Americans want to prevent criminal violence. They seem to want, rather, to punish it. Perhaps it is merely that punishment is perceived as the most effective way to prevent violence. Perhaps "prevention" programs simply are not effective enough, and punishment is a swifter and surer route.

Or is it? Psychologists have long studied punishment and its potential effectiveness in changing human behavior. Although they do not have all the answers, researchers have clearly delineated the necessary components of an effective punishment. Even a casual glance at the criminal justice system reveals several ways in which it does not punish effectively. For example, we know that for a punishment to be effective, it must follow the undesirable behavior closely in time. That is, it must be swift, or the violent individual will fail to connect the punishment to the violent behavior.

America's frustration with the slow and lengthy justice procedure is often reflected in the media. It may seem ridiculous that it can take years to prosecute someone for a violent crime, and many have called for a shortening of the criminal justice process. However, those who seek to implement the knowledge that effective punishment follows swiftly on the heels of a crime encounter an obstacle called due process. The U.S. Constitution has been interpreted to mean that all persons accused of a violent crime are entitled to a trial by their peers, and so on. Due process takes time. The choice may, in fact, be between a lawful and more violent society and a less violent society that abandons due process. Although I have spent my career to date studying behavior I personally abhor, I would never opt to abandon the judicial system as it is set out in the U.S. Constitution, which I see as a critical process protecting individuals from a lawless government. Destructive as individuals are, I still believe that a government can be much more destructive.

Given the necessary time lapse between crime and punishment, can punishment work? Perhaps to a limited extent. Can it work for people who have both a biological and learned propensity to be violent? Anecdotal evidence suggests not, although it should be pointed out that most violent felons do not commit violent crimes again: Studies on recividivism again and again find that the majority of violent felons are one-time offenders (Mednick & Kandel, 1988). This fact actually suggests that the criminal justice system is sufficiently punishing to deter most violent individuals from repeating their offenses. On the other hand, perhaps most violent individuals do not have stable behavioral tendencies to be violent. Because we run a country and not an experiment with controlled conditions, we can never know the answer to this question precisely. Does punishment work? Well, most convicted violent felons do not commit further violent felonies—for whatever reasons.

In trying to figure out ways to reduce crime, one is repeatedly drawn to the problem of recidivism. After all, it is the chronic recidivists who commit most of the violent crime we fear. What characterizes people who re-offend, who beat their wives and their children, who rape and strangle and shoot strangers, seemingly without the ability or the desire to stop? Even though they constitute only a small proportion of criminals, they commit the lion's share of crimes (Piper, 1985). Even if we could separate out the potential recidivists from the likely one-timers early in their criminal careers, could we abandon the legal principle that we cannot imprison people for crimes they may commit in the future? Some states have already begun to acknowledge that some offenders are very likely to offend again. For example, New Jersey lawmakers, in reaction to the killing of 7-year-old Megan Kanka by a convicted sex criminal, have enacted "Megan's Law," which requires notification to communities when sex offenders are released into their area (Barron, 1994). Washington State has gone further; it has enacted a law permitting authorities to indefinitely confine "habitual" sex offenders (Geyelin, 1993). These solutions are popular but not without legal problems, and judicial rulings have deemed some of them unconstitutional (Hanley, 1995). It has also proved difficult to enforce notification laws (Gladwell, 1995).

Perhaps, however, there are other ways to seek to control those individuals who are identified as stably aggressive. The best cure is prevention. Re-examining some of the research reported in this book, particularly the research on characteristics of recidivistically violent individuals, might yield some clues as to possible preventative measures.

Biological influences certainly seem stronger in such persons. They have experienced disorders prenatally and during birth; they have more health problems, more head injuries, more learning disorders, more intellectual problems, and so on. The difficulty is that biology is commonly seen as immutable. Nothing could be further from the truth. Every day, medical science proves its mutability. Unfortunately, the United States does not furnish universal access to health care. Such access—at a minimum during pregnancy and childhood—might help alleviate many of the relevant problems, like prenatal disorders and malnutrition and childhood head injuries. Could better health care reduce recidivistic violence? Research suggests that the answer may be yes.

There seems little doubt that violent recidivists are more likely to be domestic offenders than street offenders. Violence in the family arena is easier and more convenient to perpetrate, more acceptable, and less likely to land the perpetrator in serious trouble. The most straightforward way to approach this issue, it seems to me, is to reduce the social and legal acceptability of domestic violence. There are several ways society might do this. Helping families in day-to-day living might reduce the stress levels that predispose the vulnerable to violence. In addition, public education campaigns can be important. Information should be widely disseminated. Excellent models to follow are the very successful campaigns to inform the public about the dangers of driving while intoxicated.

Furthermore, despite claims that the government "can't regulate morality" the government can in fact take the lead in changing social mores. For example, in Sweden it is currently illegal to spank children. When this law was first enacted, most Swedish parents practiced, and believed in, physical punishment. Today, more than a decade after the enactment, most Swedish parents do not believe in spanking children. The important issue here is not the question of whether or not people should spank their children but rather the point that government legislation can help bring about changes in peoples' thinking about appropriate behavior. The Swedish legislation may not have regulated morality, but it clearly nudged it in a different direction. Stronger laws about domestic violence might have a similar effect in this country.

Finally, we cannot ignore the role that larger social problems play in at least some types of recidivistic violence: poverty and drug abuse (especially alcohol abuse), for example. Policy discussions of poverty and drug abuse are too often divorced from those of crime and violence. There are no simple solutions to the problems of poverty and drug abuse, which in turn are not simply related to the problem of violence. Nevertheless, to ignore them is to enormously reduce our chances of passing on to our children a safe, relatively harmonious society in which they can work and love.

References

Abbey, A., & Harnish, R. (1995). Perception of sexual intent: The role of gender, alcohol consumption, and rape supportive attitudes. *Sex Roles: A Journal of Research, 32*(5–6), 297–313.

ABC News. (1982). *Poll of public opinion on crime.* New Haven, CT: Yale University Social Science Statistical Laboratory.

Adams, D., Barnett, S., Bechtereva, N., Carter, B., Delgado, J., Diaz, J., Eliasz, A., & Genoves, S. (1990). The Seville statement on violence. *American Psychologist, 45*(10), 1167–1168.

Adler, T. (1991, December). Abuse within families emerging from closet. *American Psychological Association Monitor*, pp. 16–17.

Ageton, S. S. (1983). The dynamics of female delinquency, 1976–1980. *Criminology, 21*(4), 555–584.

Ahmed, S., & Mapletoft, S. (1989). A new approach to explain aggression. *Perceptual and Motor Skills, 69*(2), 403–408.

Akers, R. L. (1985). *Deviant behavior: A social learning approach.* Belmont, CA: Wadsworth.

Akins, K. A., & Windham, M. E. (1992). Just science? *Behavioral and Brain Sciences, 15*(2), 376–377.

Allen, M., Emmers, T., & Giery, M. (1995). Exposure to pornography and acceptance of rape myths. *Journal of Communication, 45*(1), 5–26.

Allgeier, E. R., & Wiederman, M. W. (1992). Evidence for an evolved adaptation to rape? Not yet. *Behavioral and Brain Sciences, 15*(2), 377–379.

Anderson, C. (1989). Temperature and aggression: Ubiquitous effects of heat on occurrence of human violence. *Psychological Bulletin, 106*(1), 74–96.

Anderson, J. E. (1972). *The young child in the home: A survey of three thousand families.* White House Conference on Child Health and Protection, Report of the Committee on the Infant and Preschool Child.

Anderson, K., & Anderson, D. (1976). Psychologists and spanking. *Journal of Clinical Child Psychology, Fall,* 46–49.

Arends, L. (1996, February 24). Concern about crime overflows. *The Bakersfield Californian*, pp. 1–2.

Ascher, C. (1991). School programs for African American males. *ERIC Digest, 72,* 1–3.

Associated Press. (1995a, November 21). Bid to steal baby is linked to gruesome Illinois deaths. *The Boston Globe*, p. 11.

Associated Press. (1995b, August 1). Father convicted in twins' death. *The Boston Globe*, p. 53.

Associated Press. (1995c, October). Federal death-penalty jury hears slain girl's 911 tape. *The Boston Globe*, p. 11.

Associated Press. (1995d, November 6). Graf beat his daughter, says associate of family. *The Boston Globe*, p. 56.

Associated Press. (1995e, July 10). Increase in gun use in violent crime reported. *The Boston Globe*, p. 7.

Associated Press. (1995f, August 8). Man gets 10 years for beating baby. *The Boston Globe*, p. 11.

Associated Press. (1995g, December 10). Salesman attacks Texas woman, 88. *The Boston Globe*, p. 16.

Associated Press. (1995h, November 11). Sauce jar used in assault, police say. *The Boston Globe*, p. 24.

Associated Press. (1995i, December 1). Son, 20, charged with killing father. *The Boston Globe*, p. 56.

Associated Press. (1995j, May 25). Suspect in death of woman freed. *The Boston Globe*, p. 14.

Associated Press. (1995k, October). Trial opens in I-95 killing with crossbow. *The Boston Globe*, p. 7.

Associated Press. (1995l, October 17). Youth's lawyer blames abuse for murder of Rochester family. *The Boston Globe*, p. 3.

Atkin, C. K. (1983). Effects of realistic TV violence versus fictional violence on aggression. *Journalism Quarterly, 60,* 615–621.

Atkins, M. S., Stoff, D. M., Osborne, M. L., & Brown, K. (1993). Distinguishing instrumental and hostile aggression: Does it make a difference? *Journal of Abnormal Child Psychology, 21*(4), 355–365.

Bakan, D. (1971). *Slaughter of the innocents: A study of the battered child phenomenon.* Boston: Beacon Press.

Bandura, A. (1989). Human agency in social cognitive theory. *American Psychologist, 44,* 1175–1184.

Bandura, A., & Huston, A. (1961). Identification as a process of incidental learning. *Journal of Abnormal and Social Psychology, 63,* 311–318.

Bandura, A., Ross, D., & Ross, S. (1963). Vicarious reinforcement and imitative learning. *Journal of Abnormal and Social Psychology, 67,* 601–607.

Barber, B. K., Olsen, J. E., & Shagle, S. C. (1994). Associations between parental psychological and behavioral control and youth internalized and externalized behaviors. *Child Development, 65*(4), 1120–1136.

Barrett, P. (1991, March 25). Killing of 15-year-old is part of escalation of murder by juveniles. *The Wall Street Journal,* pp. A1, A5.

Barron, J. (1994, August 3). Vigil for slain girl, 7, backs a law on offenders; a convicted sex criminal has confessed. *The New York Times*, p. B4.

Bartol, C. (1991). *Criminal behavior: A psychosocial approach* (3rd ed.). Englewood Cliffs, NJ: Prentice-Hall.

Bartol, C. (1995). *Criminal behavior: A psychosocial approach* (4th ed.). Englewood Cliffs, NJ: Prentice-Hall.

Bassuk, E., Schoonover, S., & Gelenberg, A. (1983). *The practitioner's guide to psychoactive drugs* (2nd ed.). New York: Plenum.

Bastian, L. D., & Taylor, B. M. (1991). *School crime: A national crime victimization survey report* (No. NCJ-131645). Washington, DC: U.S. Department of Justice, Bureau of Justice Statistics.

Baumrind, D. (1994). The social context of child maltreatment. *Family Relations, 43*(4), 360–368.

Becker, W., Peterson, D., Luria, Z., Shoemaker, D., & Hellmer, L. (1962). Relations of factors derived from parent-interview ratings to behavior problems of five-year-olds. *Child Development, 33*, 509–535.

Beitchman, J. H., Zucker, K. J., Hood, J. E., DaCosta, G. A., & Akman, D. (1991). A review of the short-term effects of child sexual abuse. *Child Abuse & Neglect, 14*, 537–556.

Bell, R. Q. (1979). Parent, child, and reciprocal influences. *American Psychologist, 34*(10), 821–826.

Belsky, J. (1988). Child maltreatment and the emergent family system. In K. Browne, C. Davies, & P. Strattan (Eds.), *Early prediction and prevention of child abuse* (pp. 291–302). New York: Wiley.

Bender, L. (1938). Behavior problems in the children of psychotic and criminal parents. *Genetic Psychology Monographs, 19*, 229–334.

Bender, L. (1959). Children and adolescents who have killed. *American Journal of Psychiatry, 12*(3), 34–39.

Berenbaum, S. A., & Hines, M. (1992). Early androgens are related to childhood sex-typed toy preferences. *Psychological Science, 3*(3), 203–206.

Berkow, R. (Ed.). (1987). *The Merck manual of diagnosis and therapy.* Rahway, NJ: Merck, Sharp, and Dohme.

Berkowitz, L. (1962). *Aggression: A social-psychological analysis.* New York: McGraw-Hill.

Berkowitz, L. (1983). The experience of anger as a parallel process in the display of impulsive, "angry" aggression. In R. G. Geen & E. I. Donnerstein (Eds.), *Aggression: Theoretical and empirical reviews* (Vol. 1, pp. 103–135). New York: Academic Press.

Berkowitz, L., & LePage, A. (1967). Weapons as aggression-eliciting stimuli. *Journal of Personality and Social Psychology, 7*, 202–207.

Berliner, L. (1988). Corporal punishment: Institutionalized assault or justifiable discipline? *Journal of Interpersonal Violence, June*, 222–223.

Bernard, F. (1975). An inquiry among a group of pedophiles. *Journal of Sex Research, 11*, 242–255.

Bjorkqvist, K. (1994). Sex differences in physical, verbal, and indirect aggression: A review of recent research. *Sex Roles: A Journal of Research, 30*(3–4), 177–188.

Bjorkqvist, K., Nygren, T., Bjorklund, A., & Bjorkqvist, S. (1994). Testosterone intake and aggressiveness: Real effect or anticipation. *Aggressive Behavior, 20*(1), 17–26.

Bleuler, N. (1972). *The schizophrenic disorders: Long-term patient and family studies.* New Haven, CT: Yale University Press.

Block, R. (1977). *Violent crime.* Lexington, MA: Lexington Books.

Bonfante, J. (1995). Entrepreneurs of crack: An L.A. street gang transforms itself into a cross-country cocaine empire—until the FBI busts it all over. *Time*, Vol. 8, 22–24.

Bower, B. (1994). Monkeys defy crowding-aggression link. *Science News, 146*(2), 20.

Boxley, J., Lawrance, L., & Gruchow, H. (1995). A preliminary study of eighth grade students' attitudes toward rape myths and women's roles. *Journal of School Health, 65*(3), 96–101.

Braithwaite, J. (1981). The myth of social class and criminality reconsidered. *American Sociological Review, 46*, 36–57.

Brantley, A. C., & DiRosa, A. (1994). Gangs: A national perspective. *The FBI Law Enforcement Bulletin, 63*(5), 1–6.

Bridges, G. (1978). Errors in the measurement of crime: An application of Joreskog's method for the analysis of general covariance structures. In C. F. Wellford (Ed.), *Quantitative studies in criminology* (pp. 9–30). Beverly Hills, CA: Sage.

Bridges, G. (1981). Estimating the effects of response error in self-reports of crime. In J. A. Fox (Ed.), *Methods in quantitative criminology* (pp. 29–39). New York: Academic Press.

Brown, G. (1990). CSF serotonin metabolite (5-HIAA) studies in depression, impulsivity and violence. *Journal of Clinical Psychiatry, 51*(4), 31.

Browne, A. (1984). Assault and homicide at home: When battered women kill. In *Second National Conference for Family Violence Researchers*. Durham: University of New Hampshire.

Browne, A. (1987). *When battered women kill*. New York: The Free Press.

Bryan, J., & Freed, F. (1982). Corporal punishment: Normative data and sociological and psychological correlates in a community college population. *Journal of Youth and Adolescence, 11*(2), 77–87.

Buchholz, E. S., & Korn-Bursztyn, C. (1993). Children of adolescent mothers: Are they at risk for abuse? *Adolescence, 28*(110), 361–382.

Bureau of Justice Statistics. (1992). *National update* (Vol. 1, No. 3). Washington, DC: U.S. Department of Justice.

Burne, J. (1993). When the medium's message is violent. *New Scientist, 138*(1875), 12–13.

Burrell, B. (1990). *The relationship between child abuse potential and the presence of a family member with a handicap*. Seattle, WA: National Council on Family Relations.

Busch, K., Zagar, R., Hughes, J. R., Arbit, J., & Bussell, R. B. (1990). Adolescents who kill. *Journal of Clinical Psychology, 46*, 472–485.

Caesar, P. (1988). Exposure to violence in the families-of-origin among wife-abusers and maritally nonviolent men. *Violence and Victims, 3*(1), 31–36.

Caffaro-Rouget, A., Lang, R., & vanSanten, V. (1989). The impact of child sexual abuse. *Annals of Sex Research, 2*, 29–47.

Calhoun, J. B. (1961). Phenomena associated with population density. *Proceedings of the National Academy of Sciences, 47*, 428–429.

Campbell, S. B. (1994). Hard to manage pre-school boys: Externalizing behavior, social competence, and family context: a two-year followup. *Journal of Abnormal Psychology, 22*(2), 147–166.

Carroll, J. (1977). The intergenerational transmission of family violence: The long-term effects of aggressive behavior. *Aggressive Behavior, 3*, 289–299.

Cate, R. M., Henton, J., Koval, J., Christopher, F. S., & Lloyd, S. (1982). Premarital abuse: A social psychological perspective. *Journal of Family Issues, 3*, 79–90.

Caudill, B., Hoffman, J., Hubbard, R., Flynn, P., & Luckey, J. (1994). Parental history of substance abuse as a risk factor in predicting crack smokers' substance use, illegal activities, and psychiatric status. *American Journal of Drug and Alcohol Abuse, 20*(3), 341–354.

Cazenave, N. A., & Zahn, M. A. (1992). Women, murder, and male domination: Police reports of domestic violence in Chicago and Philadelphia. In E. C. Viano (Ed.), *Intimate violence: Interdisciplinary perspectives* (pp. 83–97). Washington, DC: Hemisphere.

Centerwall, B. (1992). Television and violence: The scale of the problem and where to go from here. *Journal of the American Medical Association, 267*(22), 3059–3063.

Cervi, D. (1991). *Wife and child abuse and nonfamily violence*. Durham: Family Research Laboratory, University of New Hampshire.

Christiansen, K., & Winkler, K. C. (1992). Hormonal, anthropometrical, and behavioral correlates of physical aggression in !Kung San men of Namibia. *Aggressive Behavior, 18*(4), 271–280.

Cicchetti, D. (1990). A historical perspective on the discipline of developmental psychopathology. In J. Rolf, A. Masten, D. Cicchetti, K. Neuchterlein, & S. Weintraub (Eds.), *Risk and protective factors in the development of psychopathology* (pp. 2–29). New York: Cambridge University Press.

Cicchetti, D., & Olson, K. (1990). The developmental psychopathology of child maltreatment. In M. Lewis & S. Miller (Eds.), *Handbook of developmental psychopathology* (pp. 261–281). New York: Plenum Press.

Clay, D., & Aquila, F. (1994). Gangs and America's schools. *Phi Delta Kappan, 76*, 65–68.

Clelland, D., & Carter, T. (1980). The new myth of class and crime. *Criminology, 18*, 319–336.

Clinton, W. (1994). Proclamation 6717—National Gang Violence Prevention Week. *Weekly Compilation of Presidential Documents, 30*(37), 1750–1752.

Cohen, D. L. (1992, May 20). Children in Boston exposed early to violence. *Education Week*, pp. 11–12.

Cohen, J. M., & Cohen, M. J. (1993). *New Penguin dictionary of quotations* (p. 333). New York: Penguin Books.

Cohn, D. A. (1990). Child–mother attachment of six-year-olds and social competence at school. *Child Development, 61*(1), 152–162.

Conklin, J. (1986). *Criminology* (2nd ed.). New York: Macmillan.

Conte, J., & Schuerman, J. (1987). The effects of sexual abuse on children: A multidimensional view. *Journal of Interpersonal Violence, 2*, 380–390.

Convit, A., Isay, D., Otis, D., & Volavka, J. (1990). Characteristics of repeatedly assaultive psychiatric inpatients. *Hospital and Community Psychiatry, 41*(10), 1112–1115.

Coster, W., Gersten, M., Beeghly, M., & Cicchetti, D. (1989). Communicative functioning in maltreated toddlers. *Developmental Psychology, 25*, 1020–1029.

Curtis, G. C. (1963). Violence breeds violence. *American Journal of Psychiatry, 120*, 386–387.

Dabbs, J., & Morris, R. (1990). Testosterone, social class, and antisocial behavior in a sample of 4,462 men. *Psychological Science, 1*, 209–211.

Davis, L. V., & Carlson, B. E. (1987). Observation of spouse abuse: What happens to the children? *Journal of Interpersonal Violence, 2*(3), 278–291.

Davis, R. H. (1995). Cruising for trouble: Gang-related drive-by shootings. *The FBI Law Enforcement Bulletin, 64*(1), 16–22.

DeFrances, C. J., & Smith, S. (1994). *Crime and neighborhoods* (NCJ-147005). Washington, DC: U.S. Department of Justice.

Deley, W. (1988). Physical punishment of children: Sweden and the USA. *Journal of Comparative Family Studies, 19*(3), 419–431.

Denno, D. (1990). *Biology and violence: From birth to adulthood.* New York: Cambridge University Press.

DiLalla, L., Mitchell, C., Arthur, M., & Pagliocca, P. (1988). Aggression and delinquency: Family and environmental factors. *Journal of Youth and Adolescence, 17*(3), 233–246.

Dillingham, S. D. (1992, April). President Bush calls for "Renewed investment in fighting violent street crime." *Bureau of Justice Statistics National Update*, p. 1.

Divoky, D. (1989). Ritalin: Education's fix-it drug? *Phi Delta Kappan, 70*(8), 599.

Dodge, K., Bates, J., & Pettit, G. (1990). *Mechanisms in the cycle of violence. Science, 250*, 1678–1683.

Dodge, K. A. (1993). Attributional bias in aggressive children. In P. Kendall (Ed.), *Advances in cognitive-behavioral research and therapy* (pp. 73–110). New York: Academic.

Dodge, K. A., Bates, J., & Pettit, G. (1990). Mechanisms in the cycle of violence. *Science, 250*, 1678–1683.

Dodge, K. A., Price, J. M., Bachorowski, J., & Newman, J. P. (1990). Hostile attributional biases in severely aggressive adolescents. *Journal of Abnormal Psychology, 99*(4), 385–392.

Downey, G., & Walker, E. (1989). Social cognition and adjustment in children at risk for psychopathology. *Developmental Psychology, 25*(5), 835–845.

Egeland, B., Jacobvitz, D., & Sroufe, L. A. (1988). Breaking the cycle of abuse: Relationship predictions. *Child Development, 59*, 1080–1088.

Ellement, J. (1995, November 1). Dedham man arraigned in rape, murder of friends' disabled sister. *The Boston Globe*, p. 18.

Elliott, D., & Ageton, S. (1980). Reconciling race and class differences in self-reported and official estimates of delinquency. *American Sociological Review, 45*, 95–110.

Elliott, F. A. (1978). Neurological aspects of antisocial behavior. In W. H. Reid (Ed.), *The psychopath* (pp. 146–189). New York: Bruner/Mazel.

Ellis, E. M., Calhoun, K. S., & Atkeson, B. M. (1980). Sexual dysfunctions in victims of rape: Victims may experience a loss of sexual arousal and frightening flashbacks even one year after the assault. *Women and Health, 5*, 39–47.

Ellis, L. (1990). Left- and mixed-handedness and criminality: Explanations for a probable relationship. In S. Coren (Ed.), *Left-handedness: Behavioral implications and anomalies* (pp. 485–505). North Holland: Elsevier Science.

Ellis, L. (1991). Monoamine oxidase and criminality: Identifying an apparent biological marker for antisocial behavior. *Journal of Research in Crime and Delinquency, 28*(2), 227–251.

Engfer, A., & Schneewind, K. (1982). Causes and consequences of harsh parental punishment: An empirical investigation in a representative sample of 570 German families. *Child Abuse & Neglect, 6*(2), 129–139.

Eron, L. (1982). Parent–child interaction, television violence, and aggression of children. *American Psychologist, 37*(2), 197–211.

Eron, L. D. (1987). The development of aggressive behavior from the perspective of a developing behaviorism. *American Psychologist, 42,* 435–442.

Escovar, L., & Escovar, P. (1985). Retrospective perception of child-rearing practices in three culturally different college groups. *International Journal of Intercultural Relations, 9*(1), 31–49.

Evans, G., & Lepore, S. (1993). Household crowding and social support: A quasiexperimental analysis. *Journal of Personality and Social Psychology, 65*(2), 308–316.

Fagan, J., & Chin, K. (1989). Initiation into crack and cocaine: A tale of two epidemics. *Contemporary Drug Problems, 16*(4), 579–617.

Fagan, J., & Wexler, S. (1987). Crime at home and in the streets: The relationship between family and stranger violence. *Violence and Victims, 2*(1), 5–23.

Fagan, J. A., Stewart, D. K., & Hansen, K. V. (1983). Violent men or violent husbands: Background factors and situational correlates. In D. Finkelhor (Ed.), *The dark side of families: Current family violence research* (pp. 49–69). Beverly Hills, CA: Sage.

Farnham-Diggory, S. (1978). *Learning disabilities.* Cambridge, MA: Harvard University Press.

Farrington, D. P. (1978). The family backgrounds of aggressive youths. In L. A. Hersov, M. Berger, & D. Schaffer (Eds.), *Aggression and anti-social behavior in childhood and adolescence* (pp. 73–95). Oxford: Pergamon.

Faulk, M. (1974). Men who assault their wives. *Medicine, Science and the Law, 14*(18), 1–13.

Fergusson, D., & Horwood, L. J. (1995). Early disruptive behavior, IQ, and later school achievement and delinquent behavior. *Journal of Abnormal Child Psychology, 23*(2), 183–200.

Ferrari, J., & Parker, J. (1992). High school achievement, self-efficacy, and locus of control as predictors of freshman academic performance. *Psychological Reports, 71*(2), 515–519.

Feshbach, N. (1980). Tomorrow is here today in Sweden. *Journal of Child Clinical Psychology 9*(2), 109–112.

Finkelhor, D. (1988). An epidemiologic approach to the study of child molestation. In R. Prentky & V. Quinsey (Eds.), *Human sexual aggression: Current perspectives* (pp. 136–142). New York: Annals of the New York Academy of Sciences.

Finkelhor, D., & Yllo, K. (1985). *License to rape.* New York: Holt, Rinehart & Winston.

Fischer, M., & Newby, R. F. (1991). Assessment of stimulant response in ADHD children using a refined multimethod clinical protocol (attention deficit hyperactivity disorder). *Journal of Clinical Child Psychology, 20*(3), 232–244.

Fishbein, D. H. (1992). The psychology of female aggression. *Criminal Justice and Behavior, 19*(2), 99–126.

Flynn, J. D. (1977). Recent finds related to wife abuse. *Social Casework, 58,* 17–18.

Fogel, C. A., Mednick, S. A., & Michelsen, N. (1985). Hyperactive behavior and minor physical anomalies. *Acta Psychiatrica Scandinavia, 75,* 551–556.

Follingstad, D. (1980). A reconceptualization of issues in the treatment of abused women: A case study. *Psychotherapy: Theory, Research and Practice, 17,* 294–303.

Forsstrom-Cohen, B., & Rosenbaum, A. (1985, May). The effects of parental marital violence on young adults: An exploratory investigation. *Journal of Marriage and the Family,* 467–472.

Francis, C., Hughes, H., & Hitz, L. (1992). Physically abusive parents and the 16-PF: A preliminary psychological typology. *Child Abuse & Neglect, 16*(5), 673–691.

Frankel, M. (1992). Suicide highest in wide-open spaces. *American Demographics, 14*(4), 9.

Freedman, J. L. (1975). *Crowding and behavior.* San Francisco: Freeman.

Freedman, J. L., Levy, A., Buchanan, R. W., & Price, J. (1972). Crowding and human aggressiveness. *Journal of Experimental Social Psychology, 8,* 528–548.

Freeh, L. J. (1995). *Uniform crime report press release.* Washington, DC: U.S. Department of Justice.

Freyne, A., & O'Connor, A. (1992). XYY genotype and crime. *Medicine, Science and the Law, 32*(3), 261.

Friedrich, L., & Stein, A. H. (1973). Aggressive and prosocial television programs and the natural behavior of preschool children. *Monographs of the Society for Research in Child Development, 38,* 151.

Friedt, L., & Gouvier, W. (1989). Bender Gestalt screening for brain dysfunction in a forensic population. *Criminal Justice & Behavior, 16*(4), 455.

Frieze, I. H., & Browne, A. (1989). Violence in marriage. In L. Ohlin & M. Tonry (Eds.), *Family violence.* Chicago: University of Chicago Press.

Futterman, A., & Zirkel, S. (1992). Men are not born to rape. *Behavioral and Brain Sciences, 15*(2), 385–386.

Gaes, G. (1994). Prison crowding research reexamined. *Prison Journal, 74*(3), 329–363.

Gardner, S., & Timmons-Mitchell, J. (1990). Facilitating capable parenting among black single mothers in violent families. In E. C. Viano (Ed.), *The victimology handbook* (pp. 275–284). New York: Garland.

Garrison, W. T., & Earls, F. J. (1987). *Temperament and child psychopathology.* Newbury Park, CA: Sage.

Gaustad, J. (1990). Gangs. *ERIC Digest, 52,* 1–4.

Gaustad, J. (1991). Schools attack the root of violence. *ERIC Digest, 63,* 1–4.

Gayford, J. J. (1975). Ten types of battered wives. *Welfare Officer, 25,* 5–9.

Gayford, J. J. (1983). Battered wives. In R. J. Gelles & C. Pedrick Cornell (Eds.), *International perspectives on family violence.* Lexington, MA: Lexington Books.

Gelles, R. (1974). *The violent home: A study of physical aggression between husbands and wives.* Beverly Hills, CA: Sage Publications.

Gelles, R. (1978). Violence towards children in the United States. *American Journal of Orthopsychiatry, 48*(4), 580–592.

Gelles, R. (1985). Family violence. *Annual Review of Sociology, 11,* 347–367.

Gelles, R. J., & Pedrick Cornell, C. (Eds.). (1983). *International perspectives on family violence.* Lexington, MA: Lexington Books.

Gerbner, G. (1990). Stories that hurt: Tobacco, alcohol, and other drugs in the mass media. In H. Resnik (Ed.), *Youth and drugs: Society's mixed messages* (p. 174). Rockville, MD: Office for Substance Abuse Prevention, U.S. Department of Health and Human Services.

Geschwind, N., & Galaburda, A. M. (1987). *Cerebral lateralization: Biological mechanisms, associations, and pathology.* Cambridge, MA: MIT Press.

Geyelin, M. (1993, August 11). Sex-predator law upheld. *The Wall Street Journal,* p. B2.

Giancola, P., & Zeichner, A. (1994). Neuropsychological performance on tests of frontal-lobe functioning and aggressive behavior in men. *Journal of Abnormal Psychology, 103*(4), 832–835.

Giannini, A. J., Miller, N., Loiselle, R., & Turner, C. (1993). Cocaine-associated violence and relationship to route of administration. *Journal of Substance Abuse Treatment, 10*(1), 67–69.

Gidycz, C. A., Coble, C. N., Latham, L., & Layman, M. J. (1993). Sexual assault experience in adulthood and prior victimization experiences: A prospective analysis. *Psychology of Women Quarterly, 17*(2), 151–168.

Gidycz, C. A., Hanson, K., & Layman, M. (1995). A prospective analysis of the relationships among sexual assault experiences: An extension of previous findings. *Psychology of Women Quarterly, 19*(1), 5–30.

Gil, D. (1971). Violence against children. *Journal of Marriage and the Family, 33,* 637–648.

Gladwell, M. (1995, January 16). N.J. law on released sex offenders proves problematic; ex-inmates must report addresses, but enforcement is burdensome; some are harassed. *The Washington Post*, p. A6.

Glickauf-Hughes, C., & Wells, M. (1991). Current conceptualizations on masochism: Genesis and object relations. *American Journal of Psychotherapy, 45*(1), 53–68.

Goldman, H. (1977). The limits of clockwork: The neurobiology of violent behavior. In J. P. Conrad & S. Dinitz (Eds.), *In fear of each other* (pp. 43–77). Lexington, MA: Lexington Books.

Goldstein, A. P., Keller, H., & Erne, D. (1985). *Changing the abusive parent*. Champaign, IL: Research Press.

Gortmaker, S., Salter, C., Walker, D., & Dietz, W. (1990). The impact of television viewing on mental aptitude and achievement: A longitudinal study. *Public Opinion Quarterly, 54*(4), 594–604.

Gottfredson, M., & Hirschi, T. (1995). National crime control policies. *Society, 32*(2), 30–36.

Gove, W. R., Hughes, M., & Galle, O. R. (1979). Overcrowding in the home: An empirical investigation of its possible pathological consequences. *American Sociological Review, 44*(February), 59–80.

Grace, J. (1994). There are no children here. *Time, 144*, 44–45.

Graff, T. T. (1979). *Personality characteristics of battered women*. Unpublished doctoral dissertation, Brigham Young University, Department of Psychology, Provo, UT.

Greenfeld, L. A. (1992). *Prisons and prisoners in the United States* (No. NCJ-137002). Washington, DC: U.S. Department of Justice.

Greenwood, P. (1995). Juvenile crime and juvenile justice. In J. Q. Wilson & J. Petersilia (Eds.), *Crime* (pp. 91–117). San Francisco, CA: ICS Press

Greven, P. (1991). *Spare the child: The religious roots of physical punishment and the psychological impact of physical abuse*. New York: Knopf.

Groth, A. N. (1979). *Men who rape: The psychology of the offender*. New York: Plenum.

Grusec, J. E., & Goodnow, J. J. (1994). Impact of parental discipline methods on the child's internalization of values: A reconceptualization of current points of view. *Developmental Psychology, 30*(1), 4–19.

Gustafson, R. (1989). Human physical aggression as a function of magnitude of frustration: Indirect support and a possible confounding influence. *Psychological Reports, 64*(2), 367–375.

Haddad, J. D., Barocas, R., & Hollenbeck, A. R. (1991). Family organization and parent attitudes of children with conduct disorder. *Journal of Clinical Child Psychology, 20*(2), 152–161.

Hagedorn, J. M. (1994). Neighborhoods, markets, and gang drug organization. *Journal of Research in Crime and Delinquency. 31*(3), 264–294.

Halpern, C. T., Udry, R. J., Campbell, B., & Suchindran, C. (1993). Relationship between aggression and pubertal increases in testosterone: A panel analysis of adolescent males. *Social Biology, 40*(1–2), 8–24.

Hamberger, L. K., & Hastings, J. E. (1990). Recidivism following spouse abuse abatement counseling: Treatment program implications. *Violence and Victims, 5*, 157–169.

Hanley, R. (1995, March 1). Decision by judge in New Jersey deals setback to "Megan's Law." *The New York Times*, p. A1.

Harris, M. (1992). Television viewing, aggression, and ethnicity. *Psychological Reports, 70*(1), 137–138.

Hart, J. (1995, November 19). Teacher, 78, punched as classmates cheer. *The Boston Globe*, pp. 37–41.

Haskett, M., Johnson, C., & Miller, J. (1994). Individual differences in risk of child abuse by adolescent mothers: Assessment in the perinatal period. *Journal of Child Psychology and Psychiatry and Allied Disciplines, 35*(3), 461–476.

Hassell, R. A. (1981). *The impact of stranger versus nonstranger rape: A longitudinal study.* Paper presented at the eighth annual Conference of the Association for Women in Psychology, Boston, MA.

Hazzard, A., Celano, M., Gould, J., Lawry, S., & Webb, C. (1995). Predicting symptomatology and self-blame among child sex abuse victims. *Child Abuse and Neglect, 19*(6), 707–708.

Hegar, R. L., Zuravin, S., & Orme, J. (1994). Factors predicting severity of physical child abuse injury. *Journal of Interpersonal Violence, 9*(2), 170–183.

Heimer, K., & Matsueda, R. (1994). Role-taking, role commitment, and delinquency: A theory of differential social control. *American Sociological Review, 59*(3), 365–390.

Henderson, M. (1983). An empirical classification of non-violent offenders using the MMPI. *Personality and Individual Differences, 4,* 671–677.

Herschel, M. (1978). Dyslexia revisited. *Human Genetics, 40,* 115–134.

Hewitt, J. D. (1988). The victim–offender relationship in convicted homicide cases: 1960–1984. *Journal of Criminal Justice, 16,* 25–33.

Himelein, M. J., Vogel, R. E., & Wachowiak, D. G. (1994). Nonconsensual sexual experiences in precollege women: Prevalence and risk factors. *Journal of Counseling and Development, 72*(4), 411–415.

Hindelang, M. (1978). Race and involvement in common law personal crimes. *American Sociological Review, 43,* 93–109.

Hirschi, T. (1990). Control: Society's central notion. *The American Journal of Sociology, 96*(3), 750–752.

Horan, S. (1992). The XYY supermale and the criminal justice system: A square peg in a round hole. *Loyola of Los Angeles Law Review, 24*(4), 1343.

Horn, W. F., Ialongo, N., Greenberg, G., Packard, T., & Smith-Winberry, C. (1990). Additive effects of behavioral parent training and self-control therapy with attention deficit hyperactivity disordered children. *Journal of Clinical Child Psychology, 19*(2), 98–110.

Hotaling, G. T., Straus, M. A., & Lincoln, A. J. (1989). Intrafamily violence, and crime and violence outside the family. In L. Ohlin & M. Tonry (Eds.), *Family violence* (pp. 313–377). Chicago: University of Chicago Press.

Hotaling, G. T., & Sugarman, D. B. (1986). An analysis of risk markers in husband-to-wife violence: The current state of knowledge. *Violence and Victims, 1*(2), 101–124.

Hubbard, J. A., & Newcomb, A. F. (1991). Initial dyadic peer interaction of attention deficit hyperactivity disorder and normal boys. *Journal of Abnormal Child Psychology, 19*(2), 179–195.

Huesmann, L., Eron, L., Lefkowitz, M., & Walder, L. (1984). Stability of aggression of time and generations. *Developmental Psychology, 20*(6), 1120–1134.

Huesmann, L. R., & Eron, L. D. (1986). *Television and the aggressive child: A cross-national comparison.* Hillsdale, NJ: Lawrence Erlbaum Associates.

Hughes, J., Zagar, R., Sylvies, R. B., Arbit, J., Busch, K. G., & Bowers, N. D. (1991). Medical, family, and scholastic conditions in urban delinquents. *Journal of Clinical Psychology, 47*(3), 448–464.

Humphrey, J. A., & Palmer, S. (1987). Race, sex, and criminal homicide offender–victim relationships. *Journal of Black Studies, 18,* 45–57.

Hurley, D. (1994). Imminent danger. *Psychology Today, 27*(4), 54–62.

Huston, A., Watkins, B., & Kunkel, D. (1989). Public policy and children's television. *American Psychology, 44,* 424–433.

Huston, A., Wright, J., Rice, M., Kerkman, D., & St. Peters, M. (1990). Development of television viewing patterns in early childhood: A longitudinal investigation. *Developmental Psychology, 26*(3), 409–420.

Inciardi, J., & Pottieger, A. (1994). Crack-cocaine use and street crime. *Journal of Drug Issues, 24*(1–2), 273–292.

Jackson, J. K. (1958). Alcoholism and the family. *Annals of the American Academy of Political and Social Science, 315,* 90–98.

Jacobvitz, D., & Sroufe, L. A. (1987). The early caregiver–child relationship and attention deficit disorder with hyperactivity in kindergarten. *Child Development, 58,* 1488–1495.

Janokowski, G. (1985, September 30). Direct causal relationship between TV and undesirable behavior yet to be proven. *Television–Radio Age,* p. 65.

Jellinek, M., Murphy, J. M., Poitrast, F., Quinn, D., Bishop, S. J., & Goshko, M. (1992). Serious child mistreatment in Massachusetts: The course of 206 children through the courts. *Child Abuse & Neglect, 16,* 179–185.

Johannesson, I. (1974). Aggressive behavior among school children related to maternal practices in early childhood. In J. de Wit & W. W. Hartup (Eds.), *Determinants and origins of aggressive behavior* (pp. 413–425). The Hague: Mouton.

Johnson, J. (1991). The oldest DNA in the world. *New Scientist, 130*(1768), 44–49.

Jones, D. (1995). Editorial: Parental empathy, emotionality, and the potential for child abuse. *Child Abuse & Neglect, 19*(6), 765–766.

Jones, E., & McCurdy, K. (1992). The links between types of maltreatment and demographic characteristics of children. *Child Abuse & Neglect, 16*(2), 201–215.

Jones, J. (1990, October). Violent statistics. *American Psychological Association Monitor,* p. 4.

Jouriles, E. N., & Norwood, W. D. (1995). Physical aggression toward boys and girls in families characterized by the battering of women. *Journal of Family Psychology, 9*(1), 69–78.

Kagan, J. (1988). The meanings of personality predicates. *American Psychologist, 438,* 614–620.

Kahn, A. S., Mathie, V. A., & Torgler, C. (1994). Rape scripts and rape acknowledgement. *Psychology of Women Quarterly, 18*(1), 53–66.

Kalof, L. (1993). Rape-supportive attitudes and sexual victimization experiences of sorority and nonsorority women. *Sex Roles: A Journal of Research, 29*(11–12), 767–780.

Kandel, E. (1987). *IQ as a protective factor for subjects at high risk for anti-social behavior.* Paper presented at the Western Psychological Association Convention, Long Beach, CA.

Kandel, E. (1988). *Minor physical anomalies and parental modeling of aggression predict violent criminal behavior.* Paper presented at the meeting of the American Association for the Advancement of Science, Boston, MA.

Kandel, F. (1989). Genetic and perinatal factors in anti-social personality in a birth cohort. *Journal of Crime and Justice, 12*(2), 61–78.

Kandel, E., Brennan, P., & Mednick, S. A. (1989). Minor physical anomalies and recidivistic adult violent offending: Evidence from a birth cohort. *Acta Psychiatrica Scandinavia, 79,* 103–107.

Kandel, E., & Freed, D. (1989). Frontal lobe dysfunction and antisocial behavior: A review. *Journal of Clinical Psychology, 45*(3), 404–413.

Kandel, E., & Mednick, S. A. (1989). *The relationship between perinatal factors, hyperactivity, and violent offending.* Paper presented at the National Institute of Justice Conference on Violence, Palm Springs, CA.

Kandel, E., & Mednick, S. A. (1991). Perinatal factors predict violent offending. *Criminology, 29*(3), 101–111.

Kandel, E., Mednick, S. A., Sorensen, L. K., Hutchings, B., Knop, J., Rosenberg, R., & Schulsinger, F. (1988). High IQ as a protective factor for subjects at high risk for anti-social behavior. *Journal of Consulting and Clinical Psychology, 56*(2), 224–226.

Kandel-Englander, E. (1992). Wife-battering and violence outside the family. *Journal of Interpersonal Violence, 7*(4), 462–470.

Kang, S., Magura, S., & Shapiro, J. L. (1994). Correlates of cocaine/crack use among inner-city incarcerated adolescents. *American Journal of Drug and Alcohol Abuse, 20*(4), 413–429.

Kaufman Kantor, G., & Straus, M. A. (1990). The "drunken bum" theory of wife beating. In M. A. Straus & R. Gelles (Eds.), *Physical violence in American families* (pp. 203–219). New Brunswick, NJ: Transaction. (Original work published 1987)

Kelleher, K., Chaffin, M., Hollenberg, J., & Fischer, E. (1994). Alcohol and drug disorders among physically abusive and neglectful parents in a community-based sample. *The American Journal of Public Health, 84*(10), 1586–1590.

Kelley, S. (1992). Parenting stress and child maltreatment in drug-exposed children. *Child Abuse & Neglect, 16*(3), 317–328.

Kempe, C. H., Silverman, F. N., & Steele, B. F. (1962). The battered child syndrome. *Journal of the American Medical Association, 181*(17), 39–42.

Kemper, T., & Reichler, M. (1976). Marital satisfaction and conjugal power as determinants of intensity and frequency of rewards and punishments administered by parents. *Journal of Genetic Psychology, 129*(2), 221–234.

Kendall-Tackett, K. A., Williams, L., & Finkelhor, D. (1993). Impact of sexual abuse on children: A review and synthesis of recent empirical studies. *Psychological Bulletin, 113*(1), 164–180.

Killory, J. F. (1974). In defense of corporal punishment. *Psychological Reports, 35*, 575–581.

Kilpatrick, D. G. (1993). Rape and other forms of sexual assault. *Journal of Interpersonal Violence, 8*(2), 193–197.

Kirkegaard-Sorenson, L., & Mednick, S. A. (1977). A prospective study of predictors of criminality: 4. School behavior. In S. A. Mednick & K. O. Christiansen (Eds.), *Biosocial bases of criminal behavior* (pp. 255–266). New York: Gardner.

Klaus, K. (1994). Crime statistics. *Congressional Digest, 73*(6–7), 167–169.

Kohn, A. (1989). Suffer the restless children: Though nearly a million children are regularly given drugs to control "hyperactivity," we know little about what the disorder is, or whether it is really a disorder at all. *The Atlantic, 5*, 90–97.

Kosky, R. (1983). Childhood suicidal behavior. *Journal of Child Psychology & Psychiatry & Allied Disciplines, 24*(3), 457–468.

Koss, M. P., & Gaines, J. A. (1993). The prediction of sexual aggression by alcohol use, athletic participation, and fraternity affiliation. *Journal of Interpersonal Violence, 8*(1), 94–108.

Koss, M., Gidycz, C., & Wisniewski, N. (1987). The scope of rape: Incidence and prevalence of sexual aggression and victimization in a national sample of higher education students. *Journal of Consulting & Clinical Psychology, 55*, 162–170.

Kroeker, M., & Haut, F. (1995). A tale of two cities: The street gangs of Paris and Los Angeles. *The Police Chief, 62*(5), 32–37.

Krynicki, V. E. (1978). Cerebral dysfunction in repetitively assaultive adolescents. *Journal of Nervous and Mental Disease, 166*, 59–67.

Lane, K., & Gwartney-Gibbs, P. (1985). Violence in the context of dating and sex. *Journal of Family Issues, 6*, 45–59.

Langan, P. A., & Innes, C. A. (1986). *Preventing domestic violence against women.* Washington, DC: U.S. Government Printing Office.

Langhinrichsen-Rohling, J., Neidig, P., & Thorn, G. (1995). Violent marriages: Gender differences in levels of current violence and past abuse. *Journal of Family Violence, 10*(2), 159–175.

Larzelere, R. (1986). Moderate spanking: Model or deterrent of children's aggression in the family? *Journal of Family Violence, 1*(1), 27–36.

Lau, M., Pihl, R., & Peterson, J. (1995). Provocation, acute alcohol intoxication, cognitive performance, and aggression. *Journal of Abnormal Psychology, 104*(1), 150–155.

Lee, N. (1995). Culture conflict and crime in Alaskan native villages. *Journal of Criminal Justice, 23*(2), 177–189.

Lefkowitz, M., Eron, L., Walder, L., & Huesmann, L. (1977). *Growing up to be violent: A longitudinal study of the development of aggression.* New York: Pergamon.

Lefkowitz, M., Walder, L., & Eron, L. (1963). Punishment, identification, and aggression. *Merrill Palmer Quarterly, 9*, 159–174.

Lesnik-Oberstein, M., Koers, A. J., & Cohen, L. (1995). Parental hostility and its sources in psychologically abusive mothers: A test of the three factor theory. *Child Abuse & Neglect, 19*(1), 33–49.

Levine, M. (1975). Interparental violence and its effects on the children: A study of 50 families in general practice. *Medicine, Science and Law, 15,* 172–176.

Leviton, H. (1976). The individualization of discipline for behavior disorder pupils. *Psychology in the Schools, 13*(4), 445–448.

Lewis, D., Shanok, S., & Balla, D. (1979). Perinatal difficulties, head and face trauma, and child abuse in the medical histories of seriously delinquent children. *American Journal of Psychiatry, 1364*(A), 419–423.

Lewis, D., Moy, E., Jackson, L. D., Aaronson, R., Ritvo, H., Settu, S., & Simons, A. (1985). Biopsychosocial characteristics of children who later murder: A prospective study. *American Journal of Psychiatry, 142,* 1161–1166.

Lewis, D. O., Pincus, J. H., Bard, B., Richardson, E., Prichep, L. S., Feldman, M., & Yeager, C. (1988). Neuropsychiatric, psychoeducational, and family characteristics of 14 juveniles condemned to death in the United States. *American Journal of Psychiatry, 145*(5), 584–589.

Lewis, D. O., Pincus, J. H., Feldman, M., Jackson, L., & Bard, B. (1986). Psychiatric, neurological, and psychoeducational characteristics of 15 death row inmates in the United States. *American Journal of Psychiatry, 143*(7), 838–845.

Lindgren, C. (1990). *Justice expenditure and employment.* Washington, DC: U.S. Department of Justice.

Linz, D., Donnerstein, E., & Adams, S. (1989). Physiological desensitization and judgement about female victims of violence. *Human Communications Research, 15*(4), 509–522.

Lonsway, K. A., & Fitzgerald, L. F. (1994). Rape myths: In review. *Psychology of Women Quarterly, 18*(2), 133–164.

Los Solidos Nation. (1995). Family values: The gangster version. *Harper's, 290*(1739), 18–20.

Lowenstein, L. (1977). The value of corporal punishment. *News and Views, 3*(1), 14–15.

Lyons-Ruth, K., Alpern, L., & Repacholi, B. (1993). Disorganized infant attachment classification and maternal psychosocial problems as predictors of hostile-aggressive behavior in the preschool classroom. *Child Development, 64*(2), 572–585.

Magaw, J. (1995). ATF's role in a GREAT program (Bureau of Alcohol, Tobacco and Firearms, Gang Resistance Education training). *Juvenile Delinquency-Prevention Gangs-Study and Teaching, 62*(5), 8

Magmer, E., & Ipfling, H. (1973). On the problem of specific social class punishments. *Scientia Paedagogica Experimentalis, 10*(2), 170–192.

Makepeace, J. M. (1981). Courtship violence among college students. *Family Relations, 30*(1), 97–102.

Malamuth, N. (1992). Evolution and laboratory research on men's sexual arousal: What do the data show and how can we explain them? *Behavioral and Brain Sciences, 15*(2), 394–396.

Malamuth, N., & Brown, L. (1994). Sexually aggressive men's perceptions of women's communications: Testing three explanations. *Journal of Personality and Social Psychology, 67*(4), 699–712.

Mann, C. R. (1992). Female murderers and their motives: A tale of two cities. In E. C. Viano (Ed.), *Intimate violence: Interdisciplinary perspectives* (pp. 73–81). Washington, DC: Hemisphere.

Mannarino, A., & Cohen, J. (1986). A clinical-demographic study of sexually abused children. *Child Abuse & Neglect, 10,* 17–23.

Mark, V. H., & Ervin, F. R. (1970). *Violence and the brain.* Hagerstown, MD: Harper & Row.

Marshall, W. L., & Barbaree, H. E. (1988). An outpatient treatment program for child molesters. In R. A. Prentky & V. L. Quinsey (Eds.), *Human sexual aggression: Current perspectives* (pp. 205–215). New York: New York Academy of Sciences.

Matthys, W., Cohen-Kettenis, P., & Berkhout, J. (1994). Boys' and girls' perceptions of peers in middle childhood: Differences and similarities. *Journal of Genetic Psychology, 155*(1), 15–24.

Maurer, A. (1974). Corporal punishment. *American Psychologist, August,* 614–626.

McCahill, T., Meyer, L. C., & Fishman, A. M. (1979). *The aftermath of rape.* Lexington, MA: Heath.

McCord, J. (1979). Some child-rearing antecedents of criminal behavior in adult men. *Journal of Personality and Social Psychology, 37*(9), 1477–1486.

McCord, J. (1988). Parental aggressiveness and physical punishment in long-term perspective. In G. T. Hotaling, D. Finkelhor, J. T. Kirkpatrick, & M. A. Straus (Eds.), *Family abuse and its consequences: New directions in research* (pp. 91–98). Newbury Park, CA: Sage.

McKinney, K. C. (1988, September). Juvenile gangs: Crime and drug trafficking. *Juvenile Justice Bulletin,* 1–8.

Mednick, S. A., Gabrielli, W., & Hutchings, B. (1984). Genetic influences in criminal convictions: Evidence from an adoption cohort. *Science, 234,* 891–894.

Mednick, S. A., Harway, M., Mednik, B., & Moffitt, T. (1981). Longitudinal research: North American data sets. In T. E. Jordan (Ed.), *Child development, information and formation of public policy* (pp. 1–35). St. Louis: University of Missouri Press.

Mednick, S. A., & Hutchings, B. (1978). Genetic and psychophysiological factors in asocial behavior. *Journal of the American Academy of Child and Adolescent Psychiatry, 17,* 209–223.

Mednick, S. A., & Kandel, E. (1988). Genetic and perinatal factors in violence. In T. E. Moffitt & S. A. Mednick (Eds.), *Biological contributions to crime causation* (pp. 121–135). Dordrecht, The Netherlands: Martinus Nijhoff.

Megargee, E. I. (1966). Undercontrolled and overcontrolled personality types in extreme antisocial aggression. *Psychological Monographs, 80*(3), 149–210.

Megargee, E. I. (1982). Psychological determinants and correlates of criminal violence. In M. E. Wolfgang & N. A. Weinder (Eds.), *Criminal violence* (pp. 81–171). Beverly Hills, CA: Sage.

Meredith, W. H., Abbott, D. A., & Adams, S. L. (1986). Family violence: Its relation to marital and parental satisfaction and family strengths. *Journal of Family Violence, 1,* 299–305.

Mestel, R. (1994). What triggers the violence within? *New Scientist, 141*(1914), 30–34.

Miller, D., & Challas, G. (1981). Abused children as parents: A twenty-five year longitudinal study. In *National Conference on Family Violence Research.* Durham: University of New Hampshire.

Miller, G. E., & Prinz, R. J. (1990). Enhancement of social learning family interventions for childhood conduct disorder. *Psychological Bulletin, 108*(2), 291–317.

Milne, J. (1995, November 16). Girl, 11, testifies father watched, urged on rapist. *The Boston Globe,* p. 3.

Milner, J., Halsey, L., & Fultz, J. (1995). Empathic responsiveness and affective reactivity to infant stimuli in high- and low-risk for physical child abuse mothers. *Child Abuse & Neglect, 19*(6), 767–780.

Moeller, T. G. (1994). What research says about self-esteem and academic performance. *Education Digest, 59*(5), 34–37.

Monahan, J. (1992). Mental disorder and violent behavior: Perceptions and evidence (Awards Issue: 1991 Award Addresses). *The American Psychologist, 47*(4), 511–521.

Moore, J., Vigil, J. D., & Levy, J. (1995). Huisas of the street: Chicana gang members. *Latino Studies Journal, 6*(1), 27–49.

Morell, V. (1993). Evidence found for a possible "aggression" gene. *Science, 260*(5115), 1722–1723.

Moss, H., Mezzick, A., Yao, J., Gavaler, J., & Martin, C. (1995). Aggressivity among sons of substance-abusing fathers: Association with psychiatric disorder in the father and son, paternal personality, pubertal development, and socioeconomic status. *American Journal of Drug and Alcohol Abuse, 21*(2), 195–209.

Moyer, K. E. (1971). The physiology of aggression and the implication for aggression control. In J. L. Singer (Ed.), *The control of aggression and violence* (pp. 61–75). New York: Academic Press.

Mueller, C. W. (1983). Environmental stressors and aggressive behavior. In R. G. Geen & E. I. Donnerstein (Eds.), *Aggression: Theoretical and empirical reviews* (Vol. 2, pp. 51–77). New York: Academic Press.

Mydans, S. (1995, March 18). Gangs reach a new frontier: Reservations. *The New York Times*, 1.

Nada Raja, S., McGee, R., & Stanton, W. R. (1992). Perceived attachments to parents and peers and psychological well-being in adolescence. *Journal of Youth and Adolescence, 21*(4), 156–172.

Nagaraja, J. (1984). Non-compliance: A behavior disorder. *Child Psychiatry Quarterly, 17*(4), 127–132.

Nagin, D., & Paternoster, R. (1994). Personal capital and social control: The deterrence implications of a theory of individual differences in criminal offending. *Criminology, 32*(4), 581–606.

National Archive of Criminal Justice Data. (1991). *The national crime surveys*. Washington, DC: U.S. Bureau of Justice.

National Institute on Alcohol Abuse and Alcoholism. (1994). *Studies of alcohol-related impairment* (25 PH 351). National Institutes of Health.

National Research Council. (1993). *Understanding child abuse and neglect*. Washington, DC: National Academy Press.

Ney, P. (1992). Causes of child abuse and neglect. *Canadian Journal of Psychiatry, 37*(6), 401–405.

Nichols, P. (1987). Minimal brain dysfunction and soft signs: The collaborative perinatal project. In D. Tupper (Ed.), *Soft neurological signs* (pp. 179–200). New York: Grune & Stratton.

Nickerson, C. (1995, June 4). "Stuff of nightmares" marks Canadian trial. *The Boston Globe*, p. 2.

Offord, D. R. (1971). The natural histories of schizophrenia, depression, disorder and psychopathy: Current status. *Psychosomatics, 12*(3), 179–185.

O'Leary, K. D., Barling, J., Arias, I., Rosenbaum, A., Malone, J., & Tyree, A. (1989). Prevalence and stability of physical aggression between spouses: A longitudinal analysis. *Journal of Consulting and Clinical Psychology, 57*, 263–268.

Olweus, D. (1979). Stability of aggressive reaction patterns in males: A review. *Psychological Bulletin, 86*, 852–875.

Ostrow, R. J. (1995, December 18). Homicides in US drop sharply, FBI reports. *The Boston Globe*, p. 3.

Owens, D., & Straus, M. (1975). The social structure of violence in childhood and approval of violence as an adult. *Aggressive Behavior, 1*, 193–211.

Pagelow, M. D. (1993). Response to Hamberger's comments. *Journal of Interpersonal Violence, 8*(1), 137–139.

Parke, R., & Collmer, C. (1975). Child abuse: An interdisciplinary analysis. In E. M. Hetherington (Ed.), *Review of child development research* (pp. 509–590). Chicago: University of Chicago Press.

Parke, R., & Slaby, R. (1983). The development of aggression. In P. Mussen (Ed.), *Handbook of child psychology: Volume IV* (pp. 547–621). New York: Wiley & Sons.

Pasamanick, B., Rodgers, M. E., & Lilienfield, A. M. (1956). Pregnancy experiences and the development of behavior disorders in children. *American Journal of Psychiatry, 112*, 613–618.

Paterson, E. J. (1979). How the legal system responds to battered women. In D. M. Moore (Eds.), *Battered women*. Beverly Hills, CA: Sage.

Peele, S. (1984). The cultural context of psychological approaches to alcoholism. *American Psychologist, 39*, 1337–1351.

Perse, E. (1994). Uses of erotica and acceptance of rape myths. *Communication Research, 21*(4), 488–515.

Peterson, R., & Baily, W. (1992). Rape and dimensions of gender socioeconomic inequality in U.S. metropolitan areas. *Journal of Research in Crime and Delinquency, 29*(2), 162–177.

Pierce, C. (1984). Television and violence: Social psychiatric perspectives. *American Journal of Social Psychiatry, 3*, 41–44.

Pillemer, K., & Finkelhor, D. (1988). The prevalence of elder abuse: A random sample survey. *The Gerontologist, 28*(2), 51–57.

Piper, E. S. (1985). Violent recidivism and chronicity in the 1958 Philadelphia cohort. *Journal of Quantitative Criminology, 1*(4), 319–344.

Pirog-Good, M. (1992). Sexual abuse in dating relationships. In E. C. Viano (Ed.), *Intimate violence: Interdisciplinary perspectives* (pp. 101–110). Washington, DC: Hemisphere.

Pizzy, E. (1974). *Scream quietly or the neighbors will hear.* Great Britain: Penguin.

Pliszka, S. R. (1991). Attention-deficit hyperactivity disorder: A clinical review. *American Family Physician, 43*(4), 1267–1275.

Pope, A. W., Bierman, K. L., & Mumma, G. H. (1991). Aggression, hyperactivity, and inattention-immaturity: Behavior dimensions associated with peer rejection in elementary school. *Developmental Psychology, 27*(4), 663–671.

Porter, S., Yuille, J., & Bent, A. (1995). A comparison of the eyewitness accounts of deaf and hearing children. *Child Abuse & Neglect, 19*(1), 51–61.

Radecki, T. (1989). On picking good television and film entertainment. *NCTV News, 10*(1–2), 5.

Rand, M. R. (1991). *Crime and the nation's households, 1990.* Washington, DC: U.S. Department of Justice.

Rapaport, K., & Burkhart, B. (1984). Personality and attitudinal characteristics of sexually coercive college males. *Journal of Abnormal Psychology, 93*, 216–221.

Reed, J. (1989). Mechanical man: John Broadus Watson and the beginnings of behaviorism. *Science, 244*(4910), 1386–1388.

Reel violence (editorial). (1994). *Lancet, 343*(8890), 127.

Reiss, A. (1975). Inappropriate theories and inadequate methods as policy plagues: Self-reported delinquency and the law. In N. Demerath, O. Larsen, & K. Schulessler (Eds.), *Social policy and sociology* (pp. 211–223). New York: Academic Press.

Resick, P. A. (1993). The psychological impact of rape. *Journal of Interpersonal Violence, 8*(2), 223–255.

Resick, P. A., Calhoun, K. S., Atkeson, B. M., & Ellis, E. M. (1981). Social adjustment in victims of sexual assault. *Journal of Consulting and Clinical Psychology, 49*, 705–712.

Resick, P. A., Jordan, C. G., Girelli, S. A., Hutter, C. K., & Marhoefer-Dvorak, S. (1988). A comparative outcome study of behavior group therapy for sexual assault victims. *Behavior Therapy, 19*, 385–401.

Reuters. (1995a, November 21). Boy, 9, is charged in sister's killing. *The Boston Globe*, p. 11.

Reuters. (1995b, November 27). NY police allege copycat subway blast. *The Boston Globe*, p. 3.

Rice, M., Chaplin, T. C., Harris, G. T., & Coutts, J. (1994). Empathy for the victim and sexual arousal among rapists and nonrapists. *Journal of Interpersonal Violence, 9*(4), 435–449.

Rigdon, J., & Tapia, F. (1977). Children who are cruel to animals: A follow-up study. *Journal of Operational Psychology, 8*, 27–36.

Ritchie, K. (1989). The little woman meets son of *DSM-III. The Journal of Medicine and Philosophy, 14*(6), 695–708.

Rivera, B., & Spatz Widom, C. (1990). Childhood victimization and violent offending. *Violence and Victims, 5*(1), 19–35.

Rizzuto, A. (1991). Sigmund Freud: The secrets of nature and the nature of secrets. *The International Review of Psychoanalysis, 18*(2), 143.

Roberts, J. (1995). Sexual assault is a crime of violence. *Canadian Journal of Criminology, 37*(1), 88–93.

Robins, L. (1966). *Deviant children grown up: A sociological and psychiatric study of sociopathic personality.* Baltimore: Williams & Wilkins.

Robins, L. (1978). Sturdy childhood predictors of adult antisocial behavior: Replications from longitudinal studies. *Psychological Medicine, 84,* 611–622.

Rosenbaum, A., & Hoge, S. (1989). Head injury and marital aggression. *American Journal of Psychiatry, 146*(8), 1048–1051.

Rothbaum, B. O., Foa, E. B., Murdock, T., Riggs, D. S., & Walsh, W. (1992). A prospective examination of post-traumatic stress disorder in rape victims. *Journal of Traumatic Stress, 5,* 455–475.

Rounsaville, B. J. (1978). Theories in marital violence: Evidence from a study of battered women. *Victimology, 3*(1), 11–31.

Ruback, R. B., & Riad, J. K. (1994). The more (men), the less merry: Social density, social burden, and social support. *Sex Roles: A Journal of Research, 30*(11–12), 743–763.

Russell, D. (1983). *Rape in marriage.* New York: Collier.

Rust, J., & Kinnard, K. (1983). Personality characteristics of the users of corporal punishment in schools. *Journal of School Psychology, 21*(2), 91–98.

Sanson, A., Oberklaid, F., Pedlow, R., & Prior, M. (1991). Risk indicators: Assessment of infancy predictors of pre-school behavioural maladjustment. *Journal of Child Psychology & Psychiatry, 32*(4), 609–626.

Sargeant, G. (1994). Children with disabilities found more apt to be abused. *Trial, 30*(2), 87–88.

Saunders, D. G. (1992). A typology of men who batter: Three types derived from cluster analysis. *American Journal of Orthopsychiatry, 62*(2), 264–275.

Saunders, D. G., & Size, P. B. (1986). Attitudes about woman abuse among police officers, victims, and victim advocates. *Journal of Interpersonal Violence, 1*(1), 25–42.

Scente, D. D. (1993). RAP to street gang activity. *The Police Chief, 60*(2), 28–29.

Schneider-Rosen, K., & Cicchetti, K. (1984). The relationship between affect and cognition in maltreated infants: Quality of attachment and the development of visual self-recognition. *Child Development, 55,* 648–658.

Schuck, J. R. (1974). The use of causal nonexperimental models in aggression research. In J. de Wit & W. W. Hartup (Eds.), *Determinants and origins of aggressive behavior* (pp. 381–389). The Hague: New Babylon.

Scott, C. S., Lefley, H. P., & Hicks, D. (1993). Potential risk factors for rape in three ethnic groups. *Community Mental Health Journal, 29*(2), 133–141.

Scott, P. D. (1974). Battered wives. *British Journal of Psychiatry, 125,* 433–441.

Sears, R. (1961). Relation of early socialization experiences to aggression in middle childhood. *Journal of Abnormal and Social Psychology, 63*(3), 466–492.

Sears, R., Maccoby, E., & Levin, H. (1957). *Patterns of child rearing.* New York: Harper & Row.

Sears, R., Whiting, J., Nowlis, V., & Sears, P. (1953). Some childrearing antecedents of aggression and dependency in young children. *Genetic Psychology Monograms, 47,* 135–234.

Sechrest, D. K. (1991). The effects of density on jail assaults. *Journal of Criminal Justice, 19*(3), 211–223.

Shanok, S. S., & Lewis, D. O. (1981). Medical histories of female delinquents. *Archives of General Psychiatry, 38,* 211–213.

Sheley, J., Zhang, J., Brody, C., & Wright, J. (1995). Gang organization, gang criminal activity and individual gang members' criminal behavior. *Social Science Quarterly, 76*(1), 53–69.

Sheridan, M. (1995). A proposed intergenerational model of substance abuse, family functioning, and abuse/neglect. *Child Abuse & Neglect, 19*(5), 519–530.

Shields, N. M., McCall, G. J., & Hanneke, C. R. (1988). Patterns of family and nonfamily violence: Violent husbands and violent men. *Violence and Victims, 3*(2), 83–97.

Silverton, L. (1985). *Crime and the schizophrenia spectrum: A study of two Danish cohorts.* Unpublished doctoral dissertation, University of Southern California, Los Angeles, CA.

Singer, J., Singer, D., & Rapaczynski, W. (1984). Family patterns and television viewing as predictors of children's beliefs and aggression. *Journal of Communication, Spring,* 73–89.

Sink, C., Barnett, J., & Pool, B. (1993). Perceptions of scholastic competence in relation to middle-school achievement. *Perceptual and Motor Skills, 76*(2), 471–479.

Skodol, A. E., Oldham, J., Gallaher, P., & Bezirganian, S. (1994). Validity of self-defeating personality disorder. *American Journal of Psychiatry, 151*(4), 560–567.

Skrabanek, P. (1988). Cervical cancer in nuns and prostitutes. *Journal of Clinical Epidemiology, 41*(6), 577–582.

Snell, R. L. (1992). *Women in jail 1989.* Washington, DC: U.S. Department of Justice.

Snyder, H. N., & Sickmund, M. (1995). *Juvenile offenders and victims: A focus on violence.* Washington, DC: National Center for Juvenile Justice.

Sorenson, S., & Siegel, J. (1992). Gender, ethnicity, and sexual assaults: Findings from a Los Angeles study. *Journal of Social Issues, 48*(1), 93–104.

Sorenson, S., & White, J. (1992). Adult sexual assault: Overview of research. *Journal of Social Issues, 48*(1), 1.

Spatz Widom, C. (1989a). Child abuse, neglect, and violent criminal behavior. *Criminology, 272,* 251–271.

Spatz Widom, C. (1989b). Does violence beget violence? A critical examination of the literature. *Psychological Bulletin, 106*(1), 3–28.

Spellacy, F. (1977). Neuropsychological differences between violent and nonviolent adolescents. *Journal of Clinical Psychology, 334,* 966–969.

Spellacy, F. (1978). Neuropsychological discrimination between violent and nonviolent men. *Journal of Clinical Psychology, 341,* 49–52.

Spergel, I. A. (1989). *Youth gangs: Problem and response.* Chicago: University of Chicago Press.

Sroufe, L., Cooper, R., & DeHart, G. (1992). *Child development: Its nature and course* (2nd ed.). New York: McGraw-Hill.

Sroufe, L., Cooper, R., & DeHart, G. (1996). *Child development: Its nature and course* (3rd ed.). New York: McGraw-Hill.

Stacey, W. A., & Shupe, A. (1983). *The family secret: Domestic violence in America.* Boston: Beacon.

Steinmetz, S. (1979). Disciplinary techniques and their relationship to aggressiveness, dependency, and conscience. In W. Burr, R. Hill, F. Nye, & I. Reiss (Eds.), *Contemporary theories about the family* (pp. 405–438). London: The Free Press.

Stephan, J. J., & Jankowski, L. W. (1991). *Jail inmates, 1990.* Washington, DC: U.S. Department of Justice.

Stephens, R. D. (1994). Gangs, guns, and school violence (The young desperadoes) (Cover Story). *USA Today,* pp. 29(4).

Stets, J. E., & Straus, M. A. (1990a). Gender differences in reporting marital violence and its medical and psychological consequences. In M. A. Straus & R. J. Gelles (Eds.), *Physical violence in American families* (pp. 151–166). New Brunswick: Transaction.

Stets, J. E., & Straus, M. A. (1990b). The marriage license as a hitting license: A comparison of assaults in dating, cohabiting and married couples. In M. A. Straus & R. J. Gelles (Eds.), *Physical violence in American families* (pp. 227–241). New Brunswick: Transaction.

Stover, D. (1986). A newer threat than ever. *American School Board Journal, 173*(8), 19–24.

Strasburger, V. (1985). When parents ask about the influence of TV on their kids. *Contemporary Pediatrics, May,* 18–30.

Straus, M. (1983). Ordinary violence, child abuse, and wife-beating: What do they have in common? In D. Finkelhor, R. Gelles, G. Hotaling, & M. Straus (Eds.), *The dark side of families: Current family violence research* (pp. 213–234). Beverly Hills, CA: Sage.

Straus, M. (1985). Family training in crime and violence. In A. J. Lincoln & M. A. Straus (Eds.), *Crime and the family* (pp. 164–185). Springfield, IL: Charles C. Thomas.

Straus, M. A. (1976). Sexual inequality, cultural norms, and wife-beating. In E. C. Viano (Ed.), *Victims and society* (pp. 543–560). Washington, DC: Visage Press.

Straus, M. A. (1991). Discipline & deviance: Physical punishment of children and violence and other crime in adulthood. *Social Problems, 38*(2), 133–142.

Straus, M. A. (1992a). *Corporal punishment of children and depression and suicide in adulthood.* Philadelphia, PA: The Society for Life History Research.

Straus, M. A. (1992b). Family violence. In E. F. Borgatta & M. L. Borgatta (Eds.), *Encyclopedia of sociology* (pp. 682–689). New York: Macmillan.

Straus, M. A., & Gelles, R. J. (1986). Societal change and change in family violence from 1975 to 1985 as revealed by two national surveys. *Journal of Marriage and the Family, 48,* 465–479.

Straus, M. A., & Gelles, R. J. (1988). How violent are American families? Estimates from the National Family Violence Resurvey and other studies. In G. T. Hotaling, D. Finkelhor, J. T. Kirkpatrick, & M. A. Straus (Eds.), *Family abuse and its consequences: New directions in research* (pp. 14–37). Newbury Park, CA: Sage.

Straus, M. A., & Gelles, R. (1990). *Physical violence in American families.* New Brunswick: Transaction.

Straus, M. A., Gelles, R. J., & Steinmetz, S. K. (1980). *Behind closed doors: Violence in the American family.* New York: Doubleday.

Straus, M. A., & Hotaling, G. (1980). Culture, social organization, and irony in the study of family violence. In M. A. Straus (Ed.), *The social causes of husband–wife violence* (pp. 3–23). Minneapolis: University of Minnesota Press.

Struckman-Johnson, C., & Struckman-Johnson, D. (1992). Acceptance of male rape myths among college men and women. *Sex Roles: A Journal of Research, 27*(3/4), 85–100.

Sullivan, C. M., Davidson, W. S., Basta, J., Rumptz, M., Tan, C., & Gemi, G. (1991, August). *Women escaping abuse: Their changing needs over time.* Paper presented at the American Psychological Association Convention, San Francisco, CA.

Sutherland, E. H. (1947). *Principles of criminology* (4th ed.). Philadelphia: Lippincott.

Tauber, E., Meda, C., & Vitro, V. (1977). Child ill-treatment as considered by the Italian criminal and civil codes. *Child Abuse and Neglect, 1*(1), 149–152.

Taus, M. (1995, November 30). 20 years later, man admits to 2 murders. *The Boston Globe,* p. 24.

Taylor, S. P., Schmutte, G. T., Leonard, K. E., & Cranston, J. (1979). The effects of alcohol and extreme provocation on the use of highly noxious shock. *Motivation and Emotion, 3,* 73–81.

Taylor, S. P., & Sears, J. D. (1988). The effects of alcohol and persuasive social pressure on human physical aggression. *Aggressive Behavior, 14,* 237–244.

Thornberry, T., & Farnworth, M. (1982). Social correlates of criminal involvement: Further evidence on the relationship between social status and criminal behavior. *American Sociological Review, 47,* 505–518.

Thornhill, R., & Thornhill, N. W. (1992). The evolutionary psychology of men's coercive sexuality. *Behavioral and Brain Sciences, 15*(2), 363–375.

Tittle, C., Villemez, W., & Smith, D. (1978). The myth of social class and criminality: An empirical assessment of the empirical evidence. *American Sociological Review, 43,* 643–656.

Tong, L., Oates, K., & McDowell, M. (1987). Personality development following sexual abuse. *Child Abuse & Neglect, 11,* 371–383.

Troy, M., & Sroufe, L. A. (1987). Victimization among preschoolers: Role of attachment relationship history. *Journal of the American Academy of Child and Adolescent Psychiatry, 26,* 166–172.

Tuckman, B. W. (1965). Developmental sequences in small groups. *Psychological Bulletin, 63,* 384–399.

Turner, C. W., Hesse, B. W., & Peterson-Lewis, S. (1986). Naturalistic studies of the long-term effects of television violence. *Journal of Social Issues, 42*(3), 7–28.

United Press. (1988, October 21). Father of dead girl says beatings only "tough discipline." *The Fayetteville Observer,* p. 22.

U.S. Department of Justice. (1988). *Report to the nation on crime and justice: The data* (2nd ed.). Washington, DC: U.S. Department of Justice.

U.S. Department of Justice. (1990). *Drugs and Crime Facts, 1990.* Washington, DC: Author.

U.S. Department of Justice. (1994). *Elderly crime victims* (NCJ-147002). Washington, DC: Bureau of Justice Statistics.

Van Goozen, S., Van de Poll, N., & Frijda, N. (1994). Anger and aggression in women: Influence of sports choice and testosterone administration. *Aggressive Behavior, 20*(3), 213–222.

Vaughn, S., Hogan, A., Lancelotta, G., Shapiro, S., & Walker, J. (1992). Subgroups of children with severe and mild behavior problems: Social competence and reading achievement. *Child Psychology, 21*(2), 98–106.

Vernberg, E. M. (1990). Psychological adjustment and experiences with peers during early adolescence: Reciprocal, incidental, or undirectional relationships? *Journal of Abnormal Child Psychology, 18*(2), 187–198.

Vince, C. (1989). Assaultive injuries. In National Committee for Injury Prevention & Control & Education Development Center (Eds.), *Injury prevention: Meeting the challenge* (pp. 94–103). New York: Oxford University Press.

Virkkunen, M., & Linnoila, M. (1993). Brain serotonin, Type II alcoholism and impulsive violence. *Journal of Studies on Alcohol, 11,* 163.

Vissing, Y. M., Straus, M. A., Gelles, R. J., & Harrop, J. W. (1991). Verbal aggression by parents and psychosocial problems of children. *Child Abuse & Neglect, 15,* 223–238.

Vitaro, F., Pelletier, D., & Coutu, S. (1989). Effects of a negative social experience on the emotional and social-cognitive responses of aggressive-rejected children. *Perceptual & Motor Skills, 69*(2), 371–382.

The wages of crack. (1994). *The Economist, 332*(7879), A29.

Wagner, M., Schubert, H., & Schubert, D. (1985). Family size effects: A review. *Journal of Genetic Psychology, 146*(1), 65–78.

Waldrop, M. F., & Goering, J. D. (1971). Hyperactivity and minor physical anomalies in elementary school children. *American Journal of Orthopsychiatry, 41,* 602–607.

Walker, L. E. (1979). *The battered woman.* New York: Harper & Row.

Wang, A. Y. (1994). Pride and prejudice in high school gang members. *Adolescence, 29*(114), 279–292.

Weiss, B., Dodge, K. A., Bates, J. E., & Pettit, G. S. (1992). Some consequences of early harsh discipline: Child aggression and a maladaptive social information processing style. *Child Development, 63*(6), 1321–1335.

Weiss, G. (1990). Hyperactivity in childhood. *The New England Journal of Medicine, 323*(20), 1413–1415.

Weisz, J. R., Martin, S. L., Walter, B. R., & Fernandez, G. A. (1991). Differential prediction of young adult arrests for property and personal crimes: Findings of a cohort follow-up study of violent boys from North Carolina's Willie M Program. *Journal of Child Psychology & Psychiatry, 32*(5), 783–792.

Welsh, R. (1976). Severe parental punishment and delinquency: A developmental theory. *Journal of Clinical Child Psychology, Spring,* 17–21.

Werner, E. E., & Smith, R. S. (1982). *Vulnerable but invincible: A study of resilient children.* New York: McGraw-Hill.

Wesley, J. (1994). Effects of ability, high school achievement, and procrastinatory behavior on college performance. *Educational and Psychological Measurement, 54*(2), 404–409.

West, J., & Templer, D. I. (1994). Child molestation, rape, and ethnicity. *Psychological Reports, 75*(3), 1326.

Williams, J. H. (1987). *Psychology of women: Behavior in a biosocial context* (3rd ed.). New York: Norton.

Williams, J. W. (1992). Understanding how youth gangs operate. *Corrections Today, 54*(5), 86–87.

Wilson, J. (1995). What to do about crime: Blaming crime on root causes. *Vital Speeches, 61*(12), 373–376.

Winder, C. I., & Rau, L. (1962). Parental attitudes associated with social deviance in preadolescent boys. *Journal of Abnormal and Social Psychology, 64*(6), 418–424.

Wolfgang, M. E. (1958). *Patterns in criminal homicide.* Philadelphia: University of Pennsylvania Press.

Wolfgang, M. E. (1983). Delinquency in two birth cohorts. *American Behavioral Scientist, 27,* 75–86.

Wood, W., Wong, F., & Chachere, J. (1991). Effects of media violence on viewers' aggression in unconstrained social interaction. *Psychological Bulletin, 109*(3), 371–383.

Yanagida, E., & Ching, J. (1993). MMPI profiles of child abusers. *Journal of Child Psychology, 49*(4), 569–577.

Yarrow, M., Campbell, J. D., & Burton, R. V. (1968). *Child rearing: An inquiry into research and methods.* San Francisco: Jossey-Bass.

Yegidis, B. (1986). Date rape and other forced sexual encounters among college students. *Journal of Sex Education & Therapy, 12*(1), 51–54.

Yeudall, L. T., & Fromm-Auch, D. (1979). Neuropsychological impairments in various psychopathological populations. In J. Gruzelier & P. Flor-Henry (Eds.), *Hemisphere asymmetries of function and psychopathology* (pp. 341–363). New York: Elsevier/North Holland Biomedical Press.

Yeudall, L. T., Fromm-Auch, D., & Davies, P. (1982). Neuropsychological impairment of persistent delinquency. *The Journal of Nervous and Mental Disease, 170*(5), 257–265.

Zagar, R., Arbit, J., Hughes, J. R., Busell, R. F., & Busch, K. (1989). Developmental and disruptive behavior disorders among delinquents. *Journal of the American Academy of Child and Adolescent Psychiatry, 28*(3), 437–440.

Zagar, R., Arbit, J., Sylvies, R., Busch, K. G., & Hughes, J. R. (1990). Homicidal adolescents: A replication. *Psychological Reports, 67,* 1235–1242.

Zajonc, R. B., & Bargh, J. (1980). Birth order, family size, and decline of SAT scores. *American Psychologist, 357,* 662–668.

Zobeck, T. S., Stinson, F., Grant, B., & Bertolucci, D. (1993). *Trends in alcohol-related fatal traffic crashes, United States: 1979–1991* (26). Washington, DC: National Institute on Alcohol Abuse and Alcoholism.

Author Index

A

Abbey, A., 112, 114
Abbott, D. A., 117
Adams, S. L., 61, 84, 117
Adler, T., 88, 116, 118, 120, 149
Ageton, S., 7
Ahmed, S., 74
Akers, R. L., 69
Akins, K. A., 113
Akman, D., 143
Allen, M., 112
Allgeier, E. R., 113
Alpern, L., 68
Anderson, D., 127
Anderson, J., 89
Anderson, K. 127
Aquila, F., 107
Arbit, J., 56, 62, 91, 99
Arthur, M., 127
Ascher, C., 108
Atkeson, B. M., 146
Atkin, C. K., 80
Atkins, M. S., 68

B

Bachorowski, J., 63
Baily, W., 115

Bakan, D., 99, 145
Balla, D., 56
Bandura, A., 2, 70
Barbaree, H. E., 77
Barber, B. K., 69
Bard, B., 90
Bargh, J., 42
Barnett, J., 92
Barocas, R., 63
Barrett, P., 109
Barton, J., 153
Bartol, C., 14, 23, 32, 44, 101, 102, 103
Bassuk, E., 101, 102
Bastian, L. D., 100
Bates, J. E., 69, 75
Baumrind, D., 23
Becker, W., 130, 137
Beeghly, M., 144
Beitchman, J. H., 143
Bell, R. Q., 131
Belsky, J., 42
Bender, L., 73, 91
Bent, A. 125
Berenbaum, S. A., 88
Berkhout, J., 69
Berkow, R., 124, 125
Berkowitz, L., 73, 74
Berliner, L., 6
Bernard, F., 77
Bertolucci, D., 102

Bezirganian, S., 148
Bierman, K. L., 64
Bjorklund, A., 58
Bjorkqvist, S., 58, 86
Bjorkqvist, K., 58, 86
Bleuler, N., 73
Block, R., 41
Bonfante, J., 107
Bower, B., 45
Bowers, N. D., 46
Boxley, J., 112
Braithwaite, J., 35
Brantley, A. C., 105
Brennan, P., 55
Bridges, G., 39
Brody, C., 107
Brown, G., 57
Brown, K., 68
Brown, L., 76
Browne, A., 6, 28, 44, 118, 120, 121, 123, 149
Bryan, J., 128, 129, 134, 136
Buchanan, R. W., 45
Buchholz, E. S., 126
Burkhart, B., 27
Burne, J., 79
Burrell, B., 125
Burton, R. V., 130
Busch, K. G., 56, 62, 91, 99
Busell, R. E., 62
Bussell, R. B., 56, 99

C

Caesar, P., 130, 135, 139
Caffaro-Rouget, A., 144
Calhoun, J. B., 45, 46
Calhoun, K. S., 146
Campbell, B., 58
Campbell, S. B., 67, 68
Campbell, J. D., 130
Carlson, B. E., 149
Carroll, J., 138
Carter, T., 35
Cate, R. M., 149
Caudill, B., 104
Cazenave, N. A., 24, 25, 117, 118
Celano, M., 22
Centerwall, B., 45, 79
Cervi, D., 4, 16, 17, 28, 87
Chachere, J., 82
Chaffin, M., 125
Challas, G., 129
Chaplin, T. C., 112
Chin, K., 103
Ching, J., 125

Christiansen, K., 58
Christopher, F. S., 149
Cicchetti, D., 41, 42, 68, 144, 145
Clay, D., 107
Clelland, D., 35
Clinton, W., 105
Coble, C. N., 113
Cohen, D. L., 2, 70
Cohen, J., 144
Cohen, J. M., 76
Cohen, L., 8
Cohen, M. J., 76
Cohen-Kettenis, P., 69
Cohn, D. A., 68
Collmer, C., 130
Conklin, J., 41
Conte, J., 144
Convit, A., 77, 78
Cooper, R., 62, 144
Coster, W., 144
Coutts, J., 112
Coutu, S., 76
Cranston, J., 102
Curtis, G. C., 70, 129

D

Dabbs, J., 62
DaCosta, G. A., 143
Davies, P., 55
Davis, R. H., 105
Davis, L. V., 149
DeFrances, C. J., 8
DeHart, G., 62, 144
Deley, W., 128, 139
Denno, D., 61, 90
Dietz, W., 79
DiLalla, L., 127, 128
Dillingham, S. D., 100
DiRosa, A., 106
Divoky, D., 65
Dodge, K. A., 63, 69, 75, 76
Donnerstein, E., 84
Downey, G., 76

E

Earls, F. J., 64
Egeland, B., 42
Ellement, J., 17
Elliott, F. A., 55
Elliott, D., 41
Ellis, L., 42, 58, 64, 67, 75, 86, 88, 89, 90
Ellis, E. M., 146
Emmers, G. 112

Engfer, A., 137, 138
Erne, D., 145
Eron, L., 45, 80, 87, 127, 128, 131, 132, 134,
        136, 137, 138
Ervin, F. R., 54
Escovar, L., 138
Escovar, P., 138
Evans, G., 45

F

Fagan, J. A., 28, 36, 103
Farnham-Diggory, S., 66
Farnworth, M., 35, 38
Farrington, D. P., 53
Faulk, M., 28
Feldman, M., 90
Fergusson, D., 92
Fernandez, G. A., 62
Ferrari, J., 92
Feshbach, N., 46, 135
Finkelhor, D., 14, 22, 25, 27, 110, 11, 143
Fischer, M., 65
Fischer, E., 125
Fishbein, D. H., 58
Fishman, A. M., 147
Fitzgerald, L. F., 112
Flynn, P., 104
Flynn, J. D., 28
Foa, E. B., 146
Fogel, C. A., 55, 64, 65
Follingstad, D., 149
Forsstrom-Cohen, B., 149, 150
Francis, C., 125
Frankel, M., 45, 47
Freed, F., 128, 129, 134, 136
Freed, D., 56
Freedman, J. L., 45, 47
Frech, L. J., 8, 17, 19, 41
Freyne, A., 60
Friedrich, L., 45, 80
Friedt, L., 54, 55
Frieze, I. H., 44
Frijda, N., 58
Fromm-Auch, D., 55
Fultz, J., 126
Futterman, A., 113

G

Gabrielli, W., 59
Gaes, G., 45, 47, 48
Gaines, J. A., 102, 103, 114
Galaburda, A. M., 55, 67
Gallaher, P., 148

Gardner, S., 145
Garrison, W. T., 64
Gaustad, J., 105, 106, 108, 109
Gavaler, J., 92
Gayford, J. J., 28, 44
Gelenberg, A., 101
Gelles, R. J., 2, 3, 7, 12, 21, 29, 31, 45, 67, 87,
        88, 116, 117, 118, 120, 127, 128,
        130, 134, 135, 136, 141, 142, 149
Gerbner, G., 80
Gersten, M., 144
Geschwind, N., 55, 67
Geyelin, M., 153
Giancola, P., 56
Giannini, A. J., 103
Gidycz, C. A., 27, 113
Gil, D., 42
Girelli, S. A., 146
Gladwell, M., 154
Glickauf-Hughes, C., 148
Goerings, J. D., 54, 55, 65
Goldman, H., 54, 57
Goldstein, A. P., 103, 145
Goodnow, J. J., 67
Gortmaker, S., 79
Gottfredson, M., 43
Gould, J., 22
Gouvier, W., 54, 55
Gove, W. R., 45
Grace, J., 105
Graff, T. T., 28
Grant, B., 102
Greenberg, G., 66
Greenfeld, L. A., 2, 41, 77
Greenwood, P., 19
Greven, P., 141
Groth, A. N., 110, 111, 114
Gruchow, ., 112
Grusec, J. E., 67
Gustafson, R., 74
Gwartney-Gibbs, P., 26

H

Haddad, J. D., 63
Hagedorn, J. M., 107
Halpern, C. T., 58
Halsey, L., 126
Hamberger, L. K., 102
Hanley, R., 154
Hanneke, C. R., 5, 28
Hanson, K., 113
Harnish, ., 112, 114
Harris, M., 79
Harris, G. T., 112

Harrop, J. W., 67
Hart, J., 19
Harway, M., 77
Haskett, M., 126
Hassell, R. A., 147
Hastings, J. E., 102
Haut, F., 105
Hazzard, A., 22
Hegar, R. L., 125
Heimer, K., 43
Hellmer, L., 130
Henderson, ., 75
Henton, J., 149
Herschel, M., 66
Hesse, B. W., 80
Hewitt, J. D., 41
Hicks, D., 114
Himelein, M. J., 113
Hindelang, M., 39
Hines, M., 88
Hirschi, T., 43
Hitz, L., 125
Hoffman, J., 104
Hogan, A., 68
Hoge, S., 56, 87, 99, 101, 102
Hollenbeck, A. R., 63
Hollenberg, J., 125
Hood, J. E., 143
Horan, S., 60
Horn, W. F., 66
Horwood, L. J., 92
Hotaling, G.T., 4, 28, 35, 36, 77, 87, 90
Hubbard, R., 104
Hubbard, J. A., 64
Huesmann, L., 45, 80, 87, 127
Hughes, H., 125
Hughes, J. R., 56, 62, 64, 65, 91, 99
Hull, ., 49
Humphrey, J. A., 41
Hurley, D., 72, 73
Huston, A., 45, 70, 79, 80, 82
Hutchings, B., 59, 63
Hutter, C. K., 146

I

Ialongo, N., 66
Inciardi, J., 103, 117
Innes, C. A., 87
Ipfling, H., 138
Isay, D., 77

J

Jackson, L., 90
Jackson, J. K., 99

Jacobvitz, D., 42, 65
Jankowski, L. W., 116
Janokowski, G., 79
Jellinek, M., 77
Johannesson, I., 133
Johnson, J., 51, 126
Jones, J., 11, 24
Jones, D., 51, 126
Jones, E., 23
Jordan, C. G., 146
Jouriles, E. N., 125

K

Kagan, J., 58
Kahn, A. S., 113
Kalof, L., 113, 114
Kandel, E. (see also Kandel-Englander, E.), 39,
        41, 52, 55, 56, 58, 64, 65, 72, 77, 78,
        88, 90, 92, 153
Kandel, S., 82
Kandel-Englander, E. (see also Kandel, E.), 4,
        16, 17, 28, 29, 36, 39, 87, 91
Kang, ., 74, 103
Kaufman Kantor, G., 35, 36
Kelleher, K., 125, 126
Keller, H., 145
Kelley, S., 126
Kempe, C. H., 20
Kemper, T., 138
Kendall-Tackett, K. A., 143, 144
Kerkman, D., 80
Killory, J. F., 128
Kinnard, K., 137
Kirkegaard-Sorenson, L., 90
Klaus, K., 3
Koers, A.J., 8
Kohn, A., 65
Korn-Bursztyn, C., 126
Kosky, R., 135
Koss, M. P., 27, 102, 103, 114
Koval, J., 149
Kroeker, M., 105
Krynicki, V. E., 55
Kunkel, D., 45, 79

L

Lancelotta, G., 68
Lane, K., 26
Lang, R., 144
Langan, P. A., 87, 117
Langhinrichsen-Rohling, J., 14
Larzelere, R., 130, 131, 134, 136, 138
Latham, L., 113

Lau, M., 56
Lawrance, L., 112
Lawry, S., 22
Layman, M. J., 113
Lee, N., 43
Lefkowitz, M., 87, 127, 128, 131, 132, 133,
        134, 135, 136, 137, 138
Lefley, H.P., 114
Leonard, K.E., 102
LePage, A., 73, 74
Lesnik-Oberstein, M., 8
Levin, H., 67, 128
Levine, M., 150
Leviton, H., 127, 128
Levy, J., 105
Lewis, D., 7, 41, 56, 58, 62, 73, 90, 91, 93, 94,
        101
Lilienfield, A. M., 88
Lincoln, A. J., 4
Lindgren, C., 3, 8
Linnoila, M., 57
Linz, D., 84
Lloyd, S., 149
Loiselle, R., 103
Lonsway, K. A., 112
Lowenstein, L., 127, 128, 129
Luckey, J., 104
Luria, Z., 130
Lyons-Ruth, K., 68

M

Maccoby, E., 67, 128
Magaw, J., 109
Magmer, E., 138
Magura, S., 74, 103
Makepeace, J. M., 117, 121
Malamuth, N., 76, 112, 113
Mann, C. R., 24, 25
Mannarino, A., 144
Mapletoft, ., 74
Marhoefer-Dvorak, S., 146
Mark, V. H., 54
Marshall, W. L., 77
Martin, C., 92
Martin, S. L., 62
Mathie, V. A., 113
Matthys, W., 69
Maurer, A., 127, 135, 139
McCahill, T., 147
McCall, G. J., 5
McCord, J., 133, 139, 141
McDowell, M., 144
McGee, R., 69
McKinney, K. C., 105, 108

Meda, C., 46
Mednick, S. A., 41, 55, 58, 59, 63, 64, 153
Mednick, B., 77, 78, 88, 90
Megargee, E. I., 44, 45, 74
Meredith, W. H., 117
Mestel, R., 58
Meyer, L. C., 147
Mezzick, A., 92
Michelsen, N., 55
Miller, J., 126
Miller, N., 103
Miller, D., 129
Milne, J., 22
Milner, J., 126
Mitchell, C., 127
Moeller, T. G., 66, 92
Moffitt, T., 77
Monahan, J., 72
Moore, J., 105
Morell, V., 58, 89
Morris, R., 62
Moss, H., 92
Moyer, K. E., 57
Mueller, C. W., 43
Mumma, G. H., 64
Murdock, T., 146
Mydans, S., 105

N

Nada Raja, S., 69
Nagaraja, J., 132
Nagin, D., 43
Neidig, P., 14
Newby, R. F., 65
Newcomb, A. F., 64
Newman, J. P., 63
Ney, P., 145
Nichols, P., 55, 88
Nickerson, C., 75
Norwood, W. D., 125
Nowlis, V., 130
Nygren, T., 58

O

O'Connor, A., 60
O'Leary, K. D., 87, 117
Oates, K., 144
Oberklaid, F., 64
Offord, D. R., 73
Oldham, J., 148
Olsen, J. E., 69
Olson, K., 68, 145
Olweus, D., 53, 87

Orme, J., 125
Osborne, M. L., 68
Ostrow, R. J., 17
Otis, D., 77
Owens, D., 129, 137, 149

P

Packard, T., 66
Pagelow, M. D., 43
Pagliocca, P., 127
Palmer, S., 41
Parke, R., 128, 130, 137
Parker, J., 92
Pasamanick, B., 88
Paternoster, R., 43
Paterson, E. J., 5
Pedlow, R., 64
Pedrick Cornell, C., 45
Peele, S., 101
Pelletier, D., 76
Perse, E., 113, 115
Peterson, D., 115, 130
Peterson, J., 56
Peterson, R., 115
Peterson-Lewis, S., 80
Pettit, G. S., 69, 75
Pierce, C., 80
Pihl, R., 56
Pillemer, K., 27
Pincus, J. H., 90
Piper, E. S., 77, 78, 153
Pirog-Good, M., 148
Pizzy, E., 44, 123, 148
Pliszka, S. R., 65, 66
Pool, B., 92
Pope, A., 64
Porrieger, A., 103
Porter, S., 125
Price, J. M., 45, 63, 75
Prior, M., 64

R

Radecki, T., 80
Rand, M. R., 47
Rapaczynski, W., 45
Rapaport, K., 27
Rau, L., 70
Reed, J., 51
Reichler, M., 138
Reiss, A., 14
Repacholi, B., 68
Resick, P. A., 146, 147

Riad, J. K., 45, 48
Rice, M., 80, 112
Rigdon, J., 62, 132
Riggs, D. S., 146
Ritchie, K., 148
Rivera, B., 90
Rizzuto, A., 60
Roberts, J., 110
Robins, L., 62, 73
Rodgers, M. E., 88
Rosenbaum, A., 56, 87, 99, 101, 102, 149, 150
Ross, D., 70
Ross, S., 70
Rothbaum, B. O., 146
Rounsaville, B. J., 28
Ruback, R. B., 45, 48
Russell, D., 22, 26
Rust, J., 137

S

Salter, C., 79
Sanson, A., 64, 65
Sargeant, G., 125
Saunders, D. G., 5, 15, 30
Sccente, D. D., 107
Schmutte, G. T., 102
Schneewind, K., 137, 138
Schneider-Rosen, K., 68, 145
Schoonover, S., 101
Schubert, D., 42
Schubert, H., 42
Schuck, J. R., 130
Schuerman, J., 144
Scott, P. D., 44
Scott, C. S., 114
Sears, J. D., 99, 102
Sears, R., 67, 128, 130, 133, 134, 136
Sechrest, D. K., 45, 47
Shagle, S. C., 69
Shanok, S. S., 7, 41, 56
Shapiro, J. L., 74, 103
Shapiro, S., 68
Sheley, J., 107
Sheridan, M., 125
Shields, N. M., 5, 31
Shoemaker, D., 130
Shupe, A., 28
Sickmund, M., 106
Siegel, J., 114
Silverman, F. N., 20
Silverton, L., 73
Singer, J., 45, 132, 133
Singer, D., 45, 132, 133
Sink, C., 92

Size, P. B., 5, 15
Skodol, A. E., 148
Skrabanek, P., 129
Slaby, R., 128, 137
Smith, S., 8
Smith, D., 34, 35
Smith, R. S., 52, 53
Smith-Winberry, C., 66
Snell, R. L., 8, 99
Snyder, H. N., 106
Sorenson, S., 114, 115
Spatz Widom, C., 3, 4, 52, 58, 68, 90, 127, 128,
        129, 135
Spellacy, F., 55, 87
Spergel, I. A., 105, 106
Spunt, ., 103
Sroufe, L. A., 42, 62, 65, 67, 68, 144, 145
St.Peters, M., 80
Stacey, W. A., 28
Stanton, W. R., 69
Steele, B. F., 20
Stein, A. H., 45, 80
Steinmetz, S., 2, 127
Stephan, J. J., 116
Stephens, R. D., 99
Stets, J. E., 7, 26, 27, 117, 142, 147, 148
Stewart, D. K., 28
Stinson, F., 102
Stoff, D. M., 68
Stover, D., 108
Straaburger, V., 80
Straus, M. A., 2, 3, 4, 5, 7, 12, 15, 21, 26, 27,
        28, 29, 32, 35,
40, 46, 67, 77, 87, 88, 92, 116, 117, 118, 120,
        127, 128, 129, 130, 131, 133, 134,
        135, 136, 137, 139, 140, 141, 142,
        147, 148, 149
Struckman-Johnson, D., 112
Struckman-Johnson, C., 112
Suchindran, C., 58
Sugarman, D. B., 35, 36, 90
Sullivan, C. M., 150
Sutherland, E. H., 69, 82
Sylvies, R. B., 91

T

Tapia, F., 62, 132
Tauber, E., 46
Taus, M., 19
Taylor, B. M., 100
Taylor, S. P., 99, 102, 103
Templer, D. I., 115
Thorn, G., 14
Thornberry, T., 35, 38

Thornhill, N. W., 113
Thornhill, R., 113
Timmons-Mitchell, J., 145
Tittle, C., 35
Tong, L., 144
Torgler, C., 113
Troy, M., 68
Tuckman, B. W., 107
Turner, C. W., 80, 103

U

Udry, R. J., 58

V

Van Goozen, S., 58
Van de Poll, N., 58
VanSanten, V., 144
Vaughn, S., 68
Vernberg, E. M., 69
Vigil, J. D., 105
Villemez, W., 34, 35
Vince, C., 101
Virkkunen, M., 57
Vissings, Y. M., 67
Vitaro, F., 76
Vitro, V., 46
Vogel, R. E., 113
Volavka, J., 77

W

Wachowiak, D. G., 113
Wagner, M., 42, 138
Walder, L., 87, 127, 128
Waldrop, M. F., 54, 55, 65
Walker, E., 76
Walker, D., 79
Walker, J., 68
Walker, L. E., 28, 149
Walsh, W., 146
Walter, D. R., 62
Wang, A. Y., 108
Watkins, B., 45, 79
Webb, C., 22
Weiss, G., 54, 62, 64, 65, 89
Weiss, B., 69
Weisz, J. R., 62, 63
Wells, M., 148
Welsh, R., 131
Werner, E. E., 52, 53
Wesley, J., 92
West, J., 51, 115

Wexler, S., 28, 36
White, J., 115
Whiting, J., 130
Wiederman, ., 113
Williams, L., 143
Williams, J. H., 44
Williams, J. W., 108
Wilson, J., 45
Winder, C. L., 70
Windham, ., 113
Winkler, K. C., 58
Wisniewski, N., 27
Wolfgang, M. E., 7, 41
Wong, F., 82
Wood, W., 82
Wright, J., 80, 107

Y

Yanagida, E., 125

Yao, J., 92
Yarrow, M., 130
Yegidis, B., 27
Yeudall, L. T., 55
Yllo, K., 14, 25, 110, 111
Yuille, J., 125

Z

Zagar, R., 56, 62, 65, 67, 89, 91, 99
Zahn, M. A., 24, 25, 117, 118
Zajonc, R. B., 42
Zeichner, A., 56
Zhang, J., 107
Zirkel, S., 113
Zobeck, T. S., 102
Zucker, ., 143
Zuravin, S., 125

Subject Index

A

Addiction (*see* Substance abuse, dependency)
Aggression, 1, 2–3, 67–69
  costs of, 2–3
  development of, 67–69
  hostile aggression, 1, 68
  instrumental aggression, 1, 68
Alcohol (*see* Substance abuse)
Anti-Social Personality Disorder, 44–45, 71–72
Assault, 11–12, 16–17
Attachment, 68
Attention Deficit Disorder (*see* Hyperactivity)

B

Biological environmental influences, 51
Biology (*see also* Genetics; Biological environment influences; Hormones; Head injury; Minor physical anomalies; Neuropsychological testing; Neurotransmitters; Physiology and anatomy; Minimal brain damage), 51–52, 52–60
Biosocial model, 4, 85–95

C

Child abuse (*see also* Sexual abuse; Neglect; Emotional abuse), 20–23, 124–126, 135–137, 143–144, 144–146
  factors associated with the child, 124–125
  factors associated with the parent and the situation, 125–126
Cognitive biases (*see* Hostile interpretations)
Conduct disorders, 62–63
Crowding, 42 43, 45, 46 48

D

Date rape, 27
Dating viol0ence, 26–27
Death Row inmates, 93–95
Desensitization (*see* Television violence)
Developmental perspectives, 61–69
Displaced aggression, 61
Domestic violence (*see* Family violence)
Drugs (*see* Substance abuse)

E

Education, 37–38, 38–40, 90–93, 108–109
Elder abuse, 27
Emotional abuse, 23

F

Family size, 41–43
Family violence (*see also* Child abuse; Sexual abuse; Spouse abuse; Elder abuse; Physical punishment), 2, 4–8, 45–46, 77–78, 87–88

185

Freudian theory (*see* Psychodynamic perspectives)
Frustration and aggression, 73–74

G

Gangs, 105–109
Gender and violence, 86–90
   biological explanations of, 88–89
   socio-psychological explanations of, 89–90
Genetics, 50–51, 52, 58–60

H

Head injury, 56
Homicide (*see also* Juvenile homicide), 17, 19,
   106, 116–123
Hormones, 57–58
Hostile interpretations, 75–76
Hyperactivity, 63–66

I

Incest (*see* Sexual abuse)

J

Juvenile homicide, 106
Juvenile violence, 19

L

Learning disorders, 66–67

M

Marital rape, 25–26
Marital violence (*see* Spouse abuse)0
Mental illness, 72–73
Minimal brain damage, 54–56
Minimal brain dysfunction, 54–56
Minor physical anomalies, 54–55

N

National Crime Survey, 14–15
National Family Violence Surveys, 15, 29
Nature–Nurture Debate, 51–52
Neglect, 22–23
Neuropsychological testing, 55–56
Neurotransmitters, 56–57

O

Observational learning, 52–53, 69–70, 82
Operant conditioning, 70–71
Overcontrolled and undercontrolled violence,
   74–75

P

Pan-violence, 28–32
Physical punishment, 127–139, 140–142
   and other parenting behaviors, 137–138
   cross-sectional research, 130–132
   frequency of physical punishment, 128–129
   males versus females, 137
   prospective research, 132–134
   retrospective research, 129–130
Physiology and anatomy, 53–56
Population density (*see* Crowding)
Poverty (*see* Social class)
Protective factors, 85–86
Psychodynamic perspectives, 60–61
Psychological abuse (*see* Emotional abuse)
Psychopath (*see* Anti-Social Personality Disorder)

R

Race, 31, 40–41, 106, 108
Rape (*see* Sexual assault)
Recidivism and violence, 76–78, 153–154
Risk factors, 85–86

S

Sexual abuse (*see also* Sexual assault), 22,
   25–26, 27, 143–144, 146–147
Sexual assault (*see also* Sexual abuse), 18–19,
   25–26, 27, 71, 110–115, 143–144,
   146–147
   perpetrator characteristics, 110–113
   social conditions and, 114–115
   victim characteristics, 113–114

Social lass, 31–32, 35–37, 38–40, 154–155
Social learning perspectives, 69–71
Socioeconomic status (*see* Social class)
Sociological perspectives, 43–48
Sociopath (*see* Anti-Social Personality Disorder)
Spouse abuse, 11–12, 23–27, 30–31, 32, 44,
   142, 147–151
Spouse homicide, 116–123